Cover: *Compugraphics* by Pierre Bertrand

8 AROUND THE AMERICAS

ON A MOTORCYCLE

by

Werner Bausenhart

New York   Ottawa   Toronto

Canadian Cataloguing in Publication Data

Main entry under title:

Werner Bausenhart
  8 Around the Americas: on a motorcycle

ISBN 1-894508-02-5

     1. South America--Description and Travel. 2. North America--Description and travel. 3. Motorcycling--South America. 4. Motorcycling--North America.
     I. Title. II. Title: Eight Around the Americas. III. Title: Figure eight around the Americas.

E27.5.B38 2000   918.04'4   C00-900452-1

For further information and for orders:

LEGAS

P. O. Box 040328	68 Kamloops Ave	2908 Dufferin Street
Brooklyn, New York	Ottawa, Ontario	Toronto, Ontario
USA 11204	K1V 7C9	M6B 3S8

Printed and bound in Canada

For my very own
Lady Dulcinea,
who suffered the Old Knight
to sally forth on his quixotic adventures.

Contents

Central America and Mexico 203

Finale 227

Appendix 233

Prelude

1. *Erich*

The ugly oversize licence plate with which the German authorities succeed in defacing the otherwise beautiful rear end of a motorcycle, the large letter D, and the shiny aluminum boxes on each side of the bike parked in front of a donut shop near Wawa, Ontario cried out, "German motorcycle adventurer inside." It was eleven o'clock, and since I had been in the saddle for more than four hours, this was all the incentive I needed to stop for a coffee break. I parked my bike beside this brand new KTM motorcycle, and went inside.

He was sitting next to the entrance with his bike in full view and was holding in one hand a cup of coffee , in the other a half-eaten donut, whose icing sugar had fallen on his long curly beard, where it sparkled like snow flakes. When I asked him in German if I could sit at his table, his face lit up and he introduced himself. His name was Erich. He was from Singen, Germany, and this was his second day on the road. He had arrived in Canada by air three weeks ago with his wife. They had rented a car and had visited the main tourist attractions of Eastern Canada, Quebec City, Montreal, Ottawa, Toronto, and Niagara Falls. Yesterday his wife had gone back to Germany to her job. He himself, however, being a pensioner, had picked up his motorcycle from the cargo terminal at the Toronto airport and had started on his trip to the Yukon. This was not his first visit to Canada. He had been here three times before. On his first trip he had canoed down the Porcupine River from Old Crow to Fort Yukon. On his second visit he had bicycled on the "Dempster Highway" from Dawson to Inuvik. Last year he had paddled down the Yukon in a kayak from Dawson to Eagle.This year's trip by motorcycle had been his wife's idea. "Erich," she had said one day, "you are getting too old for these paddling and bicycling adventures. I'm giving you a motorcycle for your birthday. That'll be easier on you." This is how he got the shiny blue KTM outside.

As Erich continued with his story I was amazed at how much the two of us had in common. Both of us had been teachers, were close to sixty, and had taken early retirement. Both of us had ridden motorcycles when we were teenagers, but had stopped riding for a long time, only to start again in our fifties. Both of us liked motorcycle touring and went on our trips alone without partners. There was one big difference, however, between my situation and Erich's: he had a wife who supported, even encouraged, his adventures. My wife, on the other hand, did not like motorcycles, thought that my trips were sallies to chase windmills, and saw me off only grudgingly.

"What a lovely bike you have, Erich," I said, "and how lucky you are to have such a generous wife. How about a switch? You take mine, and I take yours."

Erich looked at my BMW R100 GS and shook his head.

"In Germany they call this kind of bike a *Gummikuh*, a rubber cow. I think it's a bit too heavy for me. Thank you, I'm quite happy with my KTM."

"No, no, Erich, I like my bike," I replied. "I was thinking of switching wives.

When I was a student back in the 1960s, I had to read a story by a medieval German writer named Hartmann. It was one of the few of the many stories I had to read that I felt had a message for me. I'm thinking of this story, because the hero is your namesake. His name was Erec, and he was one of King Arthur's Knights of the Round Table. When Erec was young he was always travelling, always looking for adventures as a true knight should, beating up bad guys and rescuing damsels in distress. But this changed drastically after he got married. He became lazy and spent more time in a horizontal position than out doing things. That displeased everyone around him, particularly his young wife Enite. While half awake one morning he overheard her complaining bitterly that her husband had become what today we would call a couch potato. Erec felt the sting, and decided that his lifestyle would have to change. Immediately he saddled up his horse and left his comfortable castle with his wife in quest of adventures. He had learned his lesson: A life without travel, without adventures on the road, is not worth living."

Erich gave me a quizzical look.

"I guess after 27 years of teaching you can't just quit from one day to the next," he said with a smile. "Indeed, my wife is like the lady in that story. Every spring she gets tired of my playing househusband, of my bossing her around. Then she tells me, 'Erich, it's time to go on one of your trips.' I agree and here I am. When I get back home I show my slides to the old folks in the Old Folks' Homes around town. That makes them happy, and gives me a purpose."

Then he looked at his watch and said that it was time for us to hit the road as dutiful knights in quest of adventures should. Erich had a sense of humor. He had graciously forgiven the old professor for delivering a lecture to a class of one.

Since it had begun to drizzle we had to put on our rain gear before we could ride off. I took the lead, and had him in my rear view mirrors for a long time. Then the rain became heavier. Then it poured, and when I could see again for any distance, Erich was no longer in view. Perhaps he had stopped at a motel for the night. I never saw him again.

2. *Preparations*

It was relatively easy for Erec, Knight of the Round Table, to go adventure travelling. All he had to do was to saddle up one of the many horses in his stable and ride off at sunrise. The present-day rider, if he chooses a motorcycle as his means of transport, usually does not have the luxury of a garage full of mounts. Furthermore, motorcycles are not as readily affordable as horses were. They are perceived as luxury items, and hence occupy a low priority in many family budgets, particularly in families where one member has no use for them. Getting one of these modern marvels of technology into the house often requires much planning, even scheming, before one can even think of riding off at sunrise.

I became proud owner of my first motorcycle only with a good deal of luck. At a neighborhood party one St. Patrick's Day I met Norbert Koch, whom I had seen the summer before riding a beautiful black BMW 600cc, when there was no chance of rain. During my teenage years in Germany, a machine such as this had represented to me the ultimate in motorcycling. For me such a machine had been as unattainable then as a Lamborghini is now. After several beers with chasers I succeeded in extracting a promise from Bert that whenever he was ready to part with his Beemer I should be the first in line to buy it. On May 5, 1989 he called me with the news that his doctor had advised him to give up motorcycling. If I were still interested I could have the bike for $500. With a bit of coaxing on my part senior management of the family could be convinced that the bike was a bargain hard to resist. So I became the owner of a 1972 BMW R 60/5 with 68,000 miles on the clock, a black beauty. It was the perfect bike to get back into the sport after not having sat on one for thirty-four years.

The following months were a period of learning. I learned to perform my own maintenance by studying service and repair manuals. I learned about what was going on inside an internal combustion engine by taking a course at a community college in small engine repair. The lawn mower had to serve as the guinea pig. It had to suffer a total disassembly, followed by a reassembly without any parts left over. I could have brought my motorcycle to class, but at this stage I would not have dared to invade the Beemer's innards. By trial and error I learned what kind of riding I liked most. I did not care for short trips to the corner store or to town to hang out with other bikers. Motorcycle rallies held little interest for me. Sunday afternoon rides of 100 miles or more were better than staying at home. I preferred round trips to going from point A to B and back to point A on the same road. In the end long round trips across country of several days or weeks duration emerged on top of the list. I had reached the point when it was time to take another look at Black Beauty. Is this the bike I want to take around the world?

With more the 80,000 miles behind it the Beemer was beginning to show signs of aging. Timing chain and clutch were due for replacement. There were several small oil leaks. Who knows what surprises were lurking in the shadows once the engine was opened up. Its gas mileage had never been good, and the size of the fuel tank did not allow a great distance between fill-ups. It was still thirsting for leaded gasoline, which was no longer available. I felt that its 600cc motor did not deliver enough power for long-distance motoring. I was ready for an upgrade. But how could I convince family management that I had outgrown Black Beauty?

In December 1990 a new factor entered the equation. My father had passed away. At the funeral in Germany my brother Heinz and I discovered that he had left a bit of money to his two sons. Most of his life Dad had been an avid motorcyclist. He had owned a number of motorcycles before the postwar German Economic Miracle induced him to buy a car. The bike I remember best was built in the same year I was born, a 1937 Zündapp 200cc with the output of a phenomenal 6 hp, a bike with which I earned my operator's licence for motorcycles at the age of sixteen. We all agreed (or at least it appeared that we all did) that Father would have liked to see me invest his bequest in a new motorcycle. Objections were overruled. So on April 4, 1991 a brand new BMW R 100 GS PD joined the household. I'm sure Dad would have approved.

Now I had two motorcycles, an expensive luxury. Selling Black Beauty was out of the question. Bert Koch, its former owner, who had passed away recently, would have turned in his grave. I would have to make sure the bike found a good home, and this was impossible with strangers. When I discussed this dilemma with my brother, he had an elegant and rather intriguing solution. As a teenager he had owned a motorcycle, which was traded in for a car when he got married, since his wife did not like motorcycles. If his own older brother were to sell him a motorcycle for the price of, say, one (1) dollar, could his wife possibly refuse such an offer, perhaps running the risk of hurting the feelings of her brother-in-law? The deal was struck as suggested, and Black Beauty returned to the place of her origin. Alas, during the years that followed my brother had outgrown Black Beauty. Furthermore, his wife seems to have undergone a conversion. In the fall of 1997 they purchased a brand new BMW R 1100 R. Now he has two motorcycles. At present he is looking for a person with good character who wants to own a motorcycle, but who has a significant other that has no use for them.

To me the BMW R 100 GS PD (PD stands for Paris-Dakar, the legendary race in which the company competed in the early 1980s), affectionately nicknamed by the Germans *Gummikuh*, rubber cow, is the ultimate machine for adventure travel. Its mechanics and electrics are relatively simple. It delivers enough power for a quick run from A to B. Its nine-gallon tank gives it a reach of some 400 miles. With only one rider there is plenty of room for luggage. It has a relatively high ground clearance and an upswept exhaust, which allows passage through deep mud and water. With a low windshield, a comfortable seat, and a slightly forward riding position it is good for twelve-hour days or more in the saddle. It is the perfect machine for long-distance riding over roads that are less than perfect (such as from Paris to Dakar). Now I had the bike for the Big One. But there was still one important element missing: time.

As a university professor I was entitled to one month of holidays, no questions asked, after eleven months of service, when it should have been the other way around. How far can one go on a motorcycle in one month? Up to Prudhoe Bay and back; down to Panama and back; perhaps from Paris to Dakar and back. One can forget going around the world. Since Jules Verne's book we know that for a circumnavigation of the globe one needs at least eighty days. In 1992, however, I was on a sabbatical leave, one whole academic year without teaching duties, one year dedicated to research leading to publication, something we academics must do in order not to perish. With a little juggling I was able to squeeze the required 80 days out of the system. However, when I started doing the calculation of the mileages involved for circumnavigating only South America, I had to admit that it could not be done in this time span, not even with a rubber cow. I decided, instead, to fly to Caracas, Venezuela, and circle South America by bus. I finished the trip in Cartagena, Colombia, 80 days and 33 buses later. Time, or the lack of it, seems to be responsible for the fact that most of us never get going on the Big One.

3. *Practising*

During the Summer of 1996 the last requirement for long-distance touring, that of time, was finally met. I decided to take up the university's offer of early retirement. In celebration of this new epoch in my life I decided to go on a long practice run for the Big One, a round trip to the Canadian Far East, to Newfoundland and Labrador.

All roads to Newfoundland, Canada's youngest and easternmost province, converge in North Sidney, Nova Scotia. From there at least two ferries depart daily to the island of Newfoundland, affectionately called "The Rock" by expatriates. A seventeen-hour ferry crosses over to Argentia in the eastern part of the province, not far from St. John's, the capital. A seven-hour ferry is headed for Channel-Port aux Basques, over 900 km west of the capital. Lewisporte, about half-way between Channel-Port aux Basques and St. John's is the port of embarcation for a twice-weekly ferry to Goose Bay, Labrador, famous for its airport, but not yet famous for being the easternmost terminus of the Trans-Labrador Highway, a newly completed road linking Goose Bay, Labrador with Eastern Quebec, making possible a round trip from Quebec City via the State of Maine, New Brunswick, Nova Scotia, Newfoundland, Labrador, and back to Quebec City. Travel guides claim that the Tanslabradoria leads through "the last pristine wilderness in North America," with "streams and lakes and ponds uncountable," "almost devoid of human habitation." What gave the final impulse to take this route was a note stating that the Translabradoria for all practical purposes can be considered to be no more than a logging road, very remote, without highway services, and very dangerous to drive. Having carefully avoided all gravel roads up to now, even a test run in the nearest sandpit, lest the bike's beautiful finish be marred, I decided that the time had come to see what this baby can do in the real world. This decision was the reason why on a beautiful evening in late July, one month into my retirement, the two of us, the Rubber Cow and its rider, had arrived at the toll booth of the ferry terminal in North Sidney, Nova Scotia.

"To Channel-Port aux Basques you say, sir?" said the friendly lady in the booth. "What is the number of your reservation?"

"Oh, so sorry," was my reply. "I didn't know that one needed a reservation. Can't I just hop on and go, me and my motorcycle?"

"Normally yes, sir, but tonight the one o'clock ferry is all booked up. But don't worry, motorcyclists are no problem. They can be stowed away easily in nooks and crannies where cars can't go. The final decision will of course rest with the boarding personnel. But I'm almost certain that they will put you on. I have to give you a stand-by boarding-card. Park your motorcycle at the head of the line of cars, and be back at twelve midnight for boarding."

The nice lady had not called me a "biker." Was it because of my dignified appearance, or because of the noble marque I was riding?

There was a four-hour wait ahead of us, and it was getting colder. An hour later a light drizzle was beginning to fall. Two hours later the announcement was made that because of rough weather the ferry would be late arriving, and that the new departure time would be 3:00 a.m. It was raining hard by now. All that waiting would have been in vain if I didn't get on. Lesson #1: Never show up at a ferry without a reservation.

Boarding at 2:00 a.m. went without a hitch. I wasn't even asked for my boarding-card. There were eight of us on motorcycles. The four Harleys somehow ended up on one side of the hold. On the other side were three Beemers (my GS, a K 75, and a brand-new R 1100 RS) and a Tokyo Chopper. Motorcycles were banished to the extreme forward section of the ship, without benefit of weather protection. The Harleys were ready to brave the elements proudly unprotected. Three of us on the other side, however, after having laboriously strapped down our steeds, covered them lovingly with raincovers, except Pat with the R 1100, who bemoaned the fact that he had failed to bring one, and that his beautiful German Metal might now be stained by a squall of seawater. This turned out to be one of Pat's least worries on this trip, for the rain kept coming down so hard by now that it would surely wash away any salt spray that might have the temerity to sneak down into the hold.

After finally settling down, we heard the announcement that because of government regulations passengers were not to occupy more than one seat, lie on the furniture, or sleep on the floor. Immediately people began to put together chairs to make beds, to lie on couches and benches, and to bed down on the floor for the night, so that the novice ferry travellers among us had a hard time finding floorspace to spend the next seven hours. Thank goodness for motion sickness pills!

Channel-Port aux Basques greeted us not only with a torrential downpour but also with gusting winds, which made vision difficult. The eight of us were strongly urged to proceed to the departure building, where I wanted to go anyway in order to make my onward reservation for Labrador: lesson learned. After we were all assembled in the departure lounge, the officials urged us strongly not to proceed on Highway #1, the Trans-Canada, saying that only 10 km from here began the worst stretch of highway in the whole of Newfoundland. For the following 25 km stretch of highway the forecast for the day and part of the night was winds gusting up to 130 km/h. As we looked on rather incredulously, out came the stories to underline their point. One RV driver reported that every year dozens, repeat, dozens of RV's get blown off the road on this stretch. A trucker mentioned that last year his rig had simply been dumped on its side, cab and all, ruining his whole cargo. One Old-Timer recalled that in the 1980s, when the train was still running, the Newfie Bullet as it was called somewhat tongue-in-cheek, it happened quite frequently that it was blown off the track by the storm, so that at times it had to be cancelled, or else tied down with steel cables. Then, to top it all, the trucker added, "As to bikers, I don't know what happens to them. Perhaps they are simply picked up, never to be seen again."

I saw the twitch of his lips, but conceded that these fear-mongers may have a point, and booked into the nearest hotel. It was only 11:00 a.m. Better to lose half a day of riding than to be abducted by a storm. Besides, this not-so-cheap hotel allowed me to sample typical Newfie cuisine, Salted Cod and Brewis, an acquired taste, to be sure. Newfie beer, however, brewed in St. John's, is excellent.

On the road again next morning I was grateful that the weather had considerably quieted down. Riding these disreputable 25 km of Hwy #1 without any problems, I noticed what was responsible for all the trouble along this stretch of road: a geographic feature of the land which shows the typical ventury effect so familiar to us from our Bing carburetors. Motorcycling does indeed open your horizon.

This was to be Stage One of the trip: Newfoundland until the time of departure of the ferry to Labrador. There were two full days left for a fleeting acquaintance with The Rock. One particular place on this side of the island had fascinated me since the late 60s, since my days as a graduate student of Germanic Studies. One of my professors of Old Icelandic, or Old Norse, had just completed a new translation from the Icelandic of the two thirteenth-century sagas recounting the Vikings' discovery of North America in the year 1000, the landing of Leif Erikson and his followers in Vînland, or Wineland, as they called it. At the same time as we were being flogged with the intricacies of Old Norse grammar, a Norwegian team headed by Helge and Anne Stine Ingstad, true believers in the written word, had discovered the exact location of Leif Erikson's legendary place of sojorn in North America, near the present village of L'Anse aux Meadows in north-western Newfoundland. The two days available would be enough to ride up the 700 km or so to the Viking site over Highway #430, fittingly named the Viking Trail, to look around, and to ride a further 700-odd km back down to Lewisporte in time to catch the ferry.

The Viking Trail leaves Highway #1 at Deer Brook, turning north, where #1 continues east. So far roads in Newfoundland had been unexpectedly good, and continued to be so. I was particularly intrigued by the local practice, which I had not noticed anywhere in the world, of signposting an upcoming pothole exactly 1 km ahead. As one approached the hole, a speed would be recommended at which it would presumably be save to hit it, usually 50 km/h. Pat, proud owner of the R 1100 RS, whom I met again that evening at the end of the Viking Trail, told me the sad story of how he probably had disregarded the suggested speed of impact. His ABS control unit had detached from the frame and had damaged the rim of his rear wheel. The question whether or not this is covered by warranty was surely the subject of numerous nightmares during the following nights. Poor Pat. I guessed that signposting the potholes in the roads is cheaper than fixing them.

The first 50 km into the Viking Trail are simply spectacular. The meticulously maintained road sweeps through Gros Morne National Park. Wide sweeping curves, rolling hills, and passing lanes on grades come together for a motorcyclist's dream course. Hiking trails, fjords with tail-slapping whales, numerous moose grazing unperturbed along both sides of the road (I counted eight in two days) invite the nature lover to linger for a while. How can this almost perfect scenery be topped? The following 400-odd km of the Viking Trail can only be somewhat of an anticlimax. The road becomes flat and straight as it hugs the south shore of the Gulf of St. Lawrence. Dozens of fishing villages, nestled in coves along the way, testify to one of the chief pursuits of the Newfoundlanders. Excitement built again as we approached the last section, when the road turns inland, and winds its way over a low mountain range up to the Viking site.

It had begun to drizzle again as we approached this last section of the Viking Trail. Low-level clouds and fog created an eerie atmosphere. We felt as if trans-ported into the realm of Old Norse mythology, into the land of people who had believed in Wodan, Thor, and Freia, no trivial deities these. After all they have given us three days of the week: Wodansday, Thorsday, and Freiasday. We seemed to be riding through the setting of Richard Wagner's *Ring*. Bring on the music, maestro. No, no, not from the *Götterdämmerung*. Something more lively, something that goes with riding a motorcycle. Yes, "The Ride of the Valkyries" is just perfect to capture the mood. Please, maestro, *da capo,* one more time, this time *fortissimo.*

The Viking site itself met all of my expectations. Those unacqainted with the background would do well to visit first the interpretation centre on the site, which introduces visitors to the settlement with a film and a life-size display of scenes from the daily life of these early visitors to North America.

A few more miles up the road lies the little village of St. Anthony, famous for its lighthouse on Fishing Point, overlooking a section of the North Atlantic aptly named Iceberg Alley, Titanic country. From the tables in the adjacent Lightkeeper's Café, while sipping your favorite brew, you can watch icebergs cruising by on their way to oblivion. On the day of my visit, however, because of the prevailing Wagnerian mood, the icebergs were hiding behind a thick wall of fog. But no matter, we will have plenty of opportunity to see icebergs en masse on our way up Iceberg Alley to Labrador.

Next day pouring rain accompanied us all the way down the Viking Trail, and east on #1, until we reached Lewisporte. Only bikers and toddlers can know the feeling of sitting all day on a wet diaper. At the Bed and Breakfast I was stay-ing at St. Anthony, I overheard the landlady complaining that they have had sev-enteen days of rain, followed by one good day, and it looked as though the cycle would be repeated. Looking around town I noticed that lilacs were still in bloom, and that you could pick your own strawberries: this at the end of July. Since her husband was a member of the local Chamber of Commerce I told him that I loved Newfoundland, but that they ought to be doing something about the weather. "We are trying," he replied, "and have been since the time of Leif Erikson. The Vikings abandoned the place as hopeless, but we're not giving up!"

At Lewisporte the trip had entered Stage Two. With a proper reservation for one rider and one motorcycle in hand, buying a ticket and boarding the Sir Robert Bond went smoothly. Strapping down the Rubber Cow posed no problem. Mine was the only motorcycle on board. The ferry carried about a dozen RVs, and several transport trucks. The rest of the available cargo space was filled with containers on temporary wheels. The crossing was scheduled to take some thirty-six hours, on a course east, i.e. outside, of Iceberg Alley.

When I handed over my credentials to the purser I was informed that I was going to "have a male birth." Not being aware that I was pregnant. I must have looked a bit stunned. Then the purser tried again, explaining to me that I was to share a room or "a cabin" with three other males. But, he added, since no one else had booked, I had the place to myself. Lucky, I thought, at least I can deliver in privacy. I caught on rather quickly though. He meant a "male berth". Why don't they call those things simply "beds" like normal people?

One hour out of Lewisporte the weather cleared up. Of course. We had left The Rock. Bright sunshine greeted us as we entered Iceberg Alley. And here they came bearing down on us. Or were we bearing down on them? Icebergs of all sizes and configurations on both sides of the ship. Whoever designed these things must have had a vivid imagination. Each one was a prime example of customization: small, large, flat, curvy, smooth, jagged, globular, triangular, etc. No assembly line production here. Harley owners, eat your hearts out! I hoped that the ship's radar was in working order, or else, Titanic, here we come! On the other hand this would probably be the last chance in my lifetime to get into the Guinness Book of Records as the first rider ever to hit an iceberg with a motorcycle. Alas the Captain did not co-operate.

As we entered Groswater Bay, at whose head lie the twin cities of Goose Bay/Happy Valley, we had left the icebergs behind in the Atlantic. Whale-watching was now on top of the entertainment list for normal passengers, but not for one about to embark on a 500-mile bike ride on pristine gravel. This rider was busy examining a kit that had come with the bike, still in its original pouch, still unopened, a kit labelled "TIP TOP Original Vulcanisation." There was a piece of chalk, slightly crumbled, a tube of "Special Cement," something that looked like a large darning needle, but was called an "Inserting Tool," little rubber rings, an "Adapter," and three metal cartridges supposedly containing CO_2. Isn't that the stuff that makes your nose wet when you drink from a glass of freshly poured Coke? I tried to commit to medium-term memory the ten steps described in the enclosed pamphlet that the victim would have to observe if disaster struck. Now, what would happen if I blew my three cartridges, and the tire was still leaking? No answer. I guessed that this would be the moment when one reverted to prayer. I should have brought a tire pump.

Another thing I had to do before embarking on Stage Three of the trip was to enquire about the road. There should be some returnees on board this ship who would know about the condition of the Translabradoria. The first person I asked shook her head in disgust, and told me that "The Road" had ripped the oil pan right off her sister's car. She hadn't even been travelling that fast. When I asked her if she herself had ever travelled on The Road, she said no, and that she had no intention to do so, ever. Others knew similar tales of disaster. The one fellow's brother had to be towed back to Goose Bay, which cost him $1,500. Another remarked that you either choked to death in the dust, or drowned in the mud. And finally, some smartass type told me, when I asked him about the condition of the roads in Labrador, that I ought to get my grammar straight: "There are no roads in Labrador. Forget about those little bits and pieces you find here and there going nowhere. There is only **one** road in Labrador, Highway #500." He laughed. "We simply call it the Labrador 500." He had no idea of its condition, but he had heard that it was in bad shape. You had to admire the sense of humour of these people: "Newfie Bullet" for a train that moved like a turtle; "Labrador 500," a name that evoked memories of the Indianapolis 500, for a road that was probably not more than a logging trail. All the reports I could gather had two things in common: (1) all were horror stories, and (2) none of the informants had actually been on The Road.

One hour before docking rain began to fall. This came as no surprise. Politically Labrador is part of the Province of Newfoundland. It follows that they had to show solidarity with The Rock in regard to the weather as well. Therefore, unpack the rainsuit, and forget about camping!

The first kilometer of the Labrador 500 is sand; beautiful, soft sand such as one would find at a beach. A big "welcoming" sign at km 0 warns the motorist of the dangers ahead: no fuel, no services, bad road conditions. A quick check confirmed that we were well-prepared for the trip: all fluids topped up, nuts and bolts where they should be and tight, tire pressure O.K. When I left this morning the owner of the Berth and Breakfast in Happy Valley had given me the only positive message so far: last week two bikers from the States had gone through. What happened to them, I wanted to know. He didn't know, he said, but that was a good sign. When I facetiously added that I might find two skeletons along the way, he was not amused. "Just be careful!" he replied.

The posted speed limit was 60 km/h. No problem. Then the sand changed to light gravel, than to deeper, more recently added, gravel, and the speed limit became an imaginary figure, to stay out of my reach until I reached Churchill Falls almost 300 km later. One positive side of the still heavily falling rain was that it kept the dust down. There was no mud, and almost no traffic. I counted fewer than twenty vehicles all day, most of them trucks. The rain, however, caused many little creeks to overflow; they were running across the road, some up to eight inches deep. Crossing these was a lot of fun. It was safe and we felt like the macho guy in the BMW advertisement. If the first third of the road was relatively dull, the second third made up for it in scenery. As far as the eye could see, virgin forest, rolling hills, at times raging rivers, then quiet lakes and bubbling brooks. The scenery was a replay of what I had seen in Gros Morne National Park. But whereas in Gros Morne everything showed the ordering hand of the caretaker, here everything was in a condition totally untouched by human hands. At times I felt that this was also true of The Road, particularly during the last third. The last 50 km before Churchill Falls were probably responsible for the horror stories I had heard. First generation gravel with head-size clunkers at times half exposed made the bike buck all over the road like a bronco on steroids, even if I slowed down to 15 km/h. One could only clench one's teeth and hope the fillings wouldn't fall out. Auto-body parts were lining The Road, many hub caps and other unidentifiable metal or plastic objects. Grading this part seemed impossible. It would have meant scraping everything off down to the bare soil. What was needed here was new gravel, hundreds and hundreds of truckloads of it. Stopping for R and R was out of the question. One nasty little surprise not mentioned in the travel guides was the voracious appetite of Labrador's bugs. When nature called it was a race against time to beat these little savages. Millions of them would zoom in for a once in a lifetime chance to ensure the survival of the species. While you fumbled with zippers, elastics, and shirt tails, these little monsters would get their pound of flesh, so to speak, no matter how fast you were. After riding off defeated time and again you would be scratching your wounds for the next several miles. After 10 hours in the saddle almost non-stop the body's caffeine level was approaching zero, blood sugar was in negative balance, and the crankiness index had reached an all-time high. The amenities of Churchill Falls were a welcome relief.

Churchill Falls is a company town, planned on a geometric pattern around its 5.4 megawatt-producing hydro-electric power plant. Gasoline is available at the convenience store: two pumps, both delivering Regular only. The Churchill Falls Inn, however, offers high octane fuel in its dining room both in liquid and in solid form, in keeping with its well-appointed rooms. Leaving this temporary haven very early next morning required a great deal of will-power.

It looked as though The Road would continue the same way it had ended yesterday. But after some 20 minutes of riding there was a marked improvement. I was thrilled to be able to reach the speed limit of 60 km/h, and even exceed it at times. Was The Road really getting better, or was I getting better on this rather tricky surface? To my delight I noticed that the faster you went the more solid the bike became. At 70 km/h you could hit a section of lose gravel without as much as getting a wiggle out of the machine, whereas the same type of gravel would be quite difficult to handle at a lower speed. Getting up the speed, of course, became a non-issue if you were riding over a washboard surface. This, fortunately, happened only rarely. At noon I had covered the remaining 250 km to the twin cities of Labrador City/Wabush, rather rusty looking places, because of the iron ore mined there.

I had memorized my TIP TOP manual for nothing, and I wasn't complaining. Labrador gravel turned out to be natural washed gravel as found on the side of the road. The pebbles were ground smooth by millions of years of glacial activity, similar to wave activity on a beach. It is tire-friendly gravel, unlike that made of crushed stone, the sharp corners of which are tire slashers.

This should actually have been the end of the trip, were it not for the fact that there were still some 250 km of gravel ahead of us before we reached asphalt. The last 15 km of The Road are paved until it crosses the border into Quebec, and becomes Quebec Highway #389, reportedly "partly paved." The next 50 km, however, were gravel, and so bumpy and slow that they may be compared with the worst section of the Labrador 500. One small compensation was the fact that the scenery was again superb. Then lo and behold, there is pavement, glorious pavement. Let me stop and kiss it! The speed limit is posted as 90 km/h. In this neck of the woods, where the next gas station is 200 km away, there are no cops, no people, and there is virtually no traffic. One marvels over how much more beautiful the scenery becomes when viewed from a vehicle running over a smooth surface. This pleasure was short-lived, however, for 75 km later it was back to gravel, this time smooth gravel, permitting a higher top speed. One very unpleasant side-effect of very fast gravel is the fact that one gets bombarded with missiles of various sizes by oncoming traffic. This is why we have that funny-looking jailhouse grill on our headlights. I heard numerous "dings" at various pitch-levels, but no glass shattering. After we reached the hydro-electric generating station of Manic 5, pavement returned for good. The rest of the 389 down to its end at Baie-Comeau was a fulfilment of the fantasies experienced during the first part, twisties all the way on excellent pavement. When finally the Golden Arches of Baie-Comeau beckoned in the distance, I knew that I was back in civilization as we know it.

The ride the rest of the way to the place I call Home was over my favorite roads north of the St. Lawrence River. In this practice run I had covered over 5,000 road km in eleven days. When I took the bike out the next morning for a wash and to examine the battle scars, it was evident that it had lost its innocence. The Rubber Cow was no longer a heifer. It had matured, and had the scars to prove it.

North America

4. *The Assault on Prudhoe Bay*

After weeks of anxiety, elation, fear, and hesitation, I decided that the First of July, 1997, Canada Day, was a good day to leave for the Big One, which was to begin with an East-West crossing of Canada, starting in my hometown, Ottawa, the Nation's Capital. Now that I had all that time, some money to spare, and a great motorcycle, my masterplan was to circumnavigate the Americas following a figure eight. The top loop, around North America, would be in a counterclockwise direction, west across Canada, up to Alaska to the end of the road, then down on the Pacific side, and through Central America. The bottom loop, around South America, would be in a clockwise direction, at first east to the Atlantic side, then south to the end of the road, up on the Pacific side, through Central America, then along the Gulf of Mexico, over to Key West, Florida, and finally, north along the Atlantic coast. Central America was to be the point of intersection of the two loops. I planned a crossing of each country along the way, and if possible a visit to each country's capital city. But few people knew about the whole plan, lest I was unable to pull it off and lost face. There was no way to avoid revealing my secret to some people, however, such, as, for instance the officers of the Canadian Automobile Association (CAA), whom I approached for a *Carnet de passage en douane*, a document required by some South American countries for customs purposes. To get this document I had to post a bond for three times the value of the vehicle, in my case for $23,160.00 Canadian, which would be returned to me when the bike was back in Canada. For the rest of the world, including family, I was going North to Alaska.

The only other preparation for the trip was fitting a new set of tires. On the day of departure the odometer read 47,300 km.

Leavetaking was a harrowing experience. As I was riding off at sunrise the last words of my wife were ringing in my ears: "I hope it rains every day!" That seemed unlikely at this time. There was not a cloud in the sky and a mild tailwind was blowing from the South. Toward noon near Val-d'Or it began to cloud over. As I crossed the Quebec border into Ontario the rain started. It came down in buckets as I reached Timmins at seven o'clock in the evening. Is the Rain Curse working already?

Having covered more than 700 km, the last 200 km in pouring rain, I had enough for my first day. Since I had read that hotel accommodation in Alaska was quite expensive I had brought my camping gear with me and was ready to try it out. But in Timmins no campground was to be found. I was told, however, that some twenty minutes west on Highway #101 there was a place where camping was possible.

The sign I was looking for hung half-obscured on a crooked flag-pole: *Fred's Half-Way*. Fred was an outfitter and guide for fishermen and hunters. There were some camping trailers for rent to overnighters, and also a small restaurant. I was allowed to pitch my tent in a convenient spot of my choosing, since I didn't need a plug-in for electricity and water. After set-up, which went rather quickly in the rain, I went looking for human contact and a beer. The restaurant was just about to close. A grey-haired fellow was sitting behind the counter shovelling in large chunks of meat and potatoes. It was Fred himself. If the name of the place had any meaning in the context of what I saw, it was certainly an understatement. Fred was gone at least three quarters of the way, as he barely managed to keep from falling face-down into his plate. Asked how much I had to pay for the night, he mumbled, "five bucks." The others in the room ignored him.

Then question period started, a routine which was to be repeated again and again in the following weeks and months. Where from? Where to? How? Why? They had almost made it to Alaska once. But then something had come up. They couldn't go, and regretted it ever since. Perhaps someday. There, at Fred's Half-Way, I had to come to terms with my new status as traveller, to validate myself, to quit looking at the watch, to let The Trip take over. It rained all night.

Packing soaking-wet camping gear is no fun, and neither is riding off in the rain without breakfast. Fred and his people must have been sleeping it off. There was no sign of life at the early hour of my departure. Breakfast in Foleyet, and finally a break in the clouds. Ontario Highway #101 is a lonely road. There was hardly any traffic until I reached Wawa at eleven o'clock, where #101 merges with #17, the Trans-Canada Highway. During the coffee break, when I met Erich, the German adventure motorcyclist, the rain started again.

Finding the campground in Nipigon was easy. A big sign showed the way to the Silverwood Park Campground. The wet camping gear got even wetter. The rain never stopped all night. At the second try I was perfecting my technique of packing wet camping gear in the rain with my rainsuit on.

Off again in the rain, but not for long. Some 60 km down the road I saw the flashing lights of two cruisers of the Ontario Provincial Police at a road block. "What have I done?" flashed through my mind. I tried to remember all the traffic violations I had committed during the past half-hour, since leaving the Silverwood Park Campground. There had been a flashing red light in Nipigon. Had I come to a full stop? I had coasted through a stop sign before entering the main highway. Passing on a solid double line? And just now I was doing 60 in a 50 km/h zone. There goes my travel money. I wondered if they take cash or Chargex? I stopped and turned off the engine.

There were only two police officers. One got out of his cruiser; the other stayed inside.

"Good morning, officer," I said with what I thought was my most winning smile. "Is anything wrong?"

He didn't hear me, for he was looking questioningly at me. I had forgotten to open the visor of my helmet. That is how nervous I was.

"You cannot continue on this highway, Sir. We're not letting anyone through," he said. "Forty kilometers from here, just this side of Thunder Bay, the road is washed out. It will take until tomorrow night to repair it. I suggest you go to the motel over there, dry out, and try again later."

It was 8.00 a.m. The motel still had a vacancy. So I followed the officer's suggestion and booked a room for two nights. I did not like to leave in the evening and perhaps have an encounter with a moose. Yesterday an old timer told me that this year alone over thirty moose had been killed by drivers. None so far by bikers. I didn't want to be the first one. It was time anyway for doing the laundry. The Grann Motel at Pass Lake Corner was as good a place as any to do it.

This was the perfect location for a road block. On the south side of the highway was the motel, a grocery store, a liquor store, and a service station. On the north side was another service station, much larger, with a giant parking lot for trucks, and a 24-hour restaurant. It was in the restaurant that all stranded motorists eventually ended up, a place to commiserate with one another, and to exchange tales of the road. I overheard one trucker mentioning the fact that this was the only place all across Canada where only one single road connected both halves of the country.

"We could be attacked, and no-one could come to our rescue," he complained. "To get to Western Canada from here you would have to go back to Sault Ste. Marie and follow the south shore around Lake Superior in the States, a detour of 2,000 miles."

A party of sixteen people, also staying at the motel, found themselves in quite a predicament. They were expected to be in Thunder Bay to attend a wedding on Friday, tomorrow afternoon. One of the men happened to be the bridegroom.

"Is this a sign from Heaven?" he wondered aloud. "Good or bad?"

Then I overheard someone else saying that this was all the fault of *El Niño*. I had not heard that word before. I knew that in Spanish it meant "the little boy." Was this perhaps the nickname for some banana republic dictator like Papa Doc, or Baby Doc, who was blamed for everything, as the Communists used to be? I knew better. If there was to be any blame assigned to anyone, how about to the one who had laid the Rain Curse on my trip? I was to hear a lot more about *El Niño* later on, in South America, where "The Little Boy" was to make newspaper headlines almost every day.

At ten o'clock the liquor store opened its doors and was doing a booming business. At one o'clock the weather was clearing up, and the police had an update on the road: it could perhaps be reopened tonight at nine. Already there were dozens of transport trucks waiting to get through, and more were arriving by the minute. There were also many RVs and private cars, only one biker so far; no sign of Erich.

After lunch I had enough hanging around in the restaurant, listening to tales of woe. I went for a long walk down the highway toward Pass Lake. But this did not help cure my frustration. The sun was shining beautifully. I could be half-way up to Alaska by now. Instead I was forced to hang around this godforsaken place, condemned to inactivity. Why couldn't I relax and just enjoy myself? I was suffering from a severe attack of performance anxiety. Having been whipped into action all my life by parents, teachers, bosses, superiors and editors, do this, do that, work, perform, deliver, meet the deadline, sitting around doing nothing made me feel guilty, almost drove me crazy. Sure, I could read something, wash the bike, listen to the radio, watch television. But all that did not advance The Trip. I was stuck in Pass Lake Corner, deactivated maybe for yet another day.

The news was released at 9.00 p.m. The road would be reopened in one hour. With all my anxiety to get going, I forced myself to spend the night in the motel. Riding past the washout next morning I noticed by the scars that a motorcycle could easily have squeezed by on the remaining asphalt. In countries south of Mexico the police would have let you through at your own risk, to jump the gap, or drown. Up here we're overprotectd by "Our Friends and Helpers." As it may be, I was glad to be on a roll again.

Breakfast in Thunder Bay, then off to Dryden and Kenora, where I met two motorcyclists from Swift Current, Saskatchewan, both on beautifully restored 1972 BMW R 75/5's. They had tried to go to Newfoundland during their two weeks of holidays, but were forced by the weather to turn around. We rode together as far as Winnipeg, where I wanted to buy some spare oil filters. Everyone who had been there told me that auto parts were very expensive in Alaska, and I had no reason to believe that this would be different for motorcycle parts, if one could get them at all. One of the mechanics at the BMW dealership told me that he had just come back from a trip to Alaska. He was ecstatic and was ready to go again. Things like these I wanted to hear.

As soon as I had set up my tent at the Portage La Prairie Campground it started to rain, and continued throughout the night. In spite of the wetness the mosquitoes kept up their barrage mercilessly. Drinking beer before retiring is not a good idea. The toilets and even the showers were full of these little pests. At noon, near the Manitoba/Saskatchewan border the weather improved somewhat. At 6.00 P.M. I arrived in Saskatoon in bright sunshine. I was happy to note that the sun still makes an appearance now and then and has not left the country for good.

As I settled down for the night, by all appearances a dry night, in a *de luxe* campground near the Saskatoon Airport, I noticed that the campground was full of Jehovah's Witnesses, who were in town for a religious convention. Could this be the reason why the weather was so good? Perhaps—. They were a great bunch of neighbours, nice to talk to. One elderly couple in a camper next to my tent told me that in their youth they had also toured the country on a motorcycle, a Matchless, and had loved it. Asked why they had chosen a motorcycle for their travels at a time when motorcyclists were less than highly regarded, they replied that they had never cared much about what "the world" was thinking about them. They had wanted some adventure in their "otherwise dull lives filled with boring routines." Their motorcycle had provided the real thing, not virtual reality as we get on television, or in movies. On their bike they had felt alive and ready to meet any challenge. Then they asked me, since I was travelling alone, if I did not feel lonely sometimes, and tempted to turn around and go home. I had to admit that at times, particularly when I was wet, cold, and tired, the thought had occurred to me that this was stupid. How nice it would be at home in my warm bed. If I looked at my watch during these moments, it would almost invariably be around five o'clock in the afternoon, time for dinner, time to warm up and elevate the blood sugar level. They knew what I was trying to say, having had similar experiences themselves. "Now," Fred added, "years later, we still have our memories, good memories, and that's what it's all about." His wife nodded approval, and with these words in our minds we decided to retire for the night.

If, indeed, Jehovah had a hand in this change of weather he/she did a good job. The air was so dry that my wet towel outside was dry in the morning. An immaculately blue sky accompanied us all the way to North Battleford, on to Highways #4 and #26 North and Northwest, then #55 West via Lac La Biche to Athabasca. But never satisfied, I had another complaint. I was getting rather bored with pencil-straight and level roads, miles and miles of bright yellow canola fields, grain elevators that all looked alike so that you began to think that you had gone in circles for the past half hour. I kept wishing for just one teeny-weeny curve. When finally on #55 there were a few twisties, the tires of the bike squealed with delight. They were already beginning to look like car tires, acquiring a square profile. The scenery, on the other hand, was magnificent. The never-ending sea of yellow canola fields we had passed earlier was giving way to forests and lakes. Some working oil wells could be seen among the trees. Bluebird Camping in Athabasca was near a golf club that I could walk over to for a snack and a beer. Toilets and showers were spotlessly clean. There were no mosquitoes. And the best yet, there was no rain in the forecast.

The scenery of *The Northern Woods and Waters Route*, Highways #54 and #2 of Northern Alberta, appeared to be stuck in an endless loop. As far as the eye could see, from horizon to horizon, the road was a straight line, at times a bit up and down, that was all. Fighting a strong gusting headwind, we arrived in Dawson Creek, British Columbia, at four o'clock in the afternoon, three o'clock local time. Traffic in town made one think that one had arrived in a southern metropolis. Motorhomes of all sizes, some towing cars, some boats, some both, were crawling through the streets, blocking intersections. Heavy semis made you look twice before you tried to sneak by. Passenger cars displayed licence plates from across Canada and the United States, including Alaska. Dawson Creek, with a population of some 12,000, not including dogs, put on a good show displaying its status as Mile "0" of the Alaska Highway, the Alcan. As a railhead during the construction of the Alcan in 1942 the town must have been bursting at the seams. Today the annual rush of tourists supplies the excitement. There are hotels, motels, and campgrounds that cater to any budget. As I pitched my tent in the Alahart RV Park almost in the center of town, I was hoping that the rest of the way up to Alaska would not be as busy as this. At this latitude it was not getting dark until 10.00 p.m. There was still plenty of time to take a few pictures at the real Mile "0" in the middle of town, as well as at the picturesque sign they put up in a large parking lot near a grain elevator, in order to alleviate road congestion downtown caused by ardent photographers. After shopping for some necessities, having dinner at the famous Alaska Cafe and Pub, I remarked to the waitress that the strong west wind had not abated, and asked her what that meant around here. She assured me that this would augur good weather for tomorrow. I hoped she was right, and gave her a generous tip. After all it took me six days and a total of 4,290 km (2,681 miles) to get here.

1) *Dawson Creek: Alaska highway Mile "0"*

2) *Watson Lake: sign forest*

At breakfast in Fort St. John the fellow next to my table asked if he could join me. Always ready for any human contact I invited him warmly. Don McLean, tall, handsome, with a greying mop of hair, owned his own business, Home Renovations. His pickup truck was parked outside. When I spelled my name for him I was teasing him about his: With the name of McLean he should be in the Hamburger business instead. He shot right back with the suggestion that I should be in the advertising business for motorbiking retirees. He had a great sense of humor. I like that in a person. We exchanged travel stories. Don had been up to Alaska and had visited most of the western Lower Forty-Eight. He bemoaned the fact that his business did not allow him more time off for travel. He added that this was one of the reasons why he was always trying to befriend passing travellers, so that at least he could dream along with them. Don had to leave and go back to work. I promised to send him a postcard from Prudhoe Bay. After I had finished my second cup of coffee and wanted to pay the bill, the waitress told me that the fellow I had been with had paid for me. A couple of days ago I had seen a bumper sticker with the message: *Commit Random Acts of Kindness.* This was one. It made the day a little brighter.

Past Fort Nelson the highway ascends into the Rocky Mountains and the scenery picks up as the traffic gets thinner. There were long stretches of road construction, and consequently long lessons in negotiating loose gravel. The scenery was so overwhelming that one tended to forget the difficult road conditions. Shortly before reaching my target for the day, Watson Lake, Yukon Territory, it started to rain, and continued unabated during tent set-up at the Downtown RV Park, and during the night. What else is new? On this day we had covered almost exactly 1,000 km, my all-time best.

Since I am a stickler for motorcycle maintenance, I had been casting anxious glances at the odometer yesterday, so as not to overshoot the interval when the bike was due to be serviced. It was due today. Someone up there must be looking kindly upon the Rubber Cow, for the rain stopped just long enough to allow me to pull off the valve covers, retorque the head-bolts, and check valve clearances. This must be done when the engine is cold. I had brought along my torque wrench and a set of sockets thinking that if I were nice to the bike, it wouldn't, couldn't possibly let me down. Everything looked as it should.

After rolling up the dripping wet camping equipment we were off to see the world-famous Watson Lake Signpost Forest. If Carl Lindley, a soldier in the U.S. Army working on the construction of the Alcan, had known in 1942 the tradition that he was establishing when in a fit of homesickness he put up a sign displaying the name of his hometown, DANVILLE, ILLINOIS, he would have put a fence around it and charged a fee to all those wishing to add their own. At the time of my visit the number of signs was estimated to exceed 30,000, and growing by the day. They were lined up on both sides of broad walkways that intersected one another like city streets. Anyone visiting the site is welcome to add a sign. There is no charge. Someone influential should make an attempt to export some of this spirit to Deadhorse, Prudhoe Bay, Alaska, which suffers from a total deficiency of it. Perhaps then the place would become a little more people-friendly.

The rain accompanied us almost all the way to Whitehorse, and stopped only after we had registered at the Sourdough Country Campsite, some ten miles south of the city. It was time for an engine oil and filter change. This has to be done while the engine is hot. Having bought the oil downtown, I tackled the job at the campground. It is a messy job. If the BMW engineers of *Sparte Motorrad* had to change their own oil and filter on the road, they would have designed a better access to the oil filter. No matter what I tried I could never manage to do this without messing up myself as well as the area surrounding the bike, creating a miniature environmental disaster. A nice dinner in town was called for to celebrate another 7,500 km of respite before the next oil and filter change was due.

It was a good time to visit Whitehorse, capital city of the Yukon Territory. The city was in the midst of its centennial celebration of the famous Klondike Gold Rush (1896-1898). Special events were put on to mark this occasion. Downtown one could see ladies in period costumes, and men sporting full beards like the '98 Stampeders. After the completion of the White Pass and Yukon Railway in 1900, it was here that the stampeders had to change from trains to riverboats to get to Dawson, their final destination. One of the stern-wheelers that made this trip down the Yukon River, the *SS Klondike,* beautifully restored, can still be seen downtown beside the Yukon River bridge. Mining for gold and other metals still plays a dominant role in the city's economy. But even more important is its role as a transportation centre for the Yukon and North West Territories. In fact during the construction of the Alcan Highway, Whitehorse served as one of the construction headquarters. Today tourism also injects a healthy amount of money into the city's purse. The shops, hotels, restaurants, cabarets, and bars live up to the expectations of most travellers, and will continue to do so even after 1998, when other anniversaries will come due.

Blue skies greeted us the next morning when we left the Alaska Highway to follow the "Klondike Loop," Yukon Highway #2, to make our way up to Dawson. It was cold. I had to stop after half an hour to walk around and warm up. Lake Laberge to our right was a place I had marked on my map as a "must-see," since it was here, on another cold day some hundred years ago around Christmas-time that a "strange" event happened, at least according to the poet Robert Service. The shore of Lake Laberge was the setting for his ballad "The Cremation of Sam McGee."

The poet, writing in the first person, and his companion, Sam McGee from Plumtree, Tennessee, had been on their way to Dawson by dogsled. The cold was unbearable. In fact it was so horribly cold that McGee could stand it no longer. Before he died he extracted the promise from his companion that the latter would cremate him, at least then he would no longer have to freeze. After days of travelling with the frozen corpse the narrator finally got a break when he reached Lake Laberge (He got the vowels mixed up, "Lake Lebarge"=Lake Laberge). There in the ice was stuck a wrecked steamer with its boiler still intact. He fired it up and shoved in the remains of Sam McGee, in order to keep his promise. After a long time he returned to take a peek. He opened the door,

> And there sat Sam, looking cool and calm, in the heart of the furnace roar;
> And he wore a smile you could see a mile, and he said: "Please close the door.
> It's fine in here, but I greatly fear you'll let in the cold and storm...
> Since I left Plumtree, down in Tennessee, it's the first time I've been warm."

The writer concludes his account with the words,

> There are strange things done in the midnight sun
> By the men who moil for gold;
> The Arctic trails have their secret tales
> That would make your blood run cold;
> The Northern Lights have seen queer sights,
> But the queerest they ever did see
> Was that night on the marge of Lake Lebarge
> I cremated Sam McGee.

This day in July was again a cold day on the shores of Lake Laberge, with a fierce northwind blowing. I did not wish to linger. I was overdue for breakfast.

A small restaurant on the left of the highway looked inviting. Inside the Cranberry Point Bed and Breakfast a woodstove was blazing. Nestling up close I ordered my favorite breakfast, French Toast. "Two pieces, please." The waitress warned me that their pieces were rather big, since they baked their own sourdough bread and the loaves were quite large. I replied that I was hungry and man enough to handle two. Why do I always have to brag? When the order arrived I didn't believe my eyes. Each of the two pieces was the size of a toilet seat. I had a hard time finishing them. But finish I did, and the honour of my manhood was safe for another day. After that and a generous helping of caffeine, the air outside no longer felt cold.

About half-way to Dawson the road was excellent. It curved gently through the northern forest, around lakes, over rivers, and low mountains, a road made for motorcycling. However, the pleasure of the second half was spoiled by two long construction zones. They had torn up the remaining asphalt, had added more fill, and were now in the process of grading it. In order to pack the surface really well they soaked it with water. Large tank trucks were flooding the whole road. There was no escape. In no time the bike was covered with mud. Mud was building up around the projecting cylinder heads of the boxer engine; it was blocking the oil cooler, and was covering man and machine from top to bottom, including the farthest recesses, in uniform Yukon brown. Back to asphalt we would have welcomed a good thunderstorm to wash away the worst. But no rain was in sight. We arrived in Dawson at 4.00 p.m. under brilliant blue skies. The first thing to do was to go to a carwash and hose down bike and rider, before we could think of looking around.

There was no doubt we were in Dawson. The giant slag heaps at the entrance of the town were a powerful reminder. Some maps call this place Dawson City, to distinguish it from Dawson Creek. I find it difficult to follow their example. The name "Dawson City" evokes memories of metropolitan centres such as Mexico City, or Panama City, both with populations in the millions. Dawson boasts a little over 2,000, and this in the summer. There were more dogs than people. On this Thursday afternoon Dawson looked to me like a ghost town.

When we were tolerably clean we looked for the campground. It was on the other side of the river. Would we be stuck there after hours? "No fear," said the bearded mariner operating the car ferry across the Yukon. "This ferry runs 24 hours a day on demand. No charge." The Yukon Territory Government Campground on the other side of the river has an idyllic setting along the river bank. I pitched my tent next to the site occupied by a large camping trailer, whose owner introduced himself as Rod.

By this time the effects of the french toast for breakfast had worn off, and the smells drifting over from my neighbour's campfire were tantalizing. I yelled over that he must be a gourmet cook judging by the smells, to which he replied with an invitation for dinner. I excused myself for not even being able to bring flowers for the charming host, but said that I would nevertheless accept the invitation, if I could invite him in return for a beer in town. No reply. Rod served a gourmet meal consisting of corn on the cob, barbecued steak with mushrooms, and roasted potatoes, washed down with lemonade.

This was the second year Rod had visited Dawson. Last year he had stayed two weeks at the same campground. This year he had planned for four. This was his second week. He said he needed more time this year for recuperation, for the past year had been a disaster for him. He had lost his job with a computer company in Prince George, British Columbia. His wife had left him taking the two children with her. Their house was up for sale. The only things he could call his own at present were his car and his camping trailer. I commiserated with him about his bad luck, and told him about my trip, and that I was interested in learning more about Dawson. He provided a wealth of information on that subject. After the seat of the Territorial Government was moved to Whitehorse in 1953, the governments, both federal and territorial, were trying to keep the place alive by restoring the old buildings and making it into a kind of museum, a tourist attraction, so that it could pay its way. This explained the big hype about the Klondike Gold Rush Centennial. There was still gold mining on a large scale in the area. In addition several hundred individual prospectors were making a living by panning or sluicing for the stuff, and of course tourism was a very important source of income. But the tourist season begins in earnest only after July 15, the following week, and will run until the middle of August. Most people living in town were directly involved in the tourist trade, which included running the gambling casino, and the various tourist attractions, such as the sites where visitors could pan for gold. It was getting late, and Rod kept looking at his watch. Then he said, "I'm sorry I can't accept your invitation for a beer. I'm due at an

Alcoholics Anonymous meeting at eight o'clock. They have a very active group here, and tonight I'm one of the speakers." We walked over to the ferry together. Rod went to his meeting, and I went to the Downtown Hotel.

The Sourdough Saloon of the hotel was sparsely populated at this early hour. Near the bar were a number of khaki-clad folk whom I judged to be tourists. In the back I saw a group of young people, probably college students here for a summer job. On the other side of the room sat a youngish looking guy with a short straggly beard, wearing a red checkered shirt, trademark of the Canadian lumberjack, grey woolen pants, and brown half-laced leather boots. He looked like a local resident. I took a seat at a table next to his, hoping that I could strike up a conversation with him. Fortified with my second bottle of Molson's I asked him what people do for excitement in this town; it looked rather dead to me. He said that on the next block was Diamond Tooth Gertie's Gambling Hall, a favorite place with many tourists. Perhaps this was my lucky day. I told him I had never won anything in my whole life, and did not see any reason why my luck should change in Dawson. He replied, judging by my outfit (I was still wearing my black leather riding gear) I didn't look that badly off. "Bikers aren't usually poor slobs." He wanted to know how much a trip like mine would cost per day. I made a quick calculation, and told him, I could manage with an average of $60, if I watched my drinking. He laughed and ordered another round for us. Of course I had to retaliate a little later. Then he insisted it was his turn, and again I retaliated, and so on. William ("Just call me Willie") said he lived much cheaper than that in his cabin in the bush. His mining operation brought in enough money for the pick-up truck outside, and for a few luxuries, like a couple of beers in the saloon, whenever he had to come to town for supplies. During the long winter months he ran a trapline, which barely paid its way, for the price of pelts was down. He was getting fed up with this kind of life. He'd rather be a biker. When I mentioned the name of one of his predecessors, George Carmack, the discoverer of the big strike along Bonanza Creek, not far from here, who had triggered the Klondike Gold Rush one hundred years ago, Willie said that he and all the prospectors he knew had dreams of some day striking it rich and becoming millionaires like Carmack. Only that kept them going. But after a while dreams wear thin. And he was ready to stop dreaming. It was not yet dark at 11.30 p.m.when I said goodnight to Willie and wished him well. To clear my head I walked up to take a look at the cabins of Robert Service and Jack London, two literary dreamers of the Gold Rush days, before heading back to the ferry. On this day my travel budget had taken quite a beating.

The next morning appeared to be the beginning of a perfect day for hitting the dirt of the Top of the World Highway, Yukon Highway #9. Immediately at the ferry stop on the north bank of the Yukon the road begins to climb to the top of a mountain range and stays up there until it merges near the border with Alaska Route #5, the Taylor Highway. The vistas from this road were simply spectacular; mountains as far as the eye could see, bordered only by the horizon, which seemed to merge with the clouds. From the point of view of scenery, this was so

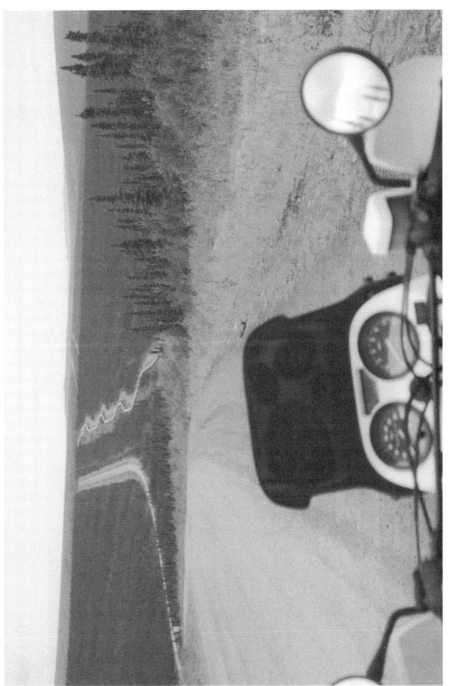

3) Dalton highway and Alaska pipeline

4) *Arctic circle monument*

far the highlight of the trip. For scenery I gave it an unqualified 10 out of 10, an A+. Alas, there was road construction for the first 30 km, and the tank trucks were pouring out load after load of water. In a few minutes the bike was covered again in familiar Yukon brown. Since there was little traffic, the rider received coverage only up to his knees. The next 40 km were paved, and the scenery looked all the more beautiful. Being able to take the twisties at a higher speed made up for the hardships suffered on the first stretch. 10 km before the Alaska border gravel returned, and became worse on the other side. The last 40 km of the Taylor Highway, before it joins the Alaska Highway, were paved.

On the roll on a dream road the rider wastes little time for coffee breaks. However, to stop for refreshments in "downtown" Chicken, Alaska, population 37, was *de rigeur*. Its popularity as a rest stop was vouched for by two busloads of tourists arriving with me. Service was slow. Service was faster in Tok, back on the Alcan, where we arrived at 3.00 p.m. Since it was still early and the road was good, we decided to go as far as Fairbanks.

After the "high" experienced on the Top of the World, this last stretch between Tok and Fairbanks proved to be an anticlimax. The long unbroken straight stretches of the road made you want to cry out for a curve, just one little curve. If it had not been for the absence of grain elevators and the presence of rather straggly looking trees, I would have thought we were back in Saskatchewan.

And then came the town of North Pole, just before Fairbanks, perhaps the tackiest piece of Alaskan real estate one can find, pure *Kitsch*. In North Pole stands, of course, Santa Claus House, where Old Ho-Ho-Ho lives with Ms. Claus, with their elves, with Rudolph and the other reindeers, where it's Christmas every day of the year, where you can plug in your motorhome at the Santaland RV Park and Campground, and where you can eat at the Elf's Den. All the grand-pas and grannies of the Lower Forty-Eight seemed to be up here lined up waiting for a spot in the Campground. Thank heavens for the four-lane highway that bypasses the town and takes you into Fairbanks quickly.

We arrived at the Fairbanks Trail's End RV Park at 6.30 p.m., set up the tent, and immediately went to a carwash to get rid of the worst mud on the bike. Night does not come at all to Fairbanks at this time of the year. There was still plenty of time to look over the Rubber Cow, to tighten nuts and bolts to specifications, to check the tires and do some laundry before the final assault on Prudhoe Bay the next day. No beer before retiring.

At breakfast near Fox, 17 km north of Fairbanks, I overheard a truckdriver who had just come down the road mentioning the fact that it had snowed the night before when he crossed Atigun Pass. Snow in the middle of July? Although it was overcast, and rather chilly, it did not look like precipitation. With enough fuel in both tank and stomach to last a while, we were looking forward to the challenges that lay ahead.

Some 45 km later, when pavement ended, there were broken clouds, and the scenery under bright sunshine looked like picture book Alaska. On hilltops the eye could follow the parallel lines of road and oil pipeline until they disappeared over the horizon. At times the pipeline zigzagged alongside the highway, presumably to slow down the flow of oil on a downgrade. Since the parking lot in front of the restaurant at the Yukon River Bridge resembled a quagmire, I decided that it was too early for a coffee stop and pushed on. So far the road was in good shape, packed gravel with some soft spots, very little dust or mud. Very soon I developed a high regard for the truckers, both oncoming and passing. After all, the Dalton Highway, Alaska Road #11, was their road, still called the Haul Road, and I felt like a trespasser. When oncoming they tried to move over on their side as far as possible, even slowing down, so as not to choke us in a desert storm, or to bombard us with missiles. They behaved like true professionals and gentlemen. At noon the clouds closed, and a light drizzle began to fall, which kept the dust down, but which was not strong enough to create mud. After a brief stop at the Arctic Circle monument for pictures, we reached Coldfoot at 3.00 p.m., and stopped for lunch at the Arctic Acres Inn. We now had a decision to make: stop for the day, or go on.

Still running on adrenalin, I decided to go for the Top. After lunch the drizzle had stopped and there was a break in the clouds. The panorama of the Brooks Range lay spread out in front of us in full splendour. We passed the last tree, duly signposted, and started to climb up Atigun Pass, where traces of the recent snowfall were still visible. It is also the Continental Divide. Once over the pass we had reached the so-called North Slope. From now on the road followed the Sagavanirktok River all the way down to Prudhoe Bay. Even though the sun was shining, it was cold. I had to stop and put on my long underwear. Still 300 km to go.

The last 200 km to Deadhorse Camp on Prudhoe Bay were sheer agony. For a long stretch of road they had put down fresh gravel which at times lay three inches deep, difficult to negotiate with the heavily loaded machine. Low clouds made for poor visibility. There was no indication that at this time of year the sun was up there somewhere 24 hours a day. It started to drizzle again, so that I had to open my face shield to be able to see the road. This was hard on the eyes. We rolled into Deadhorse a little after one o'clock in the morning, Sunday, July 13, wet, cold, and beaten. An enquiry at the Prudhoe Bay Hotel revealed that there was no camping anywhere nearby; management didn't like it. The lady at reception suggested I go "down the road" a bit to find a convenient spot. I replied that I had just come "up the road" and was unwilling to get back in the saddle. She shrugged her shoulders. I booked a room for "the night" for $75.00. Breakfast (included) was served from 5.30 until 7.30. This did not leave much time for sleeping. But then, I had not come 7,779 km for sleeping. I had made it, and that was all that mattered.

The people who run Deadhorse Camp must be some of the greediest, people-unfriendly money grabbers Corporate America has produced. The only human value welcomed on Prudhoe Bay is work, hard work. Everything else is forbidden: tourists are not welcome (the last 350 km of the Haul Road had been closed to the public until December, 1994); there is no public access to the Arctic Ocean, no alcohol, no drugs, no gambling, and no women beyond the guard house. Deadhorse Camp is run like a prison. There are no redeeming features that would make life a little more pleasant for the unfortunate inmates. They were there to work, to make money, and were continuously reminded of it.

In order to dip my hand into the ocean, I had to take a tour in a mini-van. Mary, our tour guide from Seattle, one of the few women licensed to pass through the barricade, explained some of the rules. As a licensed driver in Deadhorse she was given three chances to violate the traffic rules. After the fourth violation, for example, stopping on an open road, she would be sent packing. The inmates of Deadhorse usually worked two weeks, and then were flown out for two weeks for points south. Management wanted to avoid attacks of cabin fever. No wonder. The only living beings not under strict control in Deadhorse were the cariboos. Only they were allowed some measure of freedom.

Putting aside the people-unfriendliness of the place, one cannot help but marvel at the superhuman effort that went into this undertaking. The oil pipeline, extending all the way to Valdez, a distance of 1,300 km, is 42" in diameter and is covered by 6" of insulation. At the time it was moving 1.5 billion gallons of oil per day; it could move 2.5 billions if necessary. The oil deposit in Prudhoe Bay was estimated to last until the year 2030. But exploration has revealed other deposits nearby that could also be channelled into the pipeline. Moreover, there is a giant deposit of natural gas, which at the moment was barely exploited. Only 15 per cent was used for heating. The other 85 per cent was pumped back down for future use, and to keep up the pressure on the oil. Looking at this giant human effort, I was reminded of the Chinese Wall, which can be seen from outer space. Perhaps this is also true of the pipeline.

Back at the hotel at noon, I was told that since I hadn't had dinner yesterday, I would be entitled to a "free lunch" today. How nice. However, at the pump at one o'clock, on our way out of Deadhorse, the price of gasoline took care of the windfall.

Before leaving the hotel I had dug deeply into my saddlebags and put on all wearable items I could find. The temperature was in the low 40s; a cold wind was blowing from the south. The heavy fog lifted for a brief spell of sunshine, then the rain moved in. It rained heavily as we crossed the Brooks Range, and it continued all the way to Coldfoot. I was looking for the sign marking the first tree, but could not find it in the downpour. The gravel section that had given us problems on the way up was now the lesser of two evils. The unimproved section of the road had turned to mud, giving rise to an adrenalin rush now and then. Exchanging my road tires for a set of enduro tires before leaving home proved to be a good decision. The extra grip they afforded in the dirt was most welcome. Again I came to appreciate the courtesy of the drivers of the many 18-wheelers that came toward us, or passed us. They gave us plenty of room, allowing us to avoid the worst sink holes in the road. We arrived in Coldfoot at 9.00 p.m., again wet, cold, and beaten. Since the Arctic Acres Inn wanted $90.00 for a room, it wasn't difficult to opt for camping for $10.00. In my condition I would have been able to sleep on a rail.

The rain had stopped overnight, and the road was in a much better condition the next morning. At ten o'clock, at the Arctic Circle, the sun made an appearance just in time for picture taking. Some sections of the road had been severely chewed up the day before. Where were the road graders when they were most needed? With nothing else to do but to curse and slip and slide, I decided that I would do my own grading. Drawing on the experience of 27 years in the class-room as a teacher I gave it the grade of D, barely passable. Unfortunately, this exercise did not improve road conditions.The parking lot in front of the restau-rant near the Yukon River bridge had not improved; it looked like the road, muddy. But it was time for a coffee break. The rest of the way to the Trail's End RV Park in Fairbanks was smooth going. We arrived there at 5.00 p.m.

Recapitulating this trip up to Prudhoe Bay and back in my mind, I asked myself the question, would I do it again, knowing what it would be like? Yes, certainly. It was worth the effort, if only for the acquired bragging rights, to be able to say, I've been there, I've done it. Seeing the Alaska Pipeline snake its way over hills and across valleys was a unique experience. The scenery was great; the weather was not. But this was all part of the experience. Having accomplished what I had set out to do, the "conquest" of Prudhoe Bay, perhaps I could relax now and make the rest of the trip a pure pleasure ride, rather than a chase after a daily maximum performance.

5. *Southward Bound*

Fairbanks is a nice city gracing the banks of the Chena River. Downtown one finds a mix of the old and the new, of the historic and the modern; log cabins beside shopping malls; wooden buildings beside concrete structures. It has a prestigous university, elegant shops, many fine hotels, over one hundred bed and breakfasts, numerous churches, and a multitude of government employees. Since it is located almost in the perfect centre of the State of Alaska, it is an important distribution point, and the logical place for the seat of government. It would love to unseat the badly located state capital, Juneau. What Fairbanks lacks, however, is a distinguishing feature as a city, a landmark, an Eiffel Tower or an Empire State Building, that could be used for promotion, for example, on tourist posters. What Fairbanks has in abundance, on the other hand, is carwash facilities. Fairbanks is a city of carwashes. There are more carwashes than hotels. There are more carwashes than churches. One gets the impression that there are more carwashes in Fairbanks than hotels and churches combined. Hence, it is a paradise for motorhome owners, and should be advertised as such: *Come to Fairbanks, Carwash Capital of the Continent.* This could even lure some of the geriatric set away from Santaland.

My choice for the day was the carwash next to the Trail's End Campground, a *de luxe* facility with ten bays, high- and low- pressure guns, brushes, shampoo, wax, and hot air, presumably for blow-drying, the works. It had a great appetite for quarters, though, but what the heck! Both bike and rider needed a good scrub in order not to shock fellow motorists on our way south to Anchorage. If cleanliness is next to godliness then there is, indeed, a reason why in Fairbanks carwashes outnumber churches. Great to be back to civilization with its decadent pleasures.

The George Parks Highway, Alaska Road #3, is a pleasure to ride. This sentiment is shared by the owners of the many motorhomes clogging the road in summer, particularly in the area near Denali Park. Because of low cloud the chief attraction of the park, Mount McKinley, the continent's highest peak, remained hidden from view as we passed by. Better luck next time! Since I did not wish to abandon the bike in order to go animal-watching in the park by bus, there was no reason to hang around much longer. Hence, we arrived at Chugach State Park, just outside Anchorage, at 8.30 p.m.

There was an honor system in effect for the camping fees. I did not have the correct amount, and approached the owner of a motorhome for change. He appeared pleased to pass the time before dinner in pleasant conversation, and I learned a lot about what is involved in motorhome ownership. According to Fred, motorhomes cost anywhere between $100,000 and $1,000,000. Anything under that is a camper. Running one of these Greyhound-Bus-like giants costs around $5.00 per mile. With a cellular phone on board, a computer, and an Internet address, being on the move is no problem, even for business people. Fred believed, and his wife agreed, that the greatest problem confronting the motorhome set is too close proximity to one's partner for too long periods of time; no private space, and no place to escape to, such as a basement, a recreation room, or a garage. Fred said that one really has to like one's partner in order to get along with him or her in such close quarters. He added that I was lucky not having to step on the toes of anyone. He was right, of course. I liked my status as lone wolf, even though I had no tennis court or swimming pool on board, as some of these motorhomes seem to have.

Soon after I had set up my tent, the drawbacks of being a lone wolf in a tent became apparent. Rain began to fall and was building up to a full-blown thunderstorm. With the radio turned on and my earphones in my ears I paid little attention to the tempest outside. By chance I happened to look at the wall of the tent, and what I saw demanded immediate action. The tent was standing in three inches of water, which was rising fast. In a matter of seconds I put on my boots, rushed out, pulled out the pegs, and dragged the whole set-up onto a little hill nearby. The bike would have to fend for itself. I had a reasonably good night's sleep in spite of the deluge. But in the morning I found that I was marooned on an island in the middle of a miniature lake. The bike was standing in water eight inches deep. As I was wrestling it onto dry ground barefoot, I thought that in situations like these motorhome ownership has definite advantages.

Packing the dripping wet camping gear was no problem with all the experience I had acquired. At this stage of the trip it would probably take me longer to pack dry gear for lack of practice.

While I was eating breakfast at Elmer's Pancake and Steak House in Anchorage a local citizen convinced me that riding Alaska Route #1 to its end at Homer might be a lot of fun. So it was off to Homer. The beautiful setting of Turnagain Arm along the way, a fjord reaching up to its origin at Portage Glacier, invited many stops for picture taking. On one of these stops I was talking to two bikers on Honda Goldwings. They had been to Homer and were not impressed. They were painting a bleak picture of a place too commercialized for their taste, and clogged with motorhomes. They had liked Seward much more. Since I knew of no good reason not to change plans, Seward became the new goal.

The ride around the fjord, over the mountains and down to Seward makes one forget the terror of motorhomes on Alaska's roads. Alaska Route #9 was in great shape, and with a bit of daring on our part these behemoths could be passed quickly without much trouble. As we entered Seward the rain started. I began to wonder whether we were following the rain, or the rain was following us. This question was brought to my attention again when we stopped at a little bakery for coffee and a pastry. One of the bicyclists inside remarked that there had been beautiful sunshine all morning. The rain had just started. Were we jinxed? Would this Rain Curse follow us all the way south? The rain and the motorhomes?

With low clouds and rain there was not much to see in Seward. A cruise ship was making its way up Resurrection Bay to dock at Seward harbor. All along the shore motorhomes were lined up side by side like birds on a wire to witness this exciting event. For this motorcyclist it was time to move on.

As soon as we left Seward, the weather improved. When we made a detour to see Portage Glacier, the sun was shining. It accompanied us all the way past Anchorage as far as Palmer, where we stopped for the night at the campground near town. The setting of Palmer against the snow-covered mountains in the background was magnificent. If this were an indication of things to come there would be a big treat in store for us the next day.

The novelty of packing dry camping gear and having bright sunshine in the morning set the tone for the rest of the day. The Glenn Highway, Alaska Route #1, curves beautifully along the Matawaska River, and rises gradually to meet several glaciers, most famous among them the Matawaska Glacier. High snow-covered mountains to the North and South, the glaciers, and a multitude of lakes and rivers make one forget the dusty construction zones, the ever-present motorhomes, and the bumpy sections of the road. What a thrill. We stopped many times to take pictures. This is how I imagined the whole of Alaska to be. In my book the Glenn Highway between Palmer and Tok joins the Honors List of great rides in Alaska. Like the Top of the World it receives a straight A+.

After dinner in Tok, we were back on the Alaska Highway, got as far as the Canadian border, and spent the second dry night in a row, at the White River Motor Inn Campground.

During breakfast in Beaver Creek on the Canadian side two middle-aged gents on middle-aged Hondas in mint condition, bearing Colorado licence plates, rode up and parked their wheels beside mine. Without much ado they joined me at my table. Both were from Denver, and were on their way to Fairbanks for a double celebration: their fiftieth birthdays and their twenty-fifth year of riding together. Both had families and wives who did not ride. At one time or another most of their motorcycle buddies had been talking about the Big One, but that was as far as it went. They, on the other hand, had simply set a date and had taken off. After Fairbanks they wanted to tour Southern Alaska before heading back down. It all sounded so familiar. Almost every day at gas stations and restaurants I met people with dreams of the open road. Why didn't they just pack up and go? Because it's not that easy with family, job, mortgage, and car payments to tie you down. If it were easy the roads would be clogged not only with motorhomes but with cars and motorcycles as well. The two boys from Denver agreed with me that this would be a disaster. Let the others dream on; it's safer that way.

So far the Alaska Highway had been a big disappointment from the point of view of riding pleasure. From my reading of Danny Liska, who, in 1959, was one of the first motorcyclists to ride from the Arctic Circle to the tip of South America, I was expecting a narrow, winding ribbon snaking over mountains and through valleys. What I found instead was a road that had undergone a considerable amount of change since its construction. Like plastic surgeons the highway engineers had tucked, pinched, cut, and straightened it so many times that it had lost all the charms of a road through nature, a trail through the wilderness. The Alcan resembles an Interstate Highway, not unlike those found in the Lower Forty-Eight, with all the advantages and drawbacks, one of the latter being monotony. So far all the riding thrills had been found on roads off the Alcan, on the Top of the World, The Dalton, and The Glenn. This was about to change.

One of the most beautiful stretches of the Alcan must be the section where the road approaches Kluane Lake, half-way between the Canadian border in the north-west and Whitehorse. The road twists tortuously between the water's edge and rock outcroppings of the St. Elias Mountains, a mountain range boasting Canada's highest mountain, Mount Logan (19,545 feet), even more inaccessible than Mount McKinley, since Mount Logan is in the middle of a glaciated area best reached by airplane. The whole area is known as Kluane National Park, and has been declared a UNESCO World Heritage Site. The eastern side of Kluane Lake is flanked by another mountain range, the Ruby Range, not as high a the St. Elias Mountains, but also snow-covered. Then there is Kluane Lake itself, the largest lake in the Yukon Territory, a jewel, deep blue in color, reflecting the surrounding mountain ranges. Hence, it comes as no surprise to find that the area is a favourite with tourists.

It is also not surprising that the academic community has discovered this beautiful spot for its own use. The Arctic Institute of North America has staked out parts of this idyllic wonderland on the south shore of the lake for its Kluane Lake Research Station. During the summer the University of Calgary is the sponsor of an Arctic Studies Camp, offering a credit course in Arctic Geography, in which qualified students of any university can enrol. During the past summers my good friend and former colleague, Professor Dr. Peter Johnson, has been in charge of this course. I took him up on his invitation to drop in. Peter took me on a guided tour around the lake to several of the sites where the students do their research. This summer they were collecting core samples from lake bottoms to determine, by studying the trapped molluscs, the climatic changes that had occured during the past centuries. Back at the camp I met the students, about fifteen of them, both male and female. They were an enthusiastic bunch from various Canadian universities. They confided to me that to them this did not constitute work. This was more like play in the most idyllic setting; the most "fun-course" they had ever taken. I congratulated Peter for having contributed to this positive attitude. Perhaps *Academia* is not as bad as some would have it.

In the evening after dinner I met the superintendent, caretaker, and pilot in residence of the camp, Andy Williams. Andy flies climbers, glaciologists, or anyone interested up to the glaciers near Mount Logan in his capable turbo-prop aircraft, parked beside the runway in front of his cottage. He had flown in many parts of the world, including Punta Arenas, South America. He also served excellent Scotch Whisky, the perfect prerequisite for spinning a yarn about travelling. It was here that I finalized my plan to continue down the road as far as I could go. I am certain that both Peter and Andy would have loved to come along.

After all that barley malt I was glad that I did not have to set up my tent. As

5) *White Pass highway and railway*

a guest I was privileged to sleep in "the gazebo," a square, open-sided pavillion on the beach of Kluane Lake, half a mile from the camp. Peter warned me to speak loudly, to whistle, or to sing when approaching the gazebo, in order not to surprise prowling bears that may have dropped in. I opted for singing, since I have been told to have a singing voice that could scare anybody or anything away. It worked. There was no bear attack that night.

It did not rain, of course. It only rains when I'm camping or on the road. Leaving the Alcan at Haines Junction on our way south to Haines, Alaska, we started off in bright sunshine. One hour later up at the watershed at Klukshu Lake it got so cold that I had to put on my long underwear. The scenery on both sides of the "Haines Highway" can serve as a geography lab for glacial landforms: moraines, drumlins, eskers, and kettle lakes can be found side by side with live glaciers on the march, and all this in front of a magnificent mountain backdrop. The rain started a little later, and never stopped, not even for an instant, until the late afternoon.

Haines is at the end of the road. The alternative to backtracking is a one-hour ferry ride north via Taiya Inlet to Skagway. We had a two-hour wait for the ferry. Long lines of motorhomes were forming. Skagway (population a little over 800) will be a busy little town, perhaps busier than during the Klondike Gold Rush, when it served as the jumping off point for the miners bound for Whitehorse and Dawson. The unloading and loading of the ferry was a study in inefficiency. The "Matawaska" was built in the 1960s in the pre-motorhome era. It was side-loading and required a lot of back-and-forth before these big motorized containers with their incompetent drivers were off the boat, and the ones boarding were in place. To add insult to injury, the loading master let us, the six peasants on motorcycles, soak in the pouring rain until the nobility in their homes-on-wheels were on board. May his sons and daughters join the *Hell's Angels*. We could barely make out the shores of Skagway Fjord in the rain. Fortunately, during unloading the bikers got a break. We were the first to jump ship. Not that we were in a great hurry. Skagway turned out to be a reproduction of Dawson, a nostalgic recreation of times past, a museum-piece, even more commercialized than Dawson. It is the end of the line of the Alaska Ferry from Bellingham, Washington state, also a port of call for cruise ships. On this day two medium-size vessels lay at anchor. We gave Skagway town a quick miss in favour of a visit to the head of the Chilkoot Trail.

Maurice, on a Kawasaki 650, one of the six motorcyclists on the ferry, decided to ride with me up the Dyea Road to the trailhead, to see if there was anything left to see. In real life Maurice, 36 years old, was a workshop foreman for the Montreal Transit System. Since he had only one month of holidays, he had shipped his bike earlier by transport truck to Calgary and had flown in, in order to have more time in Alaska. The packed clay road was slick in the rain, and tricky to negotiate with my heavy machine. The Kawasaki, being much lighter, had a better time of it. A further complication was the heavy fog. All we could see was our front wheels and a little bit of road. I don't know what I expected to see at the trailhead; definitely more than I did. Here, one hundred years ago, 30,000 gold-5) seekers and as many horses, mules, dogs, even camels, had risked their lives and limbs on their trek up the mountain to Lake Bennett, where the men had to build some contrivance to float down the Yukon River to Whitehorse. Beside the sign marking the spot, we saw nothing. Now I have at least two reasons to come back to Alaska: to see Mount McKinley, and to see, and perhaps hike, the Chilkoot Trail. Maurice rode back to Skagway to find a souvenir for his 13-year-old daughter back home. We, on the other hand, took the alternative to the Chilkoot Trail, the road over White Pass.

Back on Klondike Highway #2 in the continuing rain and fog we could only guess what the scenery would be like. The road curved upward with a steep grade and numerous hairpin turns like a mountain road in the Swiss Alps. The fog was so dense at times that I had to open my visor to see the road. At the summit of White Pass, the Alaska-British Columbia border, we left fog and rain behind, and were treated to grandiose scenery of snow-covered mountains on both sides of the highway, rivers, and crystal-blue lakes. The famous White Pass & Yukon Railroad, an "International Historic Civil Engineering Landmark," ran parallel with us on the right hand side as far as Fraser, its present-day terminus. Klondike Highway #2 from Skagway to Whitehorse underlines my assertion that the best riding in Alaska and the Yukon is found on roads off the Alaska Highway.

I thought I had discovered the magic formula for good riding: staying off the Alcan as much as possible. This thinking made me decide to turn off near Watson Lake for the Cassiar Highway, British Columbia Highway #37, in spite of the fact that the maps showed long stretches of gravel, and in spite of the fact that the rain kept on coming. Big mistake. Gravel started after a brief honeymoon of a little over 100 km, at Jade City. Two factors complicated matters: in the rain much of the gravel had turned into mud, and many of the sections formerly hard-surfaced had reverted to gravel, a state of affairs not yet recorded in the available road maps. Perhaps traffic on this highway had not merited much road improvement since the closing of the Cassiar Asbestos Mine in 1992. The access road to the town of Cassiar, now a ghost town, was closed to the public. I hoped that the highway would not share the same fate as the town, for when the fog lifted we enjoyed a magnificent view: mountains, forests, lakes, and rivers, British Columbia at its best. The road, when we passed through, on the other hand, showed British Columbia at its worst. The last section before pavement reappeared was four hours of slipping, sliding, and plowing through deep mud, a dirty business. For my own satisfaction I should have graded it. However, I found myself in a quandary. The Dalton, Alaska Route #11, going north to Prudhoe Bay, had received a D, barely passable. But the Cassiar was much worse. If I were to give it an F, for total failure as a road, it would mean that I did not get through, which was not true. Moreover, it was along the Cassiar that I saw three black bears, the only bears I had spotted so far. This had to count for something. The only alternative, then, was to give it a D-, almost impassable. Done.

I took my seat on the bench at Meziadin Junction waiting my turn at the RV

Wash and Sani Dump. I felt like dumping something just to show my disgust with what I had been through during the past hours, but didn't, for I would have lost my place in the line. My reward was the chance for a good laugh at the expense of one of the members of the motorhome set, who far outnumbered the ordinary mortals on the bench. The fellow ahead of me had opened the hood of the little Toyota car he was towing behind his big rig. He was looking at the engine, shook his head in disbelief, took a second look, and rushed over to get his wife to take a look. Curious, I followed her to find out what was going on. There was no sign of an engine. Instead there was a solid block of mud filling the whole cavity under the hood. He allowed me to use the high pressure water gun ahead of him while he was considering strategy. When I rode off, a half-hour later, he was trying to unearth his little engine with the help of the waterhose and an icepick, like an archaeologist about to unearth a rare artifact. Suffer, baby, suffer! I thought, full of *Schadenfreude*. This is for holding up traffic with that unwieldy piece of machinery of yours.

That evening at the carwash of the Cassiar RV Park I met a bicyclist from Switzerland who told me that he could not usually afford the luxury of private campgrounds, but was forced to use one on this day if only to wash himself and his equipment. Claude, from Geneva, in his late twenties, French-speaking, was on his way from Prudhoe Bay to Tierra del Fuego, something we had in common. He was tall and lean, with long curly brown locks. He had been touring the world for several years; had been through Russia, Kazakhstan, China, including Tibet, and India. He agreed with me that the Cassiar was much worse than anything he had encountered on the Dalton Highway. For him on a bicycle it had been at times almost impassable. He said he would be busy tonight recording this fact on his website. Now, there was a tuned-in world traveller with his own lap-top computer with which he pays daily visits to the world wide web. He hands out his printed address on the web to everyone he meets on the road and invites them to visit him there. I was impressed, being almost completely computer illiterate. Claude asked me if I were on the way to the rally on Christmas Day in Ushuaia, Argentina, at the end of the road. This was the first time I heard of such an event. Claude had been told by someone he had met on the road, who again had heard the rumour from someone else. He knew no details. I was to hear many more hints about this "rally," always without details. With a bit of mathematics I figured out that I could, indeed, be there at Christmas. Why not go for it? It might just be fun. I thanked Claude for this interesting piece of information, and hoped that we might meet there. He shrugged his shoulders, indicating "perhaps."

In Prince George another engine oil and filter change was due, and also a change of transmission and rear drive oil. Fortunately the local RV Park and Campground provided some covered space where I could do my environmentally unfriendly thing without getting soaked. The rain accompanied us as far as the turn-off to B.C. Highway #99, which curves upward through Marble Canyon to emerge in the Fraser Valley. Past the town of Lilooet it climbs over several mountain passes with hairpin turns, a reminder of the European Alps. At times I could-

6) California redwoods

n't believe my eyes when I encountered signs beside the road in German, suggesting that this must be a favorite with German tourists. No wonder. B.C. Highway #99 passes through magnificent scenery. It, too, deserves an A+, a must-do.

*   *   *

The ferry to Victoria, on Vancouver Island, left at noon. As the Vancouver skyline was sliding by under a deep blue sky and a mild breeze was blowing, the flying mud of the Cassiar was soon forgotten. We were looking forward to being pampered by my wife's sister and brother-in-law. What luxury it was to stretch out in a real bed on a soft mattress. What luxury to gorge oneself on delicious home-cooking. Even the Rubber Cow received special treatment. It was allowed to rest in the garage/workshop, beside the family car, an honour that did not go unnoticed. The visit with family took the stress off the following day in town: to the BMW-dealer for more spare oil filters; to an ATM to get money; to the bank to get more money; to the CAA to get travellers' cheques and road maps; to a photo lab to get three films developed; to a canvas repair shop to get the zipper of my leather riding-pants replaced. (It had given up in Alaska, and the uncomfortable cold draft had to be stopped.) Ernst, my brother-in-law, acted as taxi-driver. It was a stressful day, but the reward waiting at the house, where Gisella, my sister-in-law, was the perfect hostess, more than made up for it. It did not rain all day, and there was no rain in the forecast. Did my visit with family, my wife's side of the family, neutralize The Curse?

It would have been nice to stay longer, but I had to push on if I wanted to be in Ushuaia at Christmas. The ferry to Port Angeles, Washington State, on the other side of the Strait of Juan de Fuca, left at 10.30 a.m. Waiting in the short line for motorcycles were two other bikers besides myself. Then an event happened that had all of us craning our necks. It even enticed the motorhomers to come over to take look. On an immaculately clean and sparkling Honda Goldwing SE, painted in candy apple-red, whisper-smooth like a Cadillac, arrived an elderly couple two-up, dressed in shiny black leather, wearing matching helmets in candy apple-red. The contours of this *de luxe* machinery were illuminated by a multitude of red LED's. There were headlights, foglamps, running lights, back-up lights, flood lights, everywhere. They were towing a trailer also painted candy apple red and illuminated like a Christmas tree. This grand entrance was no less than spectacular. Hardly had they parked their motorhome on two wheels when the question and answer period started. Wilbur was a retired car dealer from Lincoln, Nebraska. He and his wife Emily were realizing a dream to visit all of the 48 States of the Union on a motorcycle. Last year Wilbur had sold the business and bought the equipment, and they had started their odyssey. On their gasoline tank they had a brass plaque in the shape of the United States with the outlines of all the individual states engraved. Every state they had visited so far was marked by a little glued-in jewel. At the time they had visited 26, had made a short detour to visit friends in Victoria, Canada, and were on their way to State #27. They hoped to get all their jewels in place by the end of the year. The motorcycle drew raves of wonder. Did he have some optional equipment on his bike? No, not *some*, he had *all* the optional equipment available: electrically-heated handgrips, stereophonic radio with all bands, tape deck, CD player, CB radio, driver/passenger intercom, reverse gear, cruise control, radar detector, clock, compass, and a global positioning system, but no radar. The trailer contained a quick release tent, all of their camping gear and cooking utensils, but no microwave oven. Very soon the inevitable question was raised: how much did all this cost? Wilbur was a bit vague on this one: "An arm and a leg," was all he offered. They were a nice couple, and yet they made the three of us on rather plain-looking bikes feel like ugly ducklings beside a beautiful swan. The party broke up when it was time for boarding.

Port Angeles on U.S. Highway #101 marked the beginning of a ride not soon forgotten for its grandiose scenery, first-class road conditions, great weather, and biker-friendly fellow motorists. For the first time on this trip I felt that I had left performance anxiety behind me for good. There was no daily quota of miles to ride, no deadlines to meet, no fear of breaking down, no worry about the weather. The ride down to San Diego along the Pacific coast was unadulterated pleasure. Following the advice of Wilbur I took the east loop of Highway #101 out of Port Angeles, along Hood Canal, skirting the Olympic National Park, a ride through Washington's tourist country, a great ride.

When we crossed the Columbia River we entered Oregon's tourist playground. The road through Oregon was a dream, and in perfect condition. It generally followed the coast, but at times turned inland, climbed and descended in easy sweepers, at times in breathtaking hairpin turns that kept the adrenalin flowing. At the end of July this was the peak travel season of the year, with many hotels in the little towns posting the "no vacancy" signs. Often we had to share the road with heavily loaded logging trucks, testifying to Oregon's chief industry. The drivers of these rigs, cousins of the ones on the Dalton, knights of the road and gentlemen, never posed any danger. Along stretches exposed to the open ocean, the breeze, at times carrying fog, called for heavier gloves and warm underwear. This held as far as San Francisco.

We did not need the "Welcome to California" sign to be reminded that we had entered this state. Near the state boundary Route #101 became the Redwood Highway, winding its way through Redwood National Park. Although we were shielded from the cool ocean breeze, the redwood giants turned daylight into semi-darkness, and kept the temperature on the cool side. The biggest thrill, however, was yet to come, when at Legget we turned off U.S. Route #101 for California #1.

The first 10 miles are the overture of what is to come on California #1. It climbed immediately, with numerous hairpin turns, over the coastal mountain range. What ecstasy to ride through these heavily wooded mountains. Some curves had to be negotiated in second gear, or else—. Soon the road descended to the Pacific, but the roller coaster continued, since it had to go far inland for every cove, down and up again, on and on; slow going, but exciting. The ingredients for perfect happiness. And yet there was something that annoyed me, the rest stops.

In the Far North restaurants and coffee shops are a haven for motorists. They are generally far apart, and hence provide more than just food. They offer relaxation, good company, ambience. The owners and employees of these establishments seem to be genuinely interested in their guests. They want to know where from, where to, why and wherefore. They also offer some of their own history during these conversations. Soon everybody is talking to everybody. These are great places to meet one's fellow motorists. Down in Canada and the Forty-Eight this ambience is non-existent. No one cares whether you're coming or going. Yes, the waitresses welcome you with an implanted silicon smile. They are extremely polite as they urge you on with your food:"Is everything O.K.?" "How are we doing?" "We're doing fine!" "Good going!" " Some more coffee?" "Are we done?" "Are we going to have some dessert?" "We" are not amused to be addressed in the Royal "We." We are not children who need to be coaxed to eat their food. We are pissed off by this rather condescending treatment. But we tip anyways, a little disappointed, because we still remember the good times we had during our rest stops in Alaska.

Then there is the coffee. Why can one not get a decent cup of coffee in most restaurants in the U.S.? The stuff they are passing off as coffee might look like coffee, but certainly does not smell or taste like it. In Europe the coffee generally is excellent, and one has to go a long way to find a bad cup. In the United States and Canada it's the other way around. Is it the fault of the water being used? I don't think so. It is because the importers of coffee beans buy the cheapest beans on the market. Good enough for North American coffee junkies! Smarten up, you people out there!

In spite of these complaints, the view of the San Francisco skyline, as we rode over the Golden Gate Bridge, put a plaster over our wounded feelings. Moreover, there was more fun on #1 in store for us after we had passed Monterey. This section of the highway, passing by Big Sur, is almost as exciting as the section north of San Francisco. The road is just as scenic, curvy, and mountainous as in the earlier part, semi-desert, with sheer cliffs dropping hundreds of feet into the ocean, eroded rocks along the shore, some with holes like the *Roche Percé* in Quebec's Gaspé peninsula. But the road is wider and hence faster. There is also more traffic to cope with, motorhomes galore. The thrill continues down to William Randolph Hearst's famous castle near San Simeon. From there on it's expressway riding all the way to San Diego.

We arrived at the San Simeon State Park Campground quite late and were lucky to get the last site, normally reserved for the physically challenged, next to the toilets. Did they know what those interminable cups of coffee on the road do to a gentleman of a certain age? Whatever. It was very thoughtful of them. I had parked the bike beside the sign of the stylized wheelchair indicating the status of the spot, and was just in the process of setting up my tent, when a lady of a certain age, a bit fluffy in the hips, wearing shorts, walked by and chatted me up California-style. "Your chair doesn't look like the one on the sign," she said with a smile. "This is a German model," I replied. "The Germans are in the *avant garde* with new designs. Besides, I'd rather be riding one of these than one like the one in the picture." She wasn't finished with me yet. She looked at my tent and said, "The fellow yesterday put it right there. But he had only an itsy-bitsy one." I replied with a grin, "Mine is also only an itsy-bitsy one. But wouldn't you agree that size doesn't matter?" She looked at me a bit startled, but rewarded me with an even bigger smile and walked on.

I had called Brattin Motors, the BMW-dealer in San Diego, for an appointment on the following day, July 31. My tires had almost 16,000 km on them, and showed many little cuts, presumably courtesy of Alaska gravel. They should be replaced before the challenge of the Mexican roads. The mechanics at Brattin were ready for us. We received our new tires, had the carburetors balanced, and were out again within two hours. Real professionals these guys.

Since the day was young we turned east on Interstate #8 in the direction of Yuma. I had planned to follow #8 and #10 as far as El Paso, where I wanted to cross the border to Ciudad Juárez, then take the high road to Mexico City. I decided against using the Pacific route, for I had travelled this route before by bus, and had found it uninspiring. Another factor against the Pacific route was the time of year. The high road via Chihuahua should be much more pleasant to ride than the scorcher along the coast. But this remained to be seen. Within an hour out of San Diego we found ourselves in full desert. The countryside looked as though a giant had crumbled everything and had strewn the pieces all around.With a temperature close to 100°F I had to shed my leather riding gear, and continue in shirt and jeans. I realized that this was quite unsafe, but I was willing to take a chance with safety rather than to meet certain death by being boiled in leather. Even stripped to the bare essentials I found no relief from the heat. The heavy headwind felt as if it were coming from a blast furnace. During an air-conditioned coffee break in El Centro I decided that it would perhaps be prudent to buy bike insurance for Mexico at the local AAA. It proved to be a waste of money. We rolled into the Riverside Campground at the Arizona border near Yuma at 6.00 p.m., desiccated and exhausted, but in high spirits. This was about to change.

6. *From Yuma to Tapachula*

That night during dinner in Yuma I made up my mind that it was time to bite the bullet. It was time to inform my wife of the change of plans, a task I did not relish. I needed a longer leave of absence, say, eight more months, to ride to the end of the road in South America and back. I would be back home at the beginning of April, in time for her birthday. On the telephone after the usual greeting formalities I mentioned that I had a big surprise for her. Big mistake! I should have known that she hated surprises, surprises of any kind. When I told her the news, there was a minute of silence in the line. What followed then was a harrowing experience. The words "Don't bother coming back," stood out as one of the highlights of the conversation. Even the D-word was being invoked. Before she hung up I was told that she found my decision "totally unacceptable." I was in deep shit.

Why are some women like that? In Hartmann's story mentioned erlier, Erec's wife, Enite, actively encouraged her husband to go out adventuring. In another one of Hartmann's stories, *Iwein*, the hero, also a knight of King Arthur's Round Table, was given a one-year leave of absence by his newly wedded wife to slay as many bad guys as he could find, and to rescue as many damsels in distress as he could muster. Only after he had exceeded the deadline did she get upset. All I was asking for was a scant eight months, not even a whole year. What is the matter with women today?

Retribution was swift. The following night in the tent was a foretaste of hell. The heat was so intense that I was afraid I would be baked to a crisp by morning. I had made the mistake of setting up the tent on a concrete slab put there for the motorhomes. The slab had retained the heat like a clay oven in a bakery, and I was the bun. Sam McGee, the Klondike miner of the Robert Service poem quoted earlier, who had himself cremated to keep warm, would have been comfortable here. I vowed that from now on I would sleep in airconditioned comfort every night. No more camping. Still groggy from lack of sleep we returned to the blast furnace of the road. At 1.00 p.m. near Tucson the thermometer was again close to 100°F. But not for long, for something unexpected happened. At the time I thought that whenever I should get around to writing this down, no one will believe me, especially my former colleagues from the English Department. This could not be real. This could happen only in fiction. At 2.00 p.m. on Friday, August 1, as Interstate #10 entered Devil's Canyon, black clouds were piling up ahead of us. Thirty minutes later we were in the midst of a thunderstorm so violent that all traffic had to come to a halt for lack of vision. It had not rained since Prince George, B.C. Why now, out of the blue, as it were. Was it the telephone call last night that triggered this debacle? Was the Rain Curse still on, or on again? Was I being punished for "unacceptable" behaviour? Another motorist told me that the rains were late this year; this was the first thunderstorm of the season. Why just at the moment when I was passing through? Couldn't it wait another day? It rained hard all night and at least once every day thereafter all the way to Tapachula.

I had been to Mexico several times before, and every time I had crossed the border I found myself in shock, culture shock. The border at El Paso was no exception. This time, crossing with a vehicle, I received the first blow already at Customs and Immigration. Mexican Immigration in Ciudad Juárez was no hassle. There were several long queues. Of course I picked the wrong one, but thanks to my elementary Spanish I was shoved into the right one, and received my landing card and my *Entrada* stamp. The bike had to be cleared through Customs 31 km out of town on the road to Chihuahua. There chaos reigned supreme. First U.S.$1.00 had to be paid for parking. There was no alternative. Then again it was a matter of good luck, or many questions, until you joined the correct queue. Finally at the window you were asked for passport, landing card, driver's licence, vehicle registration, and a major credit card. These documents were copied in triplicate, which cost U.S.$3.25. They have a monopoly on this service, hence the price. After you had received this whole stack of papers you lined up for the office called "Banjercito." Finally at the window you signed a promise to reexport the vehicle within the time period specified, and the credit card was debited for U.S.$11.00. Of course they have your credit card number. If you failed to cancel out with the vehicle when leaving the country, they would charge you import duty for the estimated value of the vehicle. Then a holographic sticker was put on the windshield, which would be removed when cancelling, that is, when leaving the country. But it wasn't over yet. Having neatly put away all the papers, having wiped the sweat off your brow and having ridden off, about 1 km down the road you were stopped for a police check. Out with the documents once again. Was that it? Not yet. A further 10 km down the road was a second police check. After this the whole routine could be done with eyes closed. At the time I thought that this was the pits. But worse was to come at the borders further south.

Arriving in Ciudad Juárez from El Paso makes you realize that you are in another world, the third world. City streets are made up of a series of potholes held together by thin strands of asphalt. Channels of open sewer, sometimes up to one foot deep, run across the road. There is litter everywhere, and the smell of the sewer mixed with the stench of soot-belching Diesel trucks and buses is nauseating. Some of the cars on the road should have seen a junkyard years ago. You wondered how their brakes were as they cut in front of you, or moved up from behind? Their horns, at least, appeared to be in good working order. And all this only a short distance away, across the bridge of the Rio Grande.

My next attack of culture shock happened in Chihuahua. I arrived in town at 6.00 p.m., in pouring rain, of course. Since I had forsaken camping, I was eager to find a motel fast. The first one I stopped at was full; it was Saturday night. The next one looked even more inviting with large plastic curtains covering the parking spaces, hiding the cars from view. This would be perfect for the security of the bike. There was a vacancy. However, I was informed that a room could be booked for six hours only. The name of the motel was *Paraiso,* Paradise. It did not take me long to figure out that I had landed in a love nest. But six hours! Good Heavens! If this is the norm in Mexico, no wonder there is this myth in circulation about the "Latin Lover," who is rumoured to be indefatigable, among the world's best. I was duly impressed as I continued on down the road in the rain. We were finally lucky at the *Hotel Parador San Miguel*, a classy place with huge brick-vaulted rooms, large bathrooms, king-size beds, and, most important of all, a secure parking spot for the Rubber Cow. It was air-conditioned, and check-out was at 12.00 noon.

Perhaps in time I could get used to Mexican road conditions, if it were not for obstructions put in place on purpose, to slow you down. For long stretches the road could be quite good, but suddenly, often without warning, you would hit *topes,* literally, "moles," speed bumps that slowed you down to a crawl. This would be no problem if you had received a warning sign in time to slow down. But frequently there was no sign; you would hit these obstructions at speed and would go flying. Just to break the monotony of *topes* there would be *vibratores,* corrugations in the road surface that would rattle your bones as you rode over them. I asked myself why they had to use these devices to slow you down when entering a village or a town? The answer seems to be that the speed limit is never enforced. During all my time criss-crossing Mexico I have never met a policeman with a radar gun or seen a radar speed trap. But *topes* and *vibratores* are not unique to Mexico. Varieties of these devices can be found in almost every country south of the United States, and one learns rather quickly to look out for them.

What was more annoying than the speed bumps was the virtual absence, or the inconsistency, of road signs. Already in Ciudad Juárez I had difficulties finding my way out of town, because of the scarcity of signs pointing in the right direction. This situation got worse the farther south I traveled. Even in the more sophisticated countries, like Argentina or Chile, the sign-posting left a lot to be desired. It took me a while to realize that this was not the fault of the country. The fact that I continuously got lost was due to having been spoiled in Canada, the United States, and Europe by an over-abundance of road signs. For instance, on an expressway in Canada one would be warned 5 kilometers before a turn-off, and would receive at least three points of information, (1) the highway number, (2) the compass direction, North, South, East, West, and (3) the destination, the name of the next city. The same information would be repeated several times before the actual turn-off. At the turn-off itself there would be a sign with an arrow pointing in the direction of the turn-off, and also the word "Exit," to indicate that one was leaving the highway one was on. Immediately after the turn-off one received reconfirmation that one was on the right track by being given at least the new highway number. In Mexico and points south one would arrive at a crossroad and find no sign at all, or one without a highway number, or the name of a destination off the road that one was looking for, or any one of the names of several towns down the line in random order. Also, when highways converged for a time one would get the number of one, then the number of the other(s), at random, so that one was never sure that one had not missed a turn-off somewhere. It was absolutely imperative to stop often and ask for directions, or else run the risk of having to backtrack. I learned this the hard way. Being a man, and hence from Mars, I hated to ask for directions. I'd rather find my own way. This at times resulted in getting lost and in many time-consuming detours. Very soon I learned to adopt Venutian, i.e. more feminine, habits, and asked often, and as a reward got lost less often.

Culture shock could also be expensive. Arriving in San Luis Potosi at noon I was caught in a terrible traffic jam, aggravated by the fact that the whole town was torn up for sewer construction. Furthermore, there was a demonstration going on. Hence, instead of being able to follow the few road signs there were, I was directed by a policeman to a sidestreet, which turned into more sidestreets getting progressively narrower and narrower. Sweating profusely and rather shaken I finally succeeded in asking my way out of this maze. Hurray! Sign ahead! Left turn to Highway #57 for Mexico City. The traffic light was green. I turned left, and found myself the target of a hot pursuit by a traffic cop on a motorcycle, lights flashing. Of course I stopped immediately and put on my most winning smile, as the occasion demanded. The cop, in his early twenties, sported a Zapata mustache and the hint of a beer belly, outstanding feature of Mexican cops. Very politely he requested my *documentas*. Then we compared bikes. He said that he wouldn't mind trading his with mine. Then we enquired about our respective families. He had just married. He was curious how I, a married man, had managed to be away from home for such a long time. I informed him that it was just a matter of training. The husband has to train his wife for his absences as early as on the day of the wedding, preferably even before that. How did Christopher Columbus get away? Or Edmund Hillary? Training was the answer. Of course I didn't tell him that my stay here had been deemed "totally unaccept-able," and hence, was practically illegal, that my wife's training had been a total failure, the trainer, therefore, the candidate for an unqualified F. We had a good laugh about "the ups and downs" of married life. Then he informed me that it was his duty to give me a ticket for an illegal turn. Left turns were allowed only when the green light was flashing. Not knowing this was no excuse. This would cost me U.S.$30.00. However, there was a problem. I could pay the fine only at the office, and this happened to be closed for siesta for another two hours. He was a nice fellow. He listened patiently to my tale of poverty, of being far from home, of Mexican hospitality, and the duty we have to be nice to our foreign guests. On the latter point he was in total agreement with me. So we struck a bargain: He would not have to write out a long citation, and in return I would save time and money by being able to pay the fine on the spot. I suggested $10.00. We settled for $15.00. He gave me change for a twenty-dollar bill. We shook hands. He gave me back my *documentas*. We wished each other the best, and parted amicably. I was sure that this time "development aid" had found its way into the right pocket, where it could perhaps do some good. I hoped that he and his new wife had wine for dinner.

I had been to Mexico City several times before, and knew the lay of the town to a degree. But trying to cross this megalopolis on a motorcycle during morning rush hour was still a mindboggling experience. I was looking for Highway #190 to Oaxaca. There was indeed a road sign pointing the way. This and the following two signs were affixed to overpasses. However, the road signs on the next overpasses were used by a local politician running for a municipal office as a base for his campaign banners. All the signs were totally covered by the banners. By the time he had run out of banners, the signs to Oaxaca were nowhere to be seen. Once again I was lost and had to stop many times to ask my way out of town. I hoped that this jerk would come in last in the election.

Culture shock pursued us all the way to Oaxaca and beyond. When I had my tires put on in San Diego the mechanic told me with a smile, "You know the old saying when going to Mexico: 'Dont't drink the water.'" I must have drunk or eaten something that wreaked havoc in my gut. Fortunately, along the road to Oaxaca there were few villages, and we could stop repeatedly behind a big cactus for a call of nature, or else we would have been in big trouble. The Rubber Cow seemed to sympathize with me. Soon after filling up at one of the Pemex stations south of Mexico City, the beast started to cough and sputter and lose power, a sure sign of indigestion. It, too, must have imbibed some Mexican water, and didn't like it a bit. After cleaning out the float bowls a couple of times I noticed a slight improvement. But full recovery came only after the next fuel stop on the other side of Oaxaca. The rider had to wait yet another day before the domestic troops could destroy the foreign invader, a gut-wrenching experience.

The road from Mexico City to the Gulf of Tehuantepec via Oaxaca must be among the most thrilling rides in the country. It winds up and down tortuously over numerous mountain ranges, through villages with the obligatory *topes* and *vibratores*. Because of the changing altitude the flora varies constantly, from dry hot cactus country to humid, tropical banana groves. Traffic on this road was heavy. Numerous buses and long-haul trucks competed for the right of way. This and the many blind curves made for slow going, and the almost total absence of warning signs kept the adrenalin flowing. Many surprises were in store for the unsuspecting rider. In fact a surprise lurked behind almost every curve, in the form of a stalled vehicle, a giant pothole, a large oil slick, loose gravel, or road kill: dogs, snakes, donkeys, chicken, vultures, even cows and horses now and then. The life of a domestic animal along this road appeared to be not a happy one, certainly not a long one. It was great riding, though, and I had to give it an unqualified A+, outstanding.

After the usual afternoon thundershowers we arrived in Tehuantepec with several hours of daylight left. We were again due for an oil and filter change. Finding a place to do this was no problem. You just looked for a big oil slick on the side of the road, and you had arrived. I bought the required three liters of Castrol GTX 20W-50 and asked for permission to do it myself right there. No problem. Immediately I was surrounded by helpers. The geriatric set, parked comfortably on a nearby bench, stayed out of the way. But several teenagers competed for the privilege of being my #1 helper. I picked one of them, trying not to hurt the feelings of the others. After all, this was a highlight in their otherwise dull daily routine. Their eyes sparkled with eager anticipation when I unpacked my shiny tools and my torque wrench. Everyone wanted to make it "click" at least once. Even the oldtimers leaned forward in appreciation. Since we were parked right in the middle of the oil slick, I didn't feel too badly about our contribution to it. The boys helped to keep the mess to a minimum by placing empty containers at strategic points. The job went rather quickly amid lively conversation. Everyone seemed to be having a good time. None of my tools disappeared as I let my #1 mechanic do most of the work. He was a bright boy. His family had a farm near town. But he did not like farming. Hence, he was doing this in the hope of becoming a licensed mechanic someday. When I tipped him well he could not do enough to help me clean up with soap and water. If all oil and filter changes were so much fun, I could perhaps forgive the BMW engineers for having made the access to the oil filter so awkward.

Since this was a Thursday I was determined to arrive at the Guatemalan Embassy in Tapachula before it closed. If I needed a visa I would have the next day to get it, or else wait until Monday. I was informed that for Canadians no visa was required. During a late lunch at a restaurant on the outskirts of town the usual thundershowers came down. I waited them out so that I would not have to wear my rain suit when I went to the bank to get some Guatemalan money.

The only bank where one could get Guatemalan quetzales was downtown. When the rain stopped at 3.00 p.m. I left the restaurant in search of the bank, dressed only in shirt and jeans. The intersection in front of the bank was lower than the surrounding area, and there was about six inches of water standing from the recent downpour, black water, backed up Tapachula sewer. The traffic light had just turned green, and I was trying to cross the intersection slowly, when I was passed on the left by a taxi going full tilt. One giant tidal wave of black Tapachula water covered bike and rider from helmet to footpegs. Several pedestrians on the sidewalk shook with laughter at the sight of this baptism by sewer of a rich gringo on a shiny motorcycle. When I walked into the bank I left puddles of water behind at every step, and an evil smell announced my arrival. The teller tried to ignore me, but was urged by her boss to take my U.S. dollars and give me the requested currency. She took the money with two fingertips, handed over the quetzales, and quickly went back to shuffling papers. My odour must have overpowered her.

On our way to the Guatemalan border at Talisman it started to rain again, rather heavily. I had to put on my rain suit over my wet shirt and jeans. Very unpleasant. We were at the border at 6.00 p.m.; it was getting dark, too late to go through the formalities today.

I had read in travel guides that this border crossing was rather chaotic. It was reputedly also dangerous. Theft was said to be rife, and armed robberies had occurred in the public washrooms in broad daylight. But I was not prepared for what followed. I was still moving when about 20 teenagers stormed the bike, each one yelling at the top of his voice that he wanted to be my guide through Immigration and Customs. One of them tried to jump on the trunk in the back, almost dumping us on the side. I was livid with anger. I told them that I had no intention of crossing the border tonight. Instead I intended to stay at the hotel nearby, and cross tomorrow. They all guided us to the hotel, which did not look very trustworthy. It was surrounded by a low fence which could easily be climbed. Furthermore the doors to the units were too narrow to allow the bike to pass through. It would have to be left outside during the night. I decided to go back to Tapachula, a distance of 20 km, and find a hotel there. My would-be helpers were not pleased to see me leave. It was still raining hard.

Wet, smelly, frustrated, unnerved, and demoralized, I settled down in the Hotel Kamico, the Rubber Cow resting securely in one corner of the room. It was time to reconsider this whole affair. Even though I did not approve of my wife's disapproval of this trip, the words "totally unacceptable" still kept ringing in my ears. Then there was this humiliating baptism by sewer in the afternoon. Was this part of the Rain Curse? And then the mob scene at the border. Previously I had done quite a bit of travelling, in Australia, New Zealand, around South America by bus, four times around the world, by plane, by train, and by bus. I had been to places like Lhasa, Peshawar, and Timbuktu, and it had always been fun. But now I was having none. The bike was like a millstone around my neck, security a problem. I couldn't even go to the washroom without worrying about it. Furthermore, the hassles at the borders were frustrating. Enough was enough. I decided to call it quits now, and go back home. At least my wife would be happy. A phone-call home relayed the decision.

7. *Northward Bound*

I hated Tapachula. Freshly laundered, and, I hoped, better smelling, I saddled up next morning for the ride north. The sun was shining brilliantly, and there were no clouds in the sky. The streets were dry, except for a few puddles. Was this an immediate reward for "acceptable" behaviour? I could well imagine the smirks on the faces of my former colleagues from the English Department if they were to read this. They would never believe it. But I swear to tell the truth, and nothing but the truth. Truth is stranger than fiction. The nice weather was to continue for the following eight days, until we reached Northern Florida. The catastrophes of the day before were almost forgotten. Why had I changed my mind so quickly about the trip? Was it an act of cowardice? This question would haunt me for the next two months. Trying to find my way out of town, I got lost for the third time in two days. Why can't they put up proper signs? Or am I that stupid? I hated myself. I hated Tapachula.

In keeping with my plan to circle North America in a counterclockwise direction I turned north for the Gulf of Mexico, and followed it around all the way down to Key West. Highway #180 via Veracruz, Poza Rica, and Tampico was a delight to ride, especially in this good weather. What was I doing here? I should have been in Guatemala instead. Nevertheless, the pleasure principle had gained the upper hand once more. Now and then I had a great view of the crystal blue water and white sand beaches of the Caribbean. But at closer investigation I noticed heavy pollution, and resisted the desire for a swim. At the many roadside stalls, usually beside the *topes,* where traffic had to come to a crawl, one could gorge on the fruit the area had to offer in abundance: bananas, oranges, pineapples, mangos, coconuts, and some I had never seen before. Numerous restaurants catered to the palates of seafood- lovers: fish, crabs, and shrimps of all sizes. The multiplicity of hotels along the way suggested that the area was popular with tourists coming over from Mexico City for sun and surf. This was the beginning of August, prime holiday season. Here it was not as hot as in Acapulco, not as touristy, and hence not as expensive, and also not as polluted. Security was no problem. Veracruz emerged as my favourite among the cities to which I would gladly return.

In front of a small restaurant north of Tampico I spotted a black BMW motorcycle like the one I had "sold" to my brother. This was all the excuse I needed to stop for food and human contact. The bike looked as though it had seen better days. The paint was chipped in many places; there were some dents in the tank and fenders, and the chrome showed rust spots. Loose wires could be seen hanging near fixtures that they were supposed to supply with electricity. It had Guatemalan licence plates affixed crookedly to its rear fender. This black beauty was fading.

On one of the tables outside in the shade sat a slim and handsome young man in his early thirties accompanied by a boy no older than twelve. Exchanging greetings and introducing myself, I learned that Jim and his son were on their way to San Antonio to visit family. They had been in Guatemala for the past five years working for an American missionary church group. They loved the country and their work, and were determined to return after their holidays in the States were over.

Comparing motorcycles, I mentioned that his Beemer seemed to be getting a good workout. He agreed, and added that just before leaving Guatemala City he had taken the cylinder heads off to grind the valves. Upon reassembly he had noticed that the pistons needed new rings. However, the local BMW-dealer was short one compression ring and one oil ring. These were on order. Since his holidays were beginning the following week he did not want to wait for the order to arrive. So he had assembled the cylinders with one compression ring missing on one side, and the oil ring missing on the other. "This is why we're doing a bit of oil," he added with a grin. The bike would receive proper attention in San Antonio as soon as they arrived. I had to admire the two for their courage. I would never have dared to leave my garage with the engine in such a state. He and his son had set out for a trip of over 2,000 km through a country where support for this kind of machine was nonexistent. When I told them so, he replied that this was of no great worry to them. What was a greater worry at the moment was the fact that they were practically down to their last peso. But since they had a credit card they wanted to make a run for the border today. On the spur of the moment I decided to ride with them.

When we were ready to leave, I suggested that they go ahead and set the pace. They agreed and did not waste any time doing so. Their average speed was just under 110 km/h, and this on a road that left a lot to be desired, and with an engine that was less than perfect, to put it mildly. In spite of the many toll stations (driving in Mexico is expensive), in spite of topes and vibratores, we made good time, and stopped now and then for a drink, or simply to stretch our legs (Jim to count what was left of his money). When we were about 50 km short of Matamoros and the border, it began to get dark. Since I still had some pesos left, I decided to spend the night on the Mexican side, and cross the border the following morning. We shook hands; I wished them good luck as we parted company.

Twilight is brief in this latitude. It is dark as soon as the sun sets. This was to be my first experience riding at night in Mexico. It was an experience I did not care to repeat. There were horse-drawn vehicles on the road that did not have any lights. Some cars had headlights, others had none, or if they did have any, drivers did not bother turning them on. Those who had turned them on were not overly worried about their use of high or low beam, or where the lights were aimed, which was often straight into my eyes. In these moments of blindness I had several close encounters with potholes, which at night in the black asphalt were totally invisible. To get out of this dangerous situation, I needed to find a hotel fast.

7) Florida highway #1, Mile "0"

Arriving at the outskirts of Matamoros, I stopped at the first hotel, *Cupido*. It had curtains in front of the carports. Of course I knew where I had landed. But I was desperate enough by now to give it a try. They had a full house; no wonder, it was Sunday night. The next place was called *Jardín de delicias;* there were no curtains on the carports, since the whole establishment was surrounded by a high brick wall. It had one empty unit. However, the former occupants had plugged the toilet, and there was water covering the floor. It would take them 30 minutes to clean up. If I could wait that long, I could have the room. I learned that in the *Jardín* one could rent a room either for one hour only, or for the whole night. I found this very interesting from a cultural point of view. Presumably life moved a lot faster here than in Chihuahua, Matamoros being so close to the United States, home of the world-famous "quickie." Why waste time and money on five more hours or a whole night, if you can do the job in one. This made sense to me. Later, when I returned to Mexico, I made it a point to study rental times whenever I stopped at one of these establishments. One hour seems to be the shortest time-slot available. I have not yet found a place that catered to minute-men. I did not care to wait at the *Jardín,* and moved on.

Since by now I was practically in town and riding under streetlights, I decided to cross the border immediately. Before I knew what happened, I found myself across the bridge on the American side. I had not seen Mexican Customs and Immigration. It was necessary to go back to sign out bike and rider officially, or else be charged import duties later on. They had my VISA number. This meant paying bridge toll once again. There was another motorcycle with two up in front of me. They were searching their pockets for the 25 cents toll. It was Jim and his son. I gave them a quarter. It so happened that they had also missed Mexican Customs and Immigration and had to go back. Exit formalities at this hour of the day went fast. After having received the *Salida* stamp in the passport from Immigration, we went over to Customs to cancel the "Banjercito" document, and have the holographic sticker removed from the windshield. The Americans looked into my saddle bags while asking the routine questions. We were on the road again in 15 minutes. No hassles. Now the next thing to do was to find a cheap motel in Brownsville. *The Sands* had no big plastic curtains, no carports, and no hourly rental. Check-out time was at 11.00 a.m. The bike and I could not sleep together in the same room. We knew we had arrived in America the Good.

Riding, riding, riding, was the motto for the next few days, riding over interstates, riding over country roads, riding over anything in between that would get us closer to Key West. Corpus Christi went by on the right, then smack through the center of Houston we went during rush hour, and over to Baton Rouge, Louisiana. New Orleans I had visited with my wife the year before, but it looked different from the saddle of the Rubber Cow. Then across the state border to Gulfport, Mississippi, and on to Mobile, Alabama, and Pensacola, Florida. Down the panhandle via Panama City, Tampa, Fort Myers, Naples, and Miami. We were looking forward with eager anticipation to ride the famous Florida #1 over the islands, which they called keys, all the way to "Mile 0."

It was culture shock in reverse. Everything appeared so clean. There was no litter to be seen anywhere. The pavement was in A-1 condition no matter what the status of the road. There was no road toll. No old jalopies were puttering about. Did these vehicles have horns? By all appearances not. But all cars, buses, and trucks had lights that functioned. The horses that pulled them were to be found under the hood only, and their drivers were so law-abiding that they obeyed the speed limit most of the time, and actually came to a halt at stop signs. Red meant red, and a double line no passing. The police saw to that, a police that seemed immune to accepting "development aid"; or was I mistaken? Furthermore, there was a choice of gas stations. No oil slicks anywhere. Gasoline was free of water additives. And then there was a multitude of fast food joints that were advertised on signs before every exit, and sometimes on billboards along the way. It was a coffee junky's heaven. It felt almost like being home in Canada.

There were also some surprises in store for the unsuspecting Northerner. I had never seen a real cotton field before. The closest I had come to cotton balls was our medicine cabinet in the bathroom. Texas to me had been a state of cattle ranches and oil fields. What I saw instead were miles and miles of cotton, ready to be harvested, a beautiful sight. I had to stop and feel the fluffy little balls before taking a picture. Florida to me had been a state of citrus groves, retirement communities, and golf courses. What surprised me in Florida was that there were forests in the northern part of the state, and there was heavy logging going on. However, the greatest surprise in store for me was Florida Highway #1.

On Thursday, August 14th, during a late lunch at Denny's in Homestead, I met George, from Bismarck, North Dakota. I had parked my bike beside his shiny brand-new Harley in front of the restaurant. It turned out that both of us wanted to make the run to Key West before sunset. We decided to do it together. George was in his late forties, slightly greying at the temples, clean-shaven, wearing immaculately clean black leathers in spite of the heat; it was in the high 90s. He had quit his job in Bismarck, and was determined not to go back to work until his funds ran out. He said he had time for work the rest of his life, just not right now. For the moment riding his bike had priority. We enjoyed swapping tales of the road, until it was time to roll.

After all the hype I had read about Florida #1, perhaps I had set my expectations too high. Traffic was heavy as we entered Key Largo, and stayed that way all the way to Key West. We passed cheap housing developments, trailer parks, some of them trailer slums, strip malls of various sizes, fast-food restaurants, hotels and motels catering to all budgets, dozens of service stations, and miles and miles of car dealerships. Where was the beautiful unspoiled scenery I was expecting, the white sand beaches studded with wind-blown palms. Where was the white-crested surf breaking on the shore? Once in a while one would get a glimpse of all this, if one could take one's eyes off the road. However, the environmental pollution and the urban sprawl overpowered the little bits and pieces of untouched nature that were left. The road itself was the best feature of this whole stretch. Pencil straight and in good condition, it made its way over the numerous bridges and across keys of various sizes. The drivers, however, tried their best to spoil a good thing. They kept cutting in on us from the left and from the right. They seemed to ignore the presence of motorcycles altogether as they merrily tootled along at a snail's pace. About the presence of an inordinately large number of motorhomes in this neck of the woods I shall pass over in silence. Florida #1 turned out to be a big disappointment. I gave it a B-, O.K., but nothing to brag about.

George didn't think so. He loved the ride. Perhaps his expectations had been different from mine. He had been down here once before with his best friend. They had trucked their bikes in from Bismarck to attend Daytona Bike Week, had left the truck in Daytona, and had ridden down to Road's End. He told me that he knew "the perfect place" to stay in Key West; the place where he and his friend had stayed two years ago. I trusted his judgment and let him lead the way.

It was getting dark as we entered Key West. George's memory served him well. We arrived at our destination without getting lost. It was a Bed and Breakfast place, as I discovered the next morning, one block away from the Hemingway Estate. The main house was immaculately kept, probably restored recently. Its front was in the style of a Southern Plantation manor house, white on white, with a portico composed of four massive neoclassical columns. On the one side of the driveway two touring bikes were parked. On the other there were two cars with out-of-state licence plates. The whole place was surrounded by a six-foot-high wall with a gate, which silenced the warning bells in my head. I was impressed. At least this place lived up to my expectations of Key West, and the price was right. One "Atta boy!" for George.

Since we were not overly ravenous yet, we sauntered around the main tourist haunts of Key West. Tourism was obviously the main industry in this town. There were shops galore all selling the same type of tourist junk, T-shirts, and similar items of touristy clothing, sea shells, cheap jewellery, etc.; hundreds of bars and restaurants. I had seen all of this before in similar places, three of which that popped into my mind immediately being Bar Harbor, Maine, Lake Placid, New York, and particularly Provincetown, Cape Cod. In my mind the similarity of the latter town to Key West was striking. Both were sea-side resorts, both had a sizable yacht harbor, both were within easy reach of a large city. George listened to my revelations attentively, but seemed to be more interested in finding a good restaurant. Of course he knew "the perfect place," the same place where he and his friend had eaten two years ago, a seafood restaurant near the waterfront. I was again impressed.

During a delicious seafood dinner George filled me in a little more about his life in North Dakota. He had worked for an insurance company, selling life insurance. Since he had, as he put it, "the gift of the gab," the money was good. His friend had been in management in the same company. However, a few months ago the friend had received an offer of a promotion, which meant relocating in another city, an offer he could not refuse. The friend had moved to Fargo, and George had taken an extended leave of absence. Of course I retaliated, and told

George my tale of trials and tribulations. He did not offer any advice, and simply said, shaking his head, "Women!"— During dessert George suggested that we have our after-dinner cocktail at another place. "Don't tell me," I said with a grin, "you know 'the perfect place,' the same place you had a drink with your friend two years ago.— What is this, George, a trip down memory lane?" He just laughed, and led the way.

After all the wine I had drunk with my fish I didn't really care where we were going. It was a fairly large establishment, and at this time of the night, close to 11.00 p.m., it was crowded. But there was still room at one of the tables. I found the music, presided over by a disc jockey, too loud for my six decades-old ear drums. In the flattering dim light a number of people were dancing, some mixed couples, some women together, even some men together. Aha!—I'd had my suspicions about George all along, but now I knew for sure how the boy was wired. We ordered our drinks, but conversation was difficult because of the loud music. When the music started again after a short pause, George looked at me and said, "Let's dance!" I was stunned for a second or two. What did that mean in this context? I dance with him? (There were several male couples on the dance floor.) Or, I ask one of the women standing at the bar, and he ask another one. Or, we both ask the same woman. Or, we just get up and dance solo, as some women were doing. Not knowing what to do I took refuge in the old ruse used by women since the time of Eve after The Fall, the headache excuse. "Sorry, George, this loud music has given me a splitting headache. I think I'll just finish my drink and call it a day. But you go ahead and dance. Don't mind me." He stayed at the table until I had finished my drink. I hoped I had not hurt his feelings. Upon leaving I wished him good luck on his way home, and hoped that I would see him at breakfast. I honestly didn't feel like dancing with anyone after this long, hard day. All I wanted was a soft bed and oblivion.

At breakfast George was a no-show, presumably the victim of an all-night danceathon. Not being bright-eyed and bushy-tailed myself after all that booze the night before, I managed to check out shortly after nine o'clock. On the way back over the bridges, the keys, past the strip malls, trailer parks, and car lots, I was thinking that perhaps I had been a bit too harsh when I graded this section of Florida #1. In light of the sybaritic experiences Key West has to offer, I should upgrade it a bit: I decided to give it a straight B, O.K.

Given my precarious state of head, I had no ambition to cover a great distance. It was Friday, and traffic around Miami and Fort Lauderdale was heavy. We were aiming for Fort Pierce, but by mistake left Interstate #95 one exit too soon. Disaster of a different kind struck: we were lost in a bedroom community of identical houses, identical lawns, and identical streets, some with dead ends, others going in circles. Again my Martian nature was asserting itself, as I was determined to find my way out of this maze by myself. But I kept coming back to the same place again and again, unable to find the key. Or coming to think of it, perhaps I was in a different place each time, it just looked like the same place to me. How do the people living here manage to find their own beds after a night's carousing? A rat (rats are experts in solving mazes) would have solved this one in minutes. It took me over half an hour, and several times I had to ask humbly for directions. Finally the familiar sign of Florida Hwy #1 appeared, and we arrived in Fort Pierce in the dark.

Next day on Interstate #95, as we tried to negotiate the heavy traffic around Jacksonville, we knew that we had returned to normal when it began to rain in a manner we had become accustomed to before Tapachula: it poured. It was too dangerous to stop and put on the rain suit. So I just got wet and wetter, until the water began to rise in my boots. After 20 minutes it stopped. Half an hour later I was dry again, except for my feet, which remained water-logged for the rest of the day. Florida had kissed us good-bye with a rather wet kiss.

Thunderstorms chased us all the way across Georgia and into South Carolina. But now I was in my rain gear and felt quite snug until we turned off onto Highway #17 at Point South. Then all hell broke loose. A black wall of water descended upon us, and made for zero visibility. We had to stop for the night, forced by circumstances.

From Charleston on, which we reached at nine o'clock the next morning, everything looked familiar. We had been down here two years ago in April, following the advice of one of my friends, who was raving about the Blue Ridge Parkway. Riding the Blue Ridge had been, indeed, an unforgettable experience: the road itself, as it curved over the Blue Ridge mountains, the changing scenery at every corner, and the riot of blooms along both sides of the road, magnolias and azaleas *en masse*. This trip had also seen the appearance of the first symptoms of my motorhome phobia. These unwieldy monsters should be banned from the Blue Ridge. We had lasted as far as Asheville, North Carolina, then we turned left for Charleston and home. Now we were practically following the tire tracks we had made two years ago. This promised to be unadulterated pleasure, with the small exception, perhaps, of Myrtle Beach.

Two years ago, passing through Myrtle Beech, I couldn't believe my eyes what I saw in this holiday ghetto. The beaches and the hotels, catering to the sun and surf worshippers from the North, trying to offer something for everyone's budget, may pass as a necessary evil of today's mass tourism, but couldn't they just be content with being hotels by the sea as they were in most other places of the world? No, in their front yards they had to erect ghastly structures of steel and concrete mimicking space mountains, shrunken European castles, or fairy-tale grottoes, a Disneyesque fantasyland with animals dressed and acting like humans, little green elves, fire-breathing dragons, and giant dragon-slaying super-heroes. Myrtle Beech was as tacky as Santaland in North Pole, Alaska, pure *Kitsch*, both going after the kiddie-dollar. During the past two years it hadn't gotten any better, just bigger, with a few more atrocities added, the latter culled from recent T.V. series. So Scrooge on his Rubber Cow tried to get through Myrtle Beech as fast as possible.

One of the great rides on the Eastern Seabord starts at Jacksonville, North Carolina, where Highway #24 turns east to join #70 to Moorehead City, and on to Cedar Island, where it becomes #12. I had a two-hour wait for the ferry to

Ocracoke, and treated myself to a *de luxe* seafood dinner at the Ferry Restaurant. The crossing took two hours and fifteen minutes. It was dark when we docked. Since the temperature at this latitude was quite pleasant, I would have gladly returned to camping, if I could only find the campground. Oh, those Martian attitudes! Disgusted with myself I booked into the Bluff Shoal Motel, which was luxurious, but hard on my budget. It was a fitting end for a great day.

I knew that another great day of riding was awaiting us. It started off with a ferry ride over to Cape Hatteras, from which Highway #12 runs on a narrow spit of land called the outer banks, at times, so it seems, lower than sea-level. I had to congratulate the residents along this magnificent coastline, many of them seasonal residents only, for keeping *Kitsch* at bay. There were none of those ghastly structures that disfigured Myrtle Beech. I did not see even a single example of the well-known fast-food chains, which seem to be ubiquitous everywhere else. After a delicious breakfast at a "normal" restaurant in Nags Head, we were looking forward to another highlight awaiting us, the bridge-tunnel crossing of Chesapeake Bay at Norfolk, Virginia. Twice the highway on concrete pillars dips down under the water of the bay to let ocean-going vessels pass overhead, an experience unequalled anywhere else. What is so striking is the fact that the road appears to come to an end ahead in the middle of the bay, only to take a sudden dive underwater. A marvellous feat of engineering, more striking than the Chunnel, and great riding.

The Owl Motel near the Maryland state border fulfilled all the requirements for yet another oil and filter change. It had a large overhang in front of the rooms. I made sure to get one as far away as possible from traffic lanes, so that I could do my messy job undisturbed. To stop the draining oil from dripping all over the place, I decided to remove the strike plate protecting the oil pan from high objects on the road. This was the environmentally friendly thing to do, but it involved more work, and was rather boring, since I had no one to talk to, or so it seemed. I had put a piece of cardboard on the ground, and was in the process of lying down, when I saw an old guy —I rephrase that— when I saw a mature gentleman my age walking toward me. His name was Jim. He was a salesman for a paper company in New Jersey. Since his first appointment was at ten o'clock, he had time to kill, and obviously had decided to kill it with me. When I do mechanical things on the bike I like to focus on the job at hand. I usually don't like to chat with anyone about trivial things. Whenever I had done so in the past, I had almost always screwed up, forgetting to tighten a nut, once even forgetting to put back the oil drain plug. This had resulted in a very expensive rinse of the motor with one litre of new motor oil. But being a polite person, and one who basically likes human contact, I could not tell Jim to go take a hike and come back when it suited me. We talked as best we could with me in a horizontal position under the bike, and Jim parked on the bench in front of my room. This conversation was not job-oriented, as it had been in Tehuantepec, but it made the time fly just as fast.

Jim seemed to be genuinely interested in my trip, and asked pertinent questions about my freaking-out experience in Tapachula. "Culture shock," he said.

"Cowardice," I replied. He continued arguing against my self-accusation, but conceded that if I, *myself* was convinced that I had been a coward, there was only one thing to do: Go back and rehabilitate myself. Of course that thought had occurred to me before, but hearing it expressed in so many words by a total stranger made it all the more cogent. It took a lot of concentration on my part to put all the nuts and bolts back where they belonged, lest this motor receive another rinse job, or, horror of horrors, experience a dry run. When I was finished, we went for a coffee, since he still had an hour to kill, and I was in no particular hurry. I had enjoyed his company immensely, and told him so as we parted. I hoped he'd sell a lot of paper that day.

With my mind already back in Tapachula we headed for the last stage over what could be considered the *non plus ultra* of the highway systems of the world, the New Jersey Turnpike and the New York Thruway, very busy, very expensive, and very secure. No one ever gets lost on these toll highways with road signs in such abundance, so they say. Only idiots manage to do so in such a fool-proof environment. As we were passing by Newark Airport, New Jersey, at a fast clip, marvelling at the magnificent skyline of New York City unrolling to our right, I must have blinked for an instant, and promptly missed my access to #87, the New York Thruway. The ensuing dogleg to get this idiot on a motorcycle back on track cost us half an hour. It was great riding, nevertheless. After a few miles west on #90, we turned north for Amsterdam and #30, which leads into the Adirondack Mountains. This was the first night of camping since Yuma, which seemed ages ago. It had also been the first day in a long while when I could wear my leather jacket without courting instant death from heat stroke. We were getting close to home.

Wednesday, August 20. The ride through the Adirondacks was to be the grand finale, and it ended with a bang. I had forgotten how it felt to be cold. It was cold, in the low fifties. I had to put on my rain suit over my leathers to stop shivering. The grandiose scenery, however, the excellent road, and the light traffic almost made one forget the low mercury. Tupper Lake, close to 11.00 a.m., seemed to be a good place to raise low blood sugar and caffeine levels, and incidentally to elevate body core temperature. I backed the bike into a slot in front of the Golden Arches, what the heck. Their coffee is drinkable, if only barely. There was a mud puddle to my right, but since I get off on the left, this didn't bother me. When it was time to leave, and I was going through the ritual of dressing up, I was being watched by several people through the large window. Swollen with the pride of ownership I mounted the Rubber Cow, fired her up, shifted the weight over to my right foot to shift gear with my left, and promptly slipped in the mud puddle. Down we went with a bang, right into the mud. Scrambling out from under the machine, stopping the motor, shutting off the fuel tabs, and uprighting the bike was done in a matter of seconds. Some men walked over and asked if everything was O.K. "Oh, sure, sure," I replied wryly. "I do that all the time for dramatic effect." The loss of face, however, spoiled the ride for the next hour. This was the second time we had toppled over on this trip, the first time having been on the

Yuma campground in soft gravel. On the way home I chuckled over the thought of suing Macdonald's for mud in their parking lot, thus endangering the lives of unsuspecting motorcyclists, but decided against it, since they had a lawsuit pending with someone over having served coffee too hot for human consumption. Their lawyers obviously had enough on their plastic plates already. Hence, with a bit of dried mud on one sleeve, but otherwise in good spirits, we arrived home at 2.30 p.m., thus completing the circumnavigation of North America, the top portion of the figure eight. Total time: 51 days. Total distance: 28,864 km, or 18,040 miles.

Interlude

For it is my belief no man ever understands quite his own artful dodges to escape from the grim shadow of self-knowledge.
—Joseph Conrad, *Lord Jim*

8. *Conditioning and a Trip to Germany*

One of the episodes I can remember distinctly from my early teenage years in Germany is the street fight in which I was involved as a member of a neighbourhood gang. It took place only a few years after the fall of the totalitarian "law-and-order" regime of Hitler's Germany, when all the hoods, petty and big- time, had been in positions of authority, and street violence had been low key, since there was a war going on. During the early years after the war there was still not much violence in German cities. We went at each other with our fists. After having received several powerful punches to my face, I called it quits and walked away. My mother, when she saw my black eye and my bleeding nose, had called it good judgment. My fellow gang members, on the other hand, had called it cowardice. To avoid similar situations in the future, I tried to stay away from anything that would lead to violence. I took up boxing as a sport, just to prove that I was no coward, and yes, in the ring I was used as a punching bag on many occasions. But this never succeeded in erasing from my mind the memory of that fateful day in a back alley of my hometown. Even today I cringe whenever I think of it.

The Tapachula incident had added fresh fuel to the burning anguish carried over from my youth. I just had to go back, pick up from where I had left, and prove once again that I was no coward. The continuation of The Big One as planned originally had become more than an extended ride in the country. It had become a mission. And in order to go on that mission with something resembling a clean conscience, I had to start laying the ground work immediately, i.e. I had to prepare my wife for a second departure. This would take all the bravery I could muster.

When I arrived home I noticed with satisfaction that the house was still standing basically as I had left it. The lock of the front door had not been changed. My clothes were still hanging in my closet. Even my old toothbrush was still in its holder. Fu Fu the cat, however, gave me a dismissive tailwag, showing his disgust with having been temporarily semi-orphaned. I had made arrangements with a boy from the neighborhood to cut the lawn. He had fulfilled his contract faithfully. There were some weeds growing in the flower patch looking at me accusingly. The good thing here was the fact that they had grown so tall as to offer a good handle, which made yanking them out easier. And last, but by no means least, I was welcomed back to bed and board by my wife of twenty-eight years, grudgingly, but the D-word was not mentioned again. The first question she asked was what had happened in Tapachula. She didn't believe me when I told her that I had had second thoughts about my "surprising" her with the extension of my trip. Women seem to have a sixth sense about such things. The amount of work to be done seemed almost insurmountable.

Time was of the essence. I had told the cop in San Luis Potosi that it was never too early to start training your wife for your absences. But what if past training had not been successful? Was there such a thing as being too late? As having missed the boat, as it were? In the words of folk wisdom, *"You can't teach an old dog new tricks."* It was obvious that my training methods had failed. After twenty-seven years of professional language-teaching in the classroom I had seen teaching methods come and go: the audio-visual method, the direct method, the total immersion method, to mention but a few. I had tried them all at home, with the exception of total immersion, which, when taken to extremes, involving large bodies of water, could be considered unethical. I had to devise a new approach, and I thought that I had been led to it by the old proverb quoted above about dogs. Old dogs can indeed be taught new tricks, as demonstrated by Ivan Pavlov.

At the turn of the century the Russian physiologist Ivan Pavlov had created quite a stir in scholarly circles with his experiments involving dogs. Whenever he proceeded to feed his dogs he simultaneously rang a bell. The dogs started to salivate. After a while whenever Pavlov rang the bell the dogs salivated, whether food was given or not. Learning had taken place, learning in the form of conditioning. Salivation was the conditioned response. As a student with a male-centred view of the world I had always pictured Pavlov's dogs to be of the male variety, probably big drooling St. Bernards. But there is no reason to assume that this kind of conditioning would not work as well with the female variety, whose generic name I don't dare to mention in this context. Moreover, Pavlov had demonstrated that this learning technique could be applied to humans as well. He received a Nobel Prize for his work. Perhaps here was the answer to my prayers, applied psychology, my last chance.

As a househusband with a working wife I was put in charge of cooking on many occasions. If I were to draw on all of my culinary expertise, it would be easy to trigger instant salivation in my hungry spouse as soon as she walked into the house. But that would be too basic; it would not serve my purpose. My approach would have to be more sophisticated. The conditioned response I was after would have to be an attitude; a positive attitude toward South America and my trip, to be exact. It would mean taking Pavlovian conditioning to a higher level. It was worth a try.

In the weeks that followed, whenever I had prepared a particularly delicious meal, after we had sat down for dinner with candlelight and wine, I would mention exciting things about South America, about their food and drink, about their cultures, etc. Similarly, when we went out to a fancy restaurant I tried to create good vibes about the places down under. I don't know if all that Pavlovian bell-ringing worked in the end. In any case I tried to do my very best to follow the example of the great master. And *I* didn't expect to get a Nobel Prize for *my* work.

There were, of course, many other things to do before I could think of riding off at sunrise. The bike had to be given a good scrub. There were still layers of Yukon brown in nooks and crannies difficult to access with ordinary sponges and brushes. After many days of hard labour I had the Rubber Cow in almost mint condition, even though she now had over 76,000 km on the clock. The bike had performed flawlessly. Therefore, I did not see any reason to make modifications. It would have to do "as is," BMW off-the-shelf hard luggage and all. I should perhaps have heeded the advice given in travel guides, particularly regarding shock absorbers. But I believed in my mechanic's motto, "If it ain't broke, don't fix it." And nothing was "broke."

Another thing that needed immediate attention was my body. During the past forty years I had followed a body builder's life-style, spending at least two hours in the gym six days a week, pumping iron and doing aerobics. Some have called me an exercise addict. This may be true. However, unlike an addict I could stop my program without withdrawal symptoms as soon as I went on a trip. On the road it was just too much trouble to pursue any kind of exercise program. But at home again my gym routine had to be put back on track. I was convinced that being physically fit helped keep me alive during many hours in the saddle day in and day out even under adverse conditions. Unlike walking, running, or bicycling, motorcycling does not make you fit. It's the other way around. You have to be fit in order to ride a motorcycle. It's a matter of survival.

There were also more family responsibilities to be taken care of. My brother Heinz in Ulm, Germany was celebrating his fiftieth birthday. At the same time my niece's son was to be baptized. My wife and I were invited to attend. This promised to be no hardship. Moreover, I had been informed that Black Beauty was ready and willing to take me for a long ride if I so desired. Could one neglect such family responsibilities?

After the last party at my brother's place in Germany my wife had to go back to her job in Canada. I was free to get reacquainted with Black Beauty, now renamed affectionately "The Oldtimer," since my brother's new bike was on order. I had read a lot lately about motorcycling in the Alps, and, drawing from my experience in the past, I thought that the writers/riders were exaggerating a bit. I had crossed the Alps twice as a teenager, both times with a bicycle, the first time over the Brenner Pass via Innsbruck, and the second time over the St. Gotthard via Zürich. All I remembered was that the exercise had been hard work, much sweat and not much fun. Perhaps it was different on a motorbike. I had to find out for myself, and The Oldtimer was the perfect companion to do it with. It had received a new timing chain, an oil change, and a tune-up, and was running like a Swiss watch. I did not like the ugly oversize German licence plate defacing its beautiful rear end. This big bare piece of metal made its *derrière* look like a baboon's. But sitting in the saddle I didn't have to look at it. So what the hell. On September 10 we left the Gothic spires of the Ulm Cathedral behind for points south.

The first hour on the *Autobahn* could have been disastrous. Going around 100 km/h the two of us oldtimers were continuously being passed by traffic going at a speed that made us think we were standing still, tempting me to get off the bike. When the silhouette of the approaching mountains appeared on the horizon we

left the *Autobahn* and traffic was easier on us. From then on, as the road got twisti-
er, we were keeping up with the best of them. This Oldie still had some spunk left.

Back in my bicycling days as a teenager I always wanted to ride the
Großglockner Hochalpenstraße, if only for its reputation as being one of the greatest rides in the Alps, for its scenic beauty, for its superb highway engineering, and
for its difficulty. John Hermann's *Motorcycle Journeys Through the Alps* gives it two
stars, the highest distinction awarded, which it shares with only eight other rides
among the forty-nine described. On our way there we would have the chance to
experience another two-star ride, the *Timmels Joch,* crossing a mountain range
between Austria and Italy. Heading straight for the *Timmels Joch,* at a coffee stop
near Imst in Austria, I mentioned our goal to a cruiser rider, who was trying to
work his way through a large piece of apple strudel, something we had in common. "Once, but never again," he said. "That ride took everything I had out of
me. I was bushed at the end of it." That's what I wanted to hear. This smacked of
two-star riding. That's what we were here for. As we serpentined up on the toll
road to the top of *Timmels Joch,* I imagined what this ride would have been on a
bicycle. No, give me a motorcycle any time. It makes the magnificent scenery look
even more magnificent.

We were going to tackle the *Großglockner* the next day, so, after passing
through Merano and Bolzano, we called it a day at a little inn in the village of
Nova Levante, *Welschenofen* in German, on the *Große Dolomitenstraße.* We had
thought the *Großglockner* would be the single highlight of the trip, but we were
in for a big surprise. The next day took us through the Dolomite mountains past
the Olympic city of Cortina d'Ampezzo, an area where John Hermann finds two
more two-star rides, and even waxes poetic, describing the scenery as being
"almost a religious experience." Indeed, the jagged snow-covered peaks of the
Dolomites have no equal anywhere. This is the place where one would like to
linger awhile. But we had to push on, if we wanted to be in Tierra del Fuego at
Christmas. By now I was totally dazzled and starry-eyed by all I had seen and
experienced. Nevertheless, the *Großglockner* for me lived up to its reputation as
the ultimate in motorcycle fun. It was so much pleasure to ride that it could be
labelled decadent. As a toll road it can be ridden as often as desired, back and
forth, and back again, once the rider has paid his dues, which are quite hefty.
There were bikes of all makes and sizes flitting up and down. The two oldtimers
made a valiant effort to keep up with the flow, but an effort it remained. We were
outclassed without a doubt. But then we hadn't come here to establish a new
record for a *Großglockner* crossing. We had come to have some fun, and we got
our money's worth with interest. The grade of A+ I had to award this road took
on a new meaning. The grandiose scenery, the quality of the well-engineered
road, the never-ending hairpin turns, the quaint places along the way where one
could stop and have an excellent cappucino (there was no bad coffee available
anywhere) all taken together amounted to a nomination for a Nobel Prize, if such
an award existed for motorcycle roads.

Motorcycling in the Alps turned out to be the ultimate riding experience, the *non plus ultra* of the sport. There is no better place in the world for a rider's self-indulgence than the Alps. The books were right. Biking in the Alps is dangerous; it could become addictive.

During these days of elation, criss-crossing the Alps, I had a lot of time to think about the continuation of the trip. The next move would have to be setting a departure date. It would have to be late enough to give me enough time to winterize the house. Canadian winters can be quite cantankerous, with plenty of snow and ice, and double digit below zero temperatures. My wife would be alone in a house in the country, a forty-minute drive to her job. This would have to be taken into consideration when planning the escape. But it would have to be early enough to allow me to get away without being trapped on the way in an early snowstorm, and these arrived some years by the end of October. I decided that October 21 would be the perfect date of departure. It would fulfill both requirements. Moreover, I had returned from the Alaska portion on August 20. The trip would, therefore, continue after an interlude of exactly two months. It would still be possible to reach the end of the road in Ushuaia by Christmas.

Back in Canada the nicest time of the year had just begun, autumn with its many colours, cool nights, and falling leaves, a reminder that winter was on its way. If I wanted to be on my way, I'd better get busy. The garden had to be put to sleep. Our two cars had to be winterized, that is, the oil had to be changed, and winter tires installed. All the hatches of the house had to be closed, storm windows and doors checked. Did the heating system work? Was the plumbing protected from freezing? Someone had to be contracted to plow the snow after a snowstorm. And more conditioning had to be done.

At this stage of preparations it appeared that the object of all this attention was well-acquainted with the work of Professor Pavlov. More often than before I was treated to delicious home-cooked meals, served with candlelight and wine, a lot of wine. They were accompanied by messages about how beautiful it was in the comfort of our home in the idyllic setting of a Canadian winter wonderland; a wood fire crackling in the open fireplace; the smell of roasting chestnuts and baking cookies, the joys of Christmas, New Year's Day, Epiphany, St. Valentine's Day, Mardi Gras, St. Patrick's Day, Easter, etc. She was pulling out all the stops. The Pavlovian bell was being rung constantly. Adverse conditioning was taking place, including salivation, and it was getting more difficult each day to ride off at sunrise.

However, time is inexorable. I had done my chores as planned. The bike was loaded and ready to roll. Now all we needed was a clear morning on Monday, October 21, so that we could ride off in style.

South America

9. *Tapachula Revisited*

Leave-taking was almost a replay of a similar ceremony held on July 1. There were no tears, no hugs and kisses, no "Good luck!" wishes. When I was ready to roar away, I said, "Please, Dear, no Rain Curse this time. We had enough rain in Alaska to last us a lifetime." "Oh," she replied, smiling sweetly, "I don't worry about the weather. I have *El Niño* on my side to take care of *that*. But I wish you serious trouble at each and every border." My trip was going to take me through twenty countries, more or less. That required forty border crossings, and some countries had to be crossed twice. This was socking it to me with a double whammy, an uppercut followed by a low blow, so to speak.

By this time the term *El Niño* was beginning to mean something. It had found its way into everyone's vocabulary. Almost every night on the news there were horror stories of the damage wrought by this phenomenon of nature, particularly on the Pacific coast of Mexico (Acapulco had just been hit) and Central America, and in South America from Colombia all the way down to Chile. Floods were also reported from Brazil in the state of Pará. All of these places were on my itinerary. Moreover, I had told my wife about the niceties of crossing borders below the Forty-Eight, particularly about the border at Tapachula. And now this Border Curse. This was no longer fair play. This was hurting a guy where he was most vulnerable. Why are women like that? What had happened to the sweet young thing I married? I had promised her, "I'll be back soon!" Did she have to turn into that fury that is a woman scorned?

All that was forgotten as soon as we reached the open road. It felt great to be on the roll again. We had planned to get back to Tapachula as fast as possible, i.e. in a straight line. We crossed the United States border near Kingston, Ontario to join Interstate #81, and followed it to its end at Knoxville, Tennessee; we took #40 as far as Little Rock, Arkansas, then #30 into Dallas, Texas. In Dallas we had an appointment with the local BMW dealer to have new tires put on. From Dallas we would turn south via Waco, Victoria, and Brownsville, cross the border into Mexico, and follow the same road we had come up on in August. The morning was clear, but not for long. At noon in upper New York state it began to drizzle, which soon turned into rain. Shit was happening again. But in my warm winter riding gear, I didn't really care. Let it come down. I was ready for anything; well, almost anything.

It was smooth sailing all the way. Riding from north to south at this time of the year, I was fascinated to observe the seasons reversing themselves. In Canada all the leaves had gone, the summer flowers had been killed by early frost long ago, and the land was waiting for snow. Now, riding back into summer, I began to notice brown leaves on the trees, which slowly took on more colour until they had turned a summertime green when we reached Texas. Three days into the ride, on Wednesday evening in a motel near Memphis, I saw on the Weather Channel that Southern Ontario and Northern New York State had been hit by the first snowstorm of the season, with snow up to ten inches and drifting; chaos on the roads; many accidents. That was a close call. The next day, after a good sunny start in the morning, it turned ugly again at noon: thunderstorms, with tornado warnings in effect. "Please, madam," I thought, "no abductions by twisters. That's taking it too far." The wheels of the bike didn't leave the road that day. Perhaps somebody listened.

This was my third time on Interstate #81, and for the third time I was amazed by the amount of road kill rotting on either side of the road, mostly deer, gophers, and racoons. In Northern Ontario I had seen a handwritten sign in front of an enterprising roadside restaurant soliciting patrons with the slogan, *"Roadkill: You kill it, we grill it!"* They should open another branch in Pennsylvania south of Scranton. But business wouldn't be as good farther down the line. In Texas, for instance, you knew that you had arrived when you saw armadillos belly-up beside the road. I wondered if those little guys were edible. I didn't see them listed on any menu.

The BMW people of Plano, North Dallas, did not disappoint me. George, the head mechanic, had me out of there with my new tires on by noon. He graciously consented to store my cold weather suit until my return in April. From now on we were heading straight for the border.

This was the first serious border crossing. The American border doesn't count, since Americans and Canadians are practically first cousins, and very friendly with one another. We arrived at the border at 8.00 a.m., went through the same paper chase as at Ciudad Juárez, and paid the same amount of money, but rode into Matamoros some thirty minutes later. Everyone was friendly, everyone smiled. Even the weather was good. "Woman, eat your heart out!" I was thinking triumphantly. If this is an omen of what is to come, we'll be laughing all the way down to the tip.

Now we were on familiar ground. Again I marvelled at the smell of sewage, the bad pavement, and the run-down houses. I should be used to it by now. But I guess the shock at the border is just too great to take. I found my way out of Matamoros without getting lost, even recognized the motels I had tried unsuccessfully the last time, and made good time with the wind pushing us. I had planned to stay in Tampico for the night, but had taken a wrong turn (Oh, those road signs!), and found myself on the famous bay bridge leading out of town, committed, since there was no chance to turn around. The next hotel that came into view would be the one. The large amount of road kill and past experience made night riding unappealing.

On the way down last August I had stopped at the Hotel La Mision in Tapanatepec, which had turned out to be particularly well suited for maintenance work on the bike. Since it was time for a valve clearance check, I decided to stay there again. The elderly gentleman in charge of the grounds remembered me very well from my last visit. He even remembered that I had stayed in one of the air-conditioned units in the back. This time it was fan only in the front. What an amazing memory. It must be due to the amount of tequila they're putting away down here. Since we were getting close to Tapachula and all that implied, I was not averse to helping the old man diminish a bottle of the stuff.

* * *

We arrived in Tapachula at 2.00 p.m. To complete my maintenance routine I needed to find a place for an oil and filter change. Looking for the familiar oil slick I ended up in a side street, Oil Slick Alley, where several shops side by side were advertising their slippery business. We stopped at the one selling Castrol GTX 20W-50. Two bright-eyed teenage boys appointed themselves as my helpers. One of them immediately brandished a fourteen inch pipe wrench, tool of choice in these latitudes for an oil change. I had no difficulties convincing them that the whole procedure would be much more fun with my tools. Under the approving eyes of the boss and the obligatory geriatric set in attendance, the boys did a great job in keeping the mess to a minimum, not that it would have mattered very much if we had made one. With the new oil filter in place, each helper was allowed to make the torque wrench "click" on the drain plug. A great time was had by all when we rode off to find Hotel Kamico, the same hotel I had stayed at last time.

I was determined not to let the memory of my last stay here spoil the possibility of finding some redeeming features in this town. The hotel was first-rate, luxurious, not too expensive for my budget, and, with the bike in my room, secure; we liked each other's body odour. I had no difficulty finding a nice place for dinner. With an abundance of palm trees and other exotic plants, and under a bright blue sky, the town didn't look all that bad. In fact it looked quite nice in a seedy sort of way. The *tamales* were good, *Corona* beer was cheap; during happy hour two for the price of one; and the total bill reasonable. So what was my problem with this town? Ha! On the next day the real Tapachula revealed itself.

The road to the border at Talisman had deteriorated since my last visit. It was under construction and partly torn up. At the border the teenage mob was waiting for us, as anticipated. To pre-empt any fancy tricks on their part, I yelled at them, "Don't touch!" with a few select curse words that I had picked up along the way thrown in. Forced to make a choice I appointed a boy called Jorge to guide us through both borders. At Mexican Customs, our first stop, we were told that customs clearance for vehicles was done on the other side of Tapachula, some 5 km out of town on the highway to Mexico City. "*Hasta luego, Jorge.*" Back again we rode over 16 km of road under construction. Through the downtown maze we promptly got lost for the fourth time in three days. I ought to be more like a rat; I would have figured out this maze a long time ago. On the way out of town I almost ran down a traffic cop, whom I saw only in the last second. The man was not amused, and told me so in no uncertain terms. Lucky for me that my Spanish was poor, and he was not after "development aid." Then I almost got sided by a pickup truck, whose driver obviously had not seen me. This town did not like me;

it was out to destroy me. Mexican Customs was clearly marked, and they dispatched me in five minutes flat. Now back through this crazy town, my fifth attempt, and over 16 km of road under construction. Hurray! Success, and learning had taken place. I'll never get lost in Tapachula again as long as I live, simply because I'm not going to go back to Tapachula again, ever.

At the border Jorge and some of his little friends were waiting for us. It was bedlam. There were long line-ups of people everywhere. I parked the bike. Pay here, go there, park the bike; pay again, no receipt this time, presumably more "development aid." On to the next wicket. Park the bike; pay again, receipt this time. Photocopies of everything in triplicate. I must have paid close to US$50.00 by the time I had all my required documents and stamps, and my big plastic sticker glued to the windshield. After almost two hours of this nightmare, stressed out, I paid off my helpers, and left the border as fast as I could, lest some little nitwit think up another charge. The Border Curse seemed to be working. Or was this particular border just a quirk, an aberration, an anomaly? Let's wait and see before jumping to conclusions. At least the Crisis of Tapachula was resolved. I was on my way.

10. *Southbound Through Central America*

In Guatemala the southern route that we had chosen, CA #2, is called the Pacific Highway. It was in excellent condition, with no toll booths. It did not have many *topes,* which were called *tremulos* here, but that did not make them any less of a nuisance. In Guatemala I learned a valuable lesson in asking for directions. Near Esquintla we approached what looked like a major interchange without any road signs to point the way. There was a gas station nearby, the logical place to ask for directions, I thought. When asked for the correct turn-off for Taxisco and El Salvador the fellow selling gas pointed to the road crossing an overpass. After following this road for some 20 km, I noticed a sign showing the distance to Guatemala City. Wrong turn. I made the mistake of asking a gas-station attendant for directions only once more. I concluded that the people selling gas are morons as far as directions are concerned. The fact that they deal with many motorists does not make them knowledgeable in regard to directions. It was infinitely safer to ask car drivers, better yet truck drivers. Taxi drivers receive top honors for giving the best directions of all.

The border between Guatemala and El Salvador was less chaotic than the one in Talisman, but only slightly less. The *tramitatores,* the self-appointed helpers to guide you through, were less aggressive. One could even get away without hiring any of them. But that would be saving in the wrong place. I was just in the process of parking and locking the bike when my little helper pointed to a long queue forming in front of Immigration. There must have been around sixty people lining up. They had descended from a Tica Bus bound for San Salvador. "A long wait," I said resignedly. "Not long," replied Alberto. "The choice is yours. You give a bit of money, and we go. No wait. Otherwise at least one hour wait." What a choice for an impatient person like myself. "I pay," I announced. "Let's go." Alberto took my passport, entered the office by a side-door, slipped my passport in front of the stamping officer, who automatically continued the up-and-down movement of his right arm, without even looking at my picture. In thirty seconds flat we were on our way to Customs. This cost me US$10.00. I thought that paying this amount instead of waiting more than an hour in 90+° F heat was worth it. It did not go as fast at Customs, for several documents had to be typed up, chassis and motor numbers had to be checked on the bike, and of course photocopies had to be made of everything in triplicate. How did these people ever manage before the invention of photocopying? A mystery. The whole process took two and a half hours, with little stress on my part (except on the travel budget). Am I getting better at this? Or was it due to my knowledgeable little helper? He knew exactly where to go at every step, and we wasted no time. He had earned his generous tip. He was not only a good helper, but also a nice companion to talk to. We shook hands, and wished each other good luck.

The road into San Salvador was a pleasant surprise, with no toll, no speed bumps, and no police or army checkpoints. After Mexico and Guatemala this was a novelty. A four-lane highway led almost into the centre. At its end it split in different directions without any signs. Once again it was only by asking several times that I found my way to the hotel I had chosen from the travel guide, *Hotel Family,* two blocks from the cathedral. I had the whole afternoon, the evening, and part of the night to explore the town.

In 1961 the motorcycle adventurer Danny Liska had passed through San Salvador, and had dedicated a whole chapter of his book, *Two Wheels to Adventure,* to the ladies of this town. As a former professor and researcher by training I felt it was my duty to verify his findings. However, I did not intend to make an indepth study of the subject as Liska obviously had done. Perhaps the name of the hotel I was staying had something to do with it, at least subconsciously. An impressionistic approach would have to do.

The ladies of San Salvador were indeed a pleasure to behold. Dressed in their Sunday best seven days a week, fashionable from the tip of their coiffures to the high heels of their dainty pumps, they oozed sex appeal. To my delight I discovered that ogling was permitted, even encouraged, in this latitude. Hence, I shed my thin veneer of North American political correctness, sacrificing it for the research project at hand. By trial and error I discovered that if you looked them straight in the eyes, they would retaliate unabashedly, even mockingly, as if to say, "Are you man enough to handle me?" "Of course, sweetheart," I would reply in my mind, braggart that I am, "but my wife would probably find this 'totally unacceptable'." Based on this admittedly superficial approach, and also realizing that generalizations are dangerous, I conceded that Liska, back in 1961, might have had some credibility when he concluded his chapter with the words, *"El Salvador is famous for its coffee and whores."* I had less trouble in ascertaining that good coffee was also to be had in San Salvador.

Since I did not want to get too engrossed in my research, I dedicated much of the afternoon to general sightseeing. I found the town reminiscent of towns one might find on one of the Caribbean islands; cheap consumer goods being sold on the sidewalks, fruit vendors everywhere, and a great selection of handicrafts. I was particularly interested in buying a hammock, an essential item for boat travel on the Amazon. In San Salvador a large selection was available. First I let the street merchants praise their wares, then I submitted my specifications: size, weight, strength, and material; a natural fibre that did not scratch. Then bargaining commenced. This was a lot of fun. In the end I probably paid too much, but even at that it was a bargain. After sunset my research project received priority. It was Halloween, and I was curious to find out how San Salvador would react to the night of the witches and goblins, in light of its main exports. I had to be on guard, though, against a coffee overload before going to bed. Bar hopping in San Salvador was fun, worthy of a replay soon.

There always seems to be a price to pay, if one has overindulged the night before. It was All Saints' Day, my day, I thought, since I was convinced somehow that I would be among their number, whenever the time was right to be marchin' in, and this in spite of the sacrifices demanded by my recent research project. The road, however, reacted as though I had fallen from grace. Starting off at the out-skirts of the city as a beautiful four-lane highway, it deteriorated rapidly. Soon the potholes had become the size of cauldrons. It was horrible. The Rubber Cow jumped like a heifer, no matter what speed I tried. As I eased around a sharp curve, my rear end felt strange somehow, as though I had a flat tire. This needed to be checked. I stood on the side of the road and witnessed my first breakdown: oil was dripping down the rear end of the bike, soiling the wheel. The whole rear section of the bike was splattered with oil. I saw the very life draining out of my rear shock absorber. Since it was All Saints' Day, I thought perhaps a prayer would help, but to which one of the saints? The only one I could think of at the moment into whose domain this kind of thing might fall was St. Jude, the saint in charge of lost causes.

This pious attitude, however, soon gave way to anger. The Rubber Cow had only a little over 83,000 km on the odometer, and already things were going *kaputt*. I thought that I had bought a quality product, not some crotch rocket hastily put together in a third-world country. Later on I found out that other own-ers of this model had experienced a similar breakdown after as little as 40,000 km. In 1991 BMW had begun to install Bilstein rear shock absorbers in their Paralever rear suspension models, and the Rubber Cow had been a beneficiary. What is interesting here is the fact that the Bilstein shock was used for one year only. In 1992 BMW switched over to Showa front and rear suspensions. Obviously the Bilstein product had turned out to be a piece of junk, and, worse yet, it could not be repaired. I hoped that Mr. Bilstein himself, the genius behind this miscon-struction, was no longer working for *BMW Sparte Motorrad*, that he was demoted parhaps to their *Sparte Ochsenkarren*, to spend his remaining days designing sus-pensions for solid-wheeled ox-carts.

Of course the bike would be rideable even without a rear suspension. My father's 1937 Zündapp did not feature such a luxury. It had a "hard-tail." One of my friends, famous for his product loyalty, the owner of an elderly Harley, which he calls "The Old Hog," insists that "Real men ride on hard-tails." However, with an installed shock absorber that no longer absorbs shocks, riding becomes a bit trickier than on a hard-tail. All we had now was a coil spring, similar to the ones found in a bed mattress. If you bounce on a mattress, it continues bouncing up and down for a while after the action is stopped. This glorified bed spring at the rear end of a motorcycle does the same thing. On undulating road surfaces the bike would pitch like a boat on the high seas, the rider would become subject to seasickness. Things would really get interesting on washboard surfaces. Then the rear wheel would start bouncing up and down rapidly, with a partial, or total, loss of traction. Not nice at all on curves. But all of this was ahead of us. What had changed at this moment was my perception of the bike. From this moment on it became in my mind "The Old Cow," a bit long in the tooth, a beast that required all the attention it could get if it were to take us home again to the stable.

Just for my own satisfaction I wanted to make sure there was not some magic out there somewhere that could restore new vigour to this half-impotent rear end.

In San Miguel, a fair-sized town, we stopped at a specialist in shock absorbers. When he understood my problem, he said that there was nothing he could do to help, but that there were three motorcycle repair shops in town; perhaps they would have a solution. Raimondo offered to lead the way in his ancient VW Beetle. Off he went in a mad chase across the town, through stop signs, red lights, and back alleys, he going like the devil, the two of us bouncing along in hot pursuit. Everywhere we went, the same response. "Nothing to be done, *lo siento, Señor,* sorry." They suggested to forget Honduras, or Nicaragua. If anything could be done, our best bet would be San José, Costa Rica. After the third and last try, Raimondo stopped at a roadside coconut cart and bought a round of coconuts to replenish our body fluids. He had been extremely generous with his time. I showed my appreciation with a generous tip. Again a total stranger had committed a random act of kindness, and made the day a little brighter.

The road out of San Miguel had not improved, and since we had to get used to having a Bilstein bed spring up our rear end, going was very slow. At Santa Rosa de Lima, the last little town before the border, we decided to stop for the night. Since it was Saturday, and All Saints' Day, the whole town was having a fiesta on the square in front of the church. I joined one of the little groups, a bottle of beer in hand, to celebrate this memorable, but definitely not my lucky, day. There had been enough beer flowing to loosen tongues. I learned that almost everyone assembled had a brother, sister, cousin, uncle, or aunt either in the United States or in Canada. For a while our conversation was like a lesson in North American geography, great to improve my Spanish. I tried my best to go easy on the local brew, without much success. My excuse was that I needed this to settle my upset stomach, to recover from a bout of seasickness.

I had read in one of the guide books that it was not a good idea to cross a border during a weekend. I had crossed from the United States into Mexico on a Sunday without any problems. Things were about to change. While it only took one hour to cross the El Salvador / Honduras border at Atitlan, additional charges were levied because it was a Sunday. I paid at least $10.00 more than I would have paid on a weekday. Moreover, since banks were closed, the money changers on the street had a monopoly, and made the best of it. I should have learned my lesson then about borders and weekends. But I am notoriously slow to catch on. They need people like me in order to continue living in the style they have become accustomed to.

Tegucigalpa, the capital of Honduras, lies 80 km north of the Pan American Highway. For this reason I had originally planned to visit this city on my way back. But the Nicaraguan Embassy in Canada had told me, when they had heard of my means of transport, that the best place for me to get a visa would be in Tegucigalpa. As soon as I left the Pan Am the road began to rise, and continued to rise until we reached the city, which lies at an altitude of 1000 meters. It was a great ride over an excellent road, marred only occasionally by huge unannounced potholes. The tropical temperature prevailing along the Pacific coast had given way to a pleasantly moderate one by the time we had reached our goal. But travelling on a Sunday also had its advantages, if one didn't plan to cross borders. Downtown Tegucigalpa was a maze of one-way streets. Many of them were closed to traffic because of sewer construction. The relatively lighter Sunday traffic at least allowed one to proceed at a half-decent speed, unlike on weekdays, when traffic gridlock almost paralyzes the city. I found the hotel I had selected without much trouble, of course asking for directions at every street corner. One person asked would point one way, the next person the other, which meant that a third opinion was needed to break the deadlock. This is the Latin way. It would be unthinkable for them to admit that they really didn't know the answer. Gotta save that face, no matter what!

Settled in my hotel at 11.30 a.m. I had the remainder of the day to absorb the atmosphere of this capital city. Still in the research mode of San Salvador I tried the "look-them-straight-in- the-eye" approach with the local beauties. I noticed a similar reaction as in San Salvador, with, however, a slight difference. The local damsels seemed to be a little more reserved than the ladies of San Salvador. They were just as beautiful, though, but according to Danny Liska, not the first choice of importers in other countries. I left it at that.

Next morning a taxi deposited me in front of the Nicaraguan Consulate at nine o'clock sharp. My visa would be ready for pick-up at 2.00 p.m. The timing was perfect. It would allow me to check out from the hotel before their deadline, load the bike, and pick up the visa on my way out of town. In order not to get lost in the afternoon, I walked back to the hotel, carefully memorizing significant landmarks, buildings, street names, and intersections. But walking is one thing, riding a motorcycle through this maze, unless you're a rat, is another.

We left the hotel after lunch, at 1.20 p.m. Now the fun began. I had forgotten that virtually all streets downtown were one-way only. After some fifteen minutes of hard riding, the area began to look suspiciously familiar. We were again in front of the hotel. One more time! We arrived at the Consulate at 1.55, having missed all the memorized landmarks, with only the big Coca Cola sign on El Picacho Mountain as a rough guide for general orientation. The visa was ready. Some more fun was awaiting us as we tried to find our way out of town in the direction of Danli, via CA 6.

The Nicaraguan Consulate was on a hill overlooking the city. I could see in the distance the large soccer stadium that we had to circle in order to get to CA 6. Once we were downtown and surrounded by tall buildings, the soccer stadium was lost from view, and only the aforementioned Coca Cola sign was left as a guide. I knew that I had to get to the road leading in the other direction from where I was going. But how? One-way streets everywhere, but all going the wrong way. After coming back the second time to the same spot, I had enough, and simply made a dash for it the wrong way. A shrill police whistle was my reward. Why stop? Why ruin this poor cop's otherwise perfect day by forcing him to write a traffic ticket? I got onto the street I needed to get us out of town. That's all that mattered. *Hasta la vista, Tegucigalpa!*

On the way to the Nicaraguan border, alternately pitching, bouncing, or rolling as dictated by road conditions and the Bilstein handicap, I wondered how curses were transmitted over long distances. Would it be over airwaves, like radio signals from a tower, or like television, by satellite technology. I hoped that in the case of the Border Curse the former was true. That would mean the farther away we got from Canada, i.e. the Transmitter, the weaker the signal, i.e. the Curse, would become. The Guatemalan border had been the worst so far. San Salvador was easier. Honduras had gone faster yet. Another test case was about to come up, Las Manos.

The border at Las Manos turned out to be a breeze. With the assistance of my usual helpers we were through in forty-five minutes. No "development aid" was asked for, and the legitimate charges were moderate. This would be a test case in favour of the Radio Waves Theory. There was no hurry to jump to conclusions. However, I was ready to set up an hypothesis, a prerequisite for any solid research project:*"Over long distances curses are transmitted like radio waves."* There were many more borders to cross to test this hypothesis.

I had low expectations of Nicaragua. The country had gone through a long and bloody civil war. The economy was in shambles, and unemployment hovered around the 60 per cent mark. In conditions like this what could one expect but the worst?

But what I found was totally unexpected. The roads were excellent, particularly so east of Managua. There were no police or army checks anywhere. As a matter of fact the army remained invisible wherever I went. Traffic was very light. There were hardly any passenger cars on the road. The few heavy Diesel trucks and buses, mostly decrepit old clunkers, tried their best to pollute the atmosphere with dense, black, oily soot. I always ride with my headlights on. It's the law in Canada. They come on as soon as the ignition key is turned, and I couldn't turn them off if I tried. In Nicaragua I was continuously reminded by oncoming traffic to turn my lights off. My guess was that since auto parts were hard to get and very expensive, they considered it a waste to use up the life-span of valuable light bulbs during the daytime. This perhaps trivial experience may be a better criterion for the state of their economy and their standard of living than statistics. If road conditions are any indication of a country's economy, however, one can predict that better times are ahead for Nicaragua.

With the Christmas deadline in mind, and not knowing what Costa Rica had in store for us regarding our problem, I decided to bypass Managua on the way down, although I was determined to visit the city on the return trip. Hence, the road took us through a lush contryside, reminding us again and again of the meaning of the term "banana republic." Banana groves gave way to rich pasture land along Lakes Managua and Nicaragua. At times these pastures did not have fences, so that the cattle could roam freely from one side of the highway to the other. This, of course, was not unique to Nicaragua. It is a way of life from Mexico to the tip of South America. What I did find remarkable, though, was the fact that Nicaraguan cows were the most misbehaved bovines I have seen anywhere. They would walk across the highway at a leisurely pace, and stop in the middle to look at us with these big, stupid eyes, wondering what we were doing on their pasture. Tooting didn't help. Of course they did what cows do around the world, even the very sophisticated ones in the European Alps, they left their juicy pies all over the road, enough to decorate the area around the bike's fenders. This had serious consequences, as we were about to learn.

Another test case was approaching: the border with Costa Rica at Peñas Blancas. This time we were through in thirty minutes flat, a new record, with only a nominal charge to bypass about fifty bus passengers awaiting their turn. A little money goes a long way down here. But what an indignity was in store for us: on the Costa Rican side the Old Cow had to be sprayed with disinfectant. Was this routine procedure for all vehicles? Or had they spotted the cow shit decorating our fenders? We felt deeply hurt, insulted, even humiliated, by this undignified treatment. What were we? A couple of sickies? Well, at least we could rest assured now that we hadn't contracted foot-and-mouth disease in Nicaragua.

The elation at having made the border so quickly did not last long, for the road was in bad shape. Moreover, we were stopped by police four times during the next half-hour for document checks. Even though Costa Rica takes pride in being a democracy and boasts that it has no army, it has all the trappings of a police state. Police in their black uniforms, reminiscent of Hitler's *Schutz Staffel* the SS are omnipresent. One of their great loves seems to be to point their little radar guns at anything that moves. Having been forwarned by Jim Rogers, *The Investment Biker* who had been asked to invest in the Costa Rican economy against his will in the form of a speeding ticket, his only traffic violation on a 65,067 miles trip around the world, I scrupulously observed each and every posted speed limit. This was against my nature, and very slow-going, for in the open country the speed limit was generally set at 80 km/h, which was reasonable given the state of the roads and the heavy traffic. In towns, however, there would be a sign slowing us down to 25 km/h, 15 mph, which was ridiculous. But one could be sure that in every little town somewhere there would be lurking one of these clandestine radar gun slingers. They didn't get me in Costa Rica. But a little later one of their colleagues next door forced me to invest in the Panamanian economy.

We had not seen any serious rain since Texas, almost two weeks ago. Although we had been surrounded by thunderstorms now and then, we had somehow managed to steer around them and never got wet. Some 50 km west of San José, as we were climbing up into the Cordillera Central, we were reminded that *El Niño* was still alive and well, and doing his thing in Costa Rica. The downpour lasted until we reached the city. It stopped just in time to enable us to cope with the chaotic traffic downtown. From now on until we left Central America it rained every day, starting almost punctually at 3.00 p.m.

The checkerboard pattern of the streets in downtown San José made finding our hotel easy. The *avenidas* ran in an east-west direction, and the *calles* north-south. Both were numbered. And more remarkable, their numbers were posted on almost every street corner. I was looking for the "Garden Court," a hotel managed by the Best Western chain, and found the place without having to ask for directions even once, to the full satisfaction of my Martian ego. At US$36.00 a day this was a bargain. The hotel had recently been renovated to modern standards. It had a large covered swimming pool surrounded by luxurious vegetation next to the bar/restaurant. A delicious buffet breakfast was included in the price, and free coffee and all the bananas one wanted to eat were available throughout the day. But not enough. During "Happy Hour," between 6.00 and 7.00 p.m., the drinks were on the house. This provided a great opportunity to meet all the other guests. Could anyone resist a free drink? There was only one drawback. The hotel was located in an "unsafe" area of the city, surrounded by seedy bars and liquor stores. Management recommended that when departing or returning one take a taxi after sunset. One day I heard the sad tale of an American tourist whose wallet had been lifted from his hip pocket in the middle of the afternoon as he was walking back to the hotel. This explained why all the "extras" were thrown in; otherwise the guests would have moved to a better neighborhood. My greatest worry was parking. But the parking lot was surrounded by a ten-foot-high wire fence and had a gate that was locked at sunset. Furthermore, there was an armed guard keeping an eye on it twenty-four hours a day. It couldn't be more secure.

I had chosen this hotel because the BMW dealer was only five blocks away up the street. This was a Wednesday. I caught the *gerente*, Herbert Von Breymann, just before closing time. He said that he did not have this kind of shock absorber in stock, but would try tomorrow to order one for me from his contacts in the United States. Thus, having set the ball rolling, I could now relax back at the hotel with some Cuba Libres, rum and Coke, and half a dozen bananas.

The next morning I took a second look at the Bilstein, and what I saw almost made my heart miss a beat. The bottom loop of the shock absorber, which held the bushing for the bolt of the Paralever swing arm, had broken, and had opened up about a quarter of an inch. A few more bounces of the rear wheel and it would have come off the bolt. I didn't even want to think of what would have happened if this had occurred. To be sure the bike would be unrideable. Finding a new shock absorber was no longer optional; it was compulsory.

Herbert was busy all day Thursday trying to solve my problem. He informed me on Friday morning that he had some good news and some bad news. As usual I opted for the bad news first. His contact in Miami had told him that BMW North America had no Bilstein shock absorbers in stock, and that it would be back ordered, which would take approximately two weeks. Two weeks my foot! I knew that this was just a face- saving ploy, which in reality meant at least four weeks. Now to the good news! Herbert had called the BMW dealer in Guatemala City, an acquaintance of his, who just happened to have such an item in stock, and who had promised to send it via DHL air freight as soon as he received payment. Off we went to Western Union to transfer US$650.00 to the BMW dealer in Guatemala City. The money would arrive there the same day, which meant that the part could be in the hands of DHL in the evening, and in San José by Monday morning. Dreamer that I was, I believed this. I still hadn't learned about Latin American weekends.

Back at the coffee pot and the bananas I mulled over the options I had, if I had any at all. Plan A was the shock from Guatemala. But suppose the shipment from Guatemala never arrived, what would I do? Plan B would have to be an attempt to salvage that piece of Bilstein junk, i.e. to find someone who could weld aluminum, repair the broken loop, and press the bushing back into place. Was there a Plan C? This would be my last resort. I would have to get a steel bar machined, which would be bolted to the frame and the swing arm in place of the shock absorber. I would thus become a "Real Man," like my Hog-riding friend, riding on a "hard tail." One might as well be prepared for the unthinkable, and Plan C was almost unthinkable.

Fortunately San José is an exciting city. There were many things to do to pass the time, even though the Old Cow was now out of order. San José has a large casino that attracts the gambling crowd from North America. It has museums, parks, and a glitzy night life. If I felt adventurous, I could always take my chances in the neighborhood of the hotel. But first I should attend to business. I should visit the embassies, or consulates, of Panama, Colombia, and Venezuela.

The Panamanians and Colombians assured me that transit for man and machine would be taken care of at the border. I had learned from the travel guide that one needed a visa for Venezuela only if crossing the border overland. However, the Venezuelan embassy assured me that for Canadians no visa was required. I simply didn't believe them. It had been my experience that generally embassy employees don't know the rules and don't care what happens at the border, since they will not be around to lose face. I made a mental note to visit the Venezuelan Embassy in Panama, to find out what they had to say.

On my way back to town from embassy row I visited La Merced Park, where there was on display an example of one of the perfectly round granite spheres, this one some two-and-one-half feet in diameter, which have been found in several places throughout Costa Rica. It is correct within two millimeters. The existing balls come in various sizes, from about six inches to six feet in diameter. No one knows who made them, or for what purpose; one of those unsolved mysteries of Central and South America, of which there are many.

A visit to the gold museum downtown was next on the list, to coincide with the rain, which arrived punctually at 3.00 p.m. The amount of gold artifacts on display there is simply overwhelming. Most items dated back to a time before Columbus. The only other gold museum that could rival the wealth of this one is the one in Bogotá. In both places one is forced after a while to go outside and take a deep breath. So much gold heaped up in one place makes one dizzy.

On Saturday morning I took a local bus out to a butterfly farm near Guácima, one hour north-west of San José, reputedly the second largest in the world after the one in Taiwan. The farm was created in 1990 by an ex-Peace Corps member and his wife on one hectare of land. The tour guide showed how butterflies were bred from eggs to larvae to pupae to adult butterflies. She explained that the farm had about forty species, and that the available food supply determined which species could be bred. Male butterflies would mate with females of a different species only if no female of the same species were available. The offspring would show characteristics of both species, but would be sterile. It is interesting to note that in captivity about 80 per cent of the offspring survived, in nature only 2 per cent. Specimens were shipped to collectors all around the world. One could get philosophical contemplating the life cycle of this creature. Most of its time on earth spent in a rather ungainly form of existence is as an egg, inanimate; as a larva, ugly, a glutton; as a pupa, ugly, semi-animate; finally as a butterfly, beautiful, ethereal, but only for a short time. I liked the idea that the most beautiful stage in its metamorphosis was the very last, to be cut off sharply at death. Perhaps butterflies have something going for them. There's not much fun in getting old for members of most other species.

I had learned in Tegucigalpa that on Sunday mornings hardly anything moved. It was similar for San José. Here, too, almost nothing moved. Even the sleazy set had taken the morning off. Would my shock absorber move on such a day? I had my doubts. It probably hung suspended somewhere in mid-air between Guatemala and the Costa Rican border. I was surprised, therefore, to find that a number of people had gathered near the Gran Hotel downtown, and that the crowd was getting bigger by the minute. What was going on? Asking around I learned that there was to be a parade sponsored by the Oxcart Drivers of Costa Rica. They had their National Day during a weekend in March in San Antonio de Escazú, but on this Thanksgiving Day there was to be a rehearsal in town for the March celebration.

By the time the parade started, at noon, the crowd had lined up three deep on both sides of the street. Dozens of teams of oxen were making their way slowly down the street, oxen of all shapes, sizes, and colours, pulling little gaily painted carts with solid wooden wheels, of course all the while doing the thing oxen do best, producing juicy pies of all shapes and sizes, but in uniform colour . Some of these oxen were great pie-makers, big buggers, oxen on steroids that had built their bodies to Mr. Olympia-like proportions. At times there would be only one ox, with the driver walking in front, but most drivers had a team of two, a few even a team of three side-by-side, like a Russian *troïka*. In some of the carts were people sitting or standing. Others were loaded with an abundance of flowers and vegetables. Still others displayed a statue of a saint, or of the Virgin with Child. Prizes were awarded for the best entries, and the crowd turned out to be great judges of Costa Rican prime beef. To my North American mind, in a momentary lapse into political correctness, the thought occurred to me that here again the males had all the fun strutting their stuff, while the females had to stay at home to do all the work, i.e. produce milk. A bit of bovine liberation was needed here. But I let the locals worry about that.

Waiting, waiting, waiting. On Monday, day five into the ordeal, Herbert informed me that the part had been picked up in Guatemala City by the carrier before 5.00 p.m., and was due to arrive in San José today at 3.00 p.m.. It would be too late to be cleared by customs. I had a feeling that they would ship the thing by hot air balloon. How else could one explain a travel time of three days for such a small distance? Herbert was right.

Deeply into Cuba Libres at the hotel—I had my reasons—I met Cathy and Florette, both from Vancouver, British Columbia. Both were in their fifties, dressed in khaki calf-length dresses, wearing sensible shoes. They were down here for their annual holidays. Cathy, a social worker, was into her third kidney, smoked like a Nicaraguan Diesel truck, and was trying her best to finish off that one as well. Florette, a waitress, had tried matrimony twice without much success, and had a fifteen- year-old son as a souvenir. After they had caught up with Cuba Libres we started swapping the stories of our lives. They were great fun to talk to, and we had a few good laughs. They even took the time to commiserate with me about the slowness of the process of getting "my part" replaced. They saw a lot of humour in this. I didn't.

Tuesday, Remembrance Day. Still waiting, waiting. Does anyone know where that part actually is? I went to the shop every two hours. No news. I've never been so frustrated in my whole life, full of impotent rage. Bastards! Incompetents! It seemed that nobody really cared. That's what causes frustration. Performance anxiety had struck once again. At 5.00 p.m. Herbert received the news that the part would be released by customs tomorrow morning at 8.00 a.m. But I wasn't holding my breath.

Wednesday morning, one week after arriving in San José. I went to the shop at 9.00 a.m.. Nothing. At 10.00 a.m. Herbert sent his assistant to customs to pick up the part. Would he actually bring it back with him? I had brought the bike to the shop this morning, and was busy in the meantime taking the broken shock absorber off the bike. Lo and behold, the boy was back one hour later with a shiny brand new shock absorber, a shiny brand new Showa shock absorber that fitted 1992 and later models. The Old Cow was built in 1991 and was Bilstein- challenged. How could this happen? I could have screamed, ranted, and raved, but it wouldn't have done any good. Someone screwed up here. It was no use crying or pointing a finger, no matter which one. I had to advance to Plan B.

Herbert knew someone in town who could weld aluminum. The boy returned about one hour later with the repaired Bilstein, the bottom loop beautifully welded shut, the bushing pressed into place. Installation was a matter of minutes. But how about my money, US$650 or so, which would buy a lot of Cuba Libres? Herbert promised to try his best to fix me up in Caracas, where another one of his acquaintances managed a BMW dealership. He would return the Showa to Guatemala City, and order the correct model from the United States, to be shipped directly to Caracas. I would arrive there in ten days or so, and could pick up the new shock at the BMW dealer. Did I believe this would work out? Not really! And yet—

Rocking and rolling back to the hotel (at least the beast was rideable again), I realized that it had become too late to leave town. Another evening of free bananas, washed down with a moderate number of Cuba Libres, would not make a great difference, in light of our Christmas deadline. My frayed nerves needed a period of rest and recuperation.

That evening Rachel made her appearance during "Happy Hour." She was a filing clerk from Los Angeles, newly separated, twenty-four years old, well put together, wearing a mini-skirt that seemed a bit too short for her pudgy knees. She had come to town to make her fortune, and she had come with a plan. Her husband, a mathematician, university lecturer, and amateur gambler, had taught her all he knew about the laws of probability. Rachel was planning to have a good time in Costa Rica, and paying for it with her winnings at the casino. Wow! What a gutsy young woman, I thought, and told her so after the drinks had had an effect. I asked her to take me on as a gambler's apprentice. Perhaps I could finance *my* trip with a windfall at the casino. We left the hotel at 11.00 p.m.. Rachel said that it wasn't until this time of night that she was in the proper mindset. She also pointed out that our best odds were in Black Jack, and tried to explain the scientific approach to the game to one whose knowlege of higher mathematics, of the laws of probability, was zilch. What did she expect from a guy who had a doctorate in German Medieval Literature, but could barely manage to balance his bank account? The casino had the typical Las Vegas set-up: many slot machines, Poker tables, Baccarrat tables, Roulette tables, and Black Jack tables, which is where we ended up. At first she watched me play, and tried to give me some pointers. I won some, lost some, won again. It was obvious that my heart was not in it. I was no gambler. She began to get rather frustrated with her pupil from the slow learners' class. Obviously she had not come here to instruct one who was mathematically challenged. She wanted to play for herself. I was on my own, and went over to the one-armed bandits. There it didn't take me long to run a deficit, and I called it quits. When I left the casino at 1.00 a.m. Rachel was still going strong, and had a sizeable pile of money in front of her. I wished her luck on my way out and expressed the hope of seeing her at breakfast.

However, I could not wait until the seven o'clock breakfast. I was too eager to shake San José's dirt off my boots. The security man had to unlock the front gate for me. It felt great to be on the roll again. CA#1 out of San José was in good shape, and at six o'clock in the morning there was hardly any traffic. Even the radar gun-slingers were not out yet. We made good time to Cartago, where the road begins its climb, to reach in a short time the record height for Central America of over 9,000 feet. This was the first time for the Old Cow to reach such an altitude, and I was curious to see what would happen. I noticed that when I passed transport trucks, and there were many, I did not have quite the same acceleration as at sea level. Obviously, because of the thinner air we were running on too rich a fuel/air mixture. Moreover, whereas our idle speed of 1,100 rpm was set for sea level, the higher the altitude the lower the idle speed. At 9,000 feet the motor would stall if I didn't open the throttle a bit. I was curious about my tire pressure. I had checked it before climbing, and again at altitude, and found an increase of some 10 per cent. I was interested in this, for I planned to ride in the high Andes to La Paz, Bolivia, and wanted to know what I could expect. I concluded that high-altitude motoring was not a big deal. We could handle it.

The fabulous scenery, combined with beautiful weather, made us forget our troubles in San José. Riding up was like riding north. The vegetation changed from tropical to subtropical to temperate, and the temperature dropped sharply. After a while I had to dig out my leather jacket, which I had not worn since Mexico. Whenever I could take my eyes off the road I could see at times as far as the Atlantic, at other, as far as the Pacific. In one spot at the summit both oceans could be seen simultaneously. However, sightseeing from the rolling bike was not a good idea. There were many sections where the road dropped almost vertically from the shoulder. And at times there was not even a shoulder. Losing control here would mean the end of the trip, Endsville. At least the first 100 km of road going up were in good shape. It deteriorated rapidly thereafter on the way down. The last 100 km to the Panamanian border were again very good.

For the first time weather damage became apparent. Large sections of the highway had collapsed, and only one lane was available for traffic. In many places landslides from above had covered the whole road, and only one lane had been cleared. Although road crews were dumping fill and grading, it would take them months, if not years, to repair the damage. Was this the work of *El Niño?* At one point a steel cable had been strung across the road. A sign indicated "Road Closed." Soon a long queue of cars, trucks, and buses was forming. This was the Pan American Highway, the life-line of the country, and it was closed to traffic. The flagman did not know exactly how long it would be closed. His guess was for about an hour. Two more guys on motorcycles arrived. We looked at one another, nodded, and said, "Let's go!" When we reached the work area, they were just grading several loads of gravel. We waved, they waved, and we were through. No hard feelings. This can only happen in this neck of the woods. At home they would have gone hysterical. But would they have closed both lanes of a major highway for an undetermined amount of time? Probably not. I was curious to see if there would be any changes when I passed through this section again in February on my way back.

The timing of our arrival at the Panamanian border at Paso Canoas was not perfect. As I was digging out the documents from my top case the three o'clock downpour was just starting. Fortunately this time the process was even faster than at the last crossing, and it was also cheaper, much cheaper, for there were no little helpers offering their services and expecting to be paid. Real professionals, these border officials. When the lady at customs handed me back my pile of *doc-umentas,* she looked at me and said, "*Señor!*" "*Si, Señora?*" was my reply. She pointed at my passport and added in perfect English, "Today is your birthday: Happy Birthday!" She was right. This was my sixtieth birthday, certainly the most under-celebrated one since the moment I was born. This was another example of a "random act of kindness." It made me feel good, and I rode all the way to David in high spirits, not even noticing the rain, which came down in buckets. Even the name of the hotel in David added to my high spirits; it was called *Fiesta.* So far I found Panama very sympathetic.

8) Panama: Bridge of the Americas

In Panama the Pan Am Highway is an unmitigated pleasure to ride. It winds its way through banana groves and coffee plantations up and down the foothills of the Cordillera Central. The lush countryside, moderate traffic, and courteous drivers were responsible for a biker's high, which could easily lead into trouble. On the open highway, traffic was generally moving at 90 to 100 km/h. In towns everyone would slow down to a speed under 50 km/h. I was wondering why this was so. The road was wide open, there were no traffic lights or stop signs, and people and animals stayed clear of the road, so I let it rip. Suddenly in one of the little towns a cop popped up, as though from nowhere, and flagged me down. I was a long way past him, but since he had his cruiser parked on the side of the road, I considered it prudent to turn around. We exchanged greetings, and he asked me politely for my *documentas*. He wanted to know how I liked it down here in his country, and I told him the truth, that I was enchanted. Then he pointed to a battered radar gun lying on the hood of his cruiser and said that he had clocked me at 85 km/h. I did not deny this. He was right. Then he added that this was unfortunately a 45 km/h zone, and according to his price list, which he showed me, this would cost me US$50.00. What could I say? I pleaded my well-rehearsed stupid tourist situation, not having seen the sign, not knowing the local laws, and being far away from home; finally I suggested that one should be nice to one's guests and not take money from them. He listened patiently to my psychobabble for a while, then he asked me my profession. I told him I was a teacher. So he said, "You are a teacher and a teacher teaches students. That's your job. Look at this uniform. I am a policeman and a policeman gives tickets to speeders. That's my job. I have no choice. But you have the choice of a number of towns down the line to pay your fine. *Touché!* This made sense to me. I had to try another tack. I pointed out to him that in my country if one paid cash on the spot for something instead of paying later, one would usually get a huge discount. Would this also be true in Panama? If so, I would suggest that US$20.00 would be just punishment for my crime. To this he replied quickly, "Make it 25." We shook hands, and once again "development aid" had found a worthy (and witty) recipient. Of course I would not be able to claim this "travel expense" for income tax purposes, since I did not get a receipt. What was happening here? Was the whole Latin world now in possession of radar guns? Bad news. I vowed that from now on I would obey all speed limits. Not doing so would be too hard on my budget.

Heavy clouds were piling up as we rode over the Bridge of the Americas spanning the Pacific exit of the Panama Canal. There were many ships in the bay waiting for their time to enter the canal. From a taxi driver I got directions to the hotel we had selected. We arrived at Hotel Costa Inn, in the Bella Vista area of town, minutes before the first drops began to fall. This was the end of the line in Central America. The next problem to be solved was how to get across the Darién Gap, a stretch of roadless jungle between Panama and Colombia.

11. *From Panama to Brazil*

To get from Panama to Colombia the motorist has three options. The first is to continue on the road until its termination at Yaviza, some 240 km east of Panama City. From Yaviza to the first town in Colombia one would have to hack one's way through the jungle and float the vehicle on some of the rivers. This had been done several times, and had involved a large investment in time and money. In 1961 Danny Liska had shipped the bike and walked through. The first recorded crossing on a motorcycle from north to south had been made by Ed Culberson in 1986 on his second try. He described his ordeal in *Obsessions Die Hard.* Two years later, Helge Pederson had crossed from south to north, and written about it in *10 Years on 2 Wheels.* Both had been "riding" BMW R 80 G/S motorcycles. But in fact they had not really been "riding" through the Gap. The bikes had to be dragged and floated by helpers, some of whom of course also had to be paid. Culberson had emerged relatively unscathed. His motorcycle, however, which had accidentally fallen into the water, broke down later, on the Pan American Highway in South America. Pederson, on the other hand, had paid a heavy personal price in the form of a broken hand and rib, and infected legs. Both had gone through the Gap during the dry season. To attempt a crossing during the wet season would be suicidal. The wet season was still in progress when we arrived in Panama. Hence, option one for me was not really an option.

The second option would be by sea, either from Balboa on the Pacific side or from Colón on the Caribbean side. However, having lost eight days in Costa Rica, and wanting to be in Ushuaia at Christmas, I was looking for a faster way to get to Colombia. This was the third option, by air.

Looking for ways to make contacts with shipping agencies in Panama City, I thought there was nothing to be lost by beginning the process right at the hotel, at the Florencia Travel Agency on ground level. Katia Sole, one of the agents, discovered that none of the scheduled air carriers carried motorcycles. The bike would have to be shipped by air cargo. One of her acquaintances, Alfredo, was working for Serbi Cargo. He promised to meet me next day at 8.00 a.m. sharp at the cargo terminal of Tocumen Airport, where he would assist me in loading the bike on a cargo flight to Bogotá, Colombia. Even though it would be a Saturday, the bike would still be shipped the same day. Perfect. I booked a flight to Bogotá on Avianca for Sunday morning at 9.30. Everything was working out perfectly, or so I thought. I had not counted on Latin American weekends.

I never did meet Alfredo. I waited for him for two hours at Serbi Cargo, but Alfredo did not show up. Apparently he was busy downtown. Serbi Cargo sent me over to Challenge Air Cargo (CAC), which they should have done two hours earlier. The CAC people appeared to be true professionals. They had my waybill typed up in a few minutes, and advised me to remove my rear-view mirrors. Gasoline, oil, and battery did not need to be removed. I paid US$295.00. The bike would be strapped onto a pallet and leave tonight at 11.00 p.m. on a Boeing 757 freighter for Bogotá. All I had to do now was to go over to customs with my way-bill, and clear the bike for export (a record of temporary import had been stamped into my passport at the border). Customs was just around the corner, so I jumped on the bike without a helmet for this two-minute ride. Customs was closed. It was a Saturday. But the officers on duty at the entrance to the cargo airport told me that, althought they could not clear the bike, it could be done tomorrow morning at the passenger terminal before I boarded my flight. I wanted to believe this, and had no reason to suspect that they were just telling me what I wanted to hear. Back to CAC. Unfortunately the daily rain was early. It came down with its usual intensity, and since I had neither helmet nor rain gear, I was dripping wet by the time I got back. I left the bike in CAC's care and hitched a ride back to town, since there were no taxis near the cargo terminal. There was still plenty of time to go sightseeing in the older part of the city, and have a nice meal and a few drinks to celebrate my good fortune.

At seven o'clock on Sunday morning Tocumen Airport looked deserted. It took a while to find someone from Customs. *"Señor,"* he said, "This is Sunday, and on Sundays Customs is closed, *lo siento,* sorry." The Old Cow would have to wait for me until I arrived in Bogotá Monday night.

I had planned to look at the Panama Canal on our way back, but with all that involuntary extra time to spend I decided that I might as well take this day to do my sightseeing. I arrived on a local bus at the Miraflores Locks, the first set of locks on the Pacific side of the Canal, as a big ocean liner was lifted into Lake Miraflores on its way to the Atlantic. In the morning, traffic moves from the Pacific side to the Atlantic side; in the afternoon in the reverse direction. It takes twenty-four hours for a ship to clear the Canal. At this time the Panamanians were already operating the Canal, but under American supervision. By the turn of the century Panama would be in full control. Would there be any traffic on the Canal during the weekend? I doubted it. That would be against their nature.

On the bus back to town I met Riccardo. He recognized the gringo in me, and told me that he had worked several years in California. He had come back to Panama for several reasons. His new wife did not like to live so far away from her family, nor did she like to live in California. They had two little girls, and since his father-in-law, with connections in the lumbering industry, had found a job for him as a truck driver, Riccardo had returned. He had regretted it ever since. His job was hauling logs for a lumber company in the Darién. But this was a season-al job only. During the rainy season, from May to December, there was little work, since the roads were impassable. Soon they had money problems, and his wife and daughters had gone back to live with her parents. Now on his own, Riccardo was trying to get back to the United States. But it was difficult. He was waiting for his papers. He showed me some interesting sights in the old part of the city, west of Bella Vista, the *Casco viejo,* the Old Compound, where I would not have dared to walk by myself, especially after dark. Of particular interest to me were *Las Bóvedas,* the Vaults, the former prison, where once a day during high tide the inmates had to stand in water up to their necks. Perhaps the modern Panamanian prison is a bit less grim. But just to be on the safe side, I made a mental note to stay out of it. Since Riccardo was again unemployed, I invited him for dinner. He in turn, being a proud person, took me to a bar for a drink. The place was packed with both males and females. Loud music made conversation impossible. It looked seedy to me. The ladies present could have been from San Salvador. I didn't want to find out. Riccardo strongly urged me to take a taxi back to the hotel. He did not have to do much urging. The Old Compound of Panama City is not a safe place to be after dark, even for locals.

On Monday morning I explained my problem with customs to the receptionist at the hotel, and asked her to find out for me where I would have to go. After several telephone calls she was not any the wiser. Florencia Travel opened at 8.00 a.m. Katia had more luck. She informed me that I would have to go to Balboa, *Aduana, Control de Vehiculos.* I was there at opening time, at 8.30. Once I had tracked down the official in charge, the whole process took thirty minutes. I had a stamp in my passport proclaiming that I was permitted to leave Panama without my vehicle, and was US$23.00 poorer; still, better than being in a Panamanian jail. Now I had to get my ticket to Bogotá rewritten. The next flight would be on Aces, leaving Tocumen at 8.00 p.m. Was there anything else that could go wrong?

The foreign embassies were in the New City, east of Bella Vista. This part of Panama City could have been located anywhere in North America. It had a number of high-rise office buildings, high-rise hotels, stately mansions from an earlier period, and a little farther out the suburban jungle. The Colombian Embassy told me that all the paperwork would be done in Bogotá. The Venezuelans insisted again that even for overland entry, no visa was required. Again I didn't believe them. I spent the rest of the afternoon in this part of town, which was considerably safer than the old part. This was a good place to stock up on American cash, since Panama uses American paper money as its official currency. However, a "buck" is not a "buck" here. It looks the same, but is called a "Balboa."

When the flight to Bogotá took off at exactly 8.00 p.m., I breathed a sigh of relief. At least we were out of the clutches of Panama Customs. The Panamanians had been milking me until the very end: 20.00 Balboas Departure Tax seemed exorbitant.

Cash continued to flow in Bogotá; my cash. The taxi driver asked for US$20.00 to take me to my designated hotel. I knew these devils; birds of a feather all of them, no matter where in the world. I countered with an offer of $10.00. He bluntly refused. I tried several others with the same result. Then one explained to me that this was the going rate for two reasons: (1) it was nighttime, and in Bogotá a danger allowance has to be paid at night; and (2) the day was an official holiday, "Independence of Cartagena Day." Hence, a holiday supplement had to be paid. "Did anyone work today?" I asked the driver. "*No, Señor,* holiday for everybody. Everything closed." Where was my bike? shot through my mind. Perhaps still sitting out on the apron, with no one here working to unload the plane. I could hardly wait until next morning to discover the truth. I had a feeling it would be bitter.

Out at the cargo terminal the next morning, I got to hear what I had feared since last night. The bike had not arrived from Panama yet, because of the holiday. "Call us tomorrow morning, Sir, then we'll know more." "Shit, shit, shit!" Was this an instant replay of Costa Rica? To be sitting around, to be condemned to inactivity again, waiting, waiting! I would not have expected that from CAC, an American company based in Miami. Fortunately, the weather in Bogotá was much more pleasant than that in Panama, in the low seventies Fahrenheit, sunny and dry. Furthermore, I had been here in 1992, and knew the city quite well. What does one do in a frustrating situation like this? One goes sightseeing.

Experience had taught me to approach sightseeing in Bogotá with caution. A little imprudence five years ago had almost bought me a good beating, or worse. In the centre of town, on a traffic island, I had witnessed an interesting scene: about a dozen street people, all in their early twenties, dirty as iron-mongers, were cooking their breakfast over an open fire of discarded cardboard boxes and wooden crates. In order to get a bird's eye view of this idyll, I walked up to the second floor of a nearby office building, and took a picture from the balcony. One of the boys must have seen me, or perhaps the flash of my camera. Before I could tuck away my camera, I was surrounded by five of them, each one brandishing a piece of firewood. They started tearing at my clothes, all the while yelling, *"Non photographía!"* I yelled back at them that I had taken a photo of the buildings behind them. That did not make much of an impression. Before they could start swinging their clubs, I dashed into a stationery store nearby. The sales clerks there had seen the action, and were not happy at all to have the cause of the disturbance behind their sales counter. They wagged their fingers at me and told me, *"Never, ever take picture of these people. Stay away from them, far away!"* Well, I knew that by now. But how to get myself out of this mess? I was not going to move, no matter what. In the meantime one of the clerks had called the police. They arrived shortly after, Uzis slung over their shoulders, Colt 45s on their hips. They offered to walk me back to my hotel, admonishing me all the way to be a bit more careful. I still had vivid memories of this nightmare, five years later.

But Bogotá had changed. There were still street people, still pan-handlers, but relatively few young ones. The older ones were sitting on street corners and were usually selling something. The area around Plaza Bolívar, the square in the centre of the city, was devoid of the heavy police and military presence that had been very much in evidence during my last visit. I did not feel threatened anywhere I walked, not even in the side streets. Bogotá had cleaned up its act. It had become a relatively safe city, like most big cities in North America. Since the majority of the population was of Caucasian origin, I could put my head down and pretend I was one of them. Of course I was careful where I aimed my camera.

The Gold Museum, with perhaps the best collection of gold artifacts in the world, was a great place to get inspired for the peace offering that would have to be made to the management of the house in Canada upon my return. In 1992 after the "Around-South-America-in-Eighty-Days" trip I had brought back an emerald necklace from Bogotá. Colombia is the world's chief producer of emeralds, and the jewellery shops in town were almost bursting with the greatest selection any-where of emerald jewellery. This time I was aiming for matching earrings, to be bought on my way back. I had all day to make my choice. After a day of muse-um-hopping and window shopping, I was actually looking forward to my return visit next year. Now, if I could only get my bike out of customs and get rolling.

"Don't worry," said the man from CAC at the Air Cargo Terminal on Wednesday morning. "Your bike is here. Now we have to wait for Customs." How long that would take? He couldn't say, perhaps two to three hours. Waiting again! I had the feeling that most of the time so far on this part of the trip had been spent waiting for something or somebody. After three hours of counting the flies on the walls, bored silly, I checked with the front office. "Yes, they are here." Why didn't they tell me that before? The two gentlemen from Customs filled in sever-al standard forms with my vital statistics and the bike's . "What's next, *Señores?*" "Now we wait for an inspector to clear the bike." "At what time will that be?" "Probably around four or five o'clock." Since I had counted all the flies there were, I decided to go back to town to do some more window shopping. At least something was happening.

At four o'clock back at CAC they gave me a stack of papers, relieved me of US$39.00, and sent me over to the Customs building some 600 yards across the Airport Expressway. There were several active wickets. The one I needed had, of course, the longest queue. I hoped they did not close at 5.00 p.m. No, they were open 24 hours a day. Suddenly I saw a whole bunch of people leaving the build-ing. Asking what was happening, I was told they had gone with the inspector over to Air Cargo; I should follow them. Having caught up with the group, I asked who was the inspector. It was a lady. She checked my documents on the march, and told me to wait for her at CAC. She would be there in about two hours. Again waiting.

The CAC people had brought the bike to the front of the building. I was in the process of installing the rear-view mirrors when the inspector arrived. She had started her round on the other side of the hall, and was about to leave the premis-es. She had totally forgotten about me. I had to run after her to jolt her memory. She checked the chassis number without a problem. The engine number of this machine, however, had been stamped in the worst location possible. Hidden behind exhaust pipe and frame members, it could hardly be seen in daylight. In the dim light of the freight shed the lady had to get down on her hands and knees and use her cigarette lighter to do her duty. I hoped that the person at *BMW Sparte Motorrad* responsible for this stupidity would be put to work full-time reading engine numbers in the dim light of an open fire when he, or she, arrived in Hell. I decided that henceforth I would simply say that there was no engine number. But we were not done yet.

The final paperwork had to be completed back at the Customs Office, some 600 yards across the Airport Expressway. But first the lady had to have a cup of coffee, some pastry, and two cigarettes. Back at the office she disappeared with my papers to make several photocopies of everything. What else is new! Then I helped her fill in the *Carnet de passage en douane* the document issued by the Canadian Automobile Association to guarantee the export of the vehicle. At 8.00 p.m. I had all my papers in order and rushed back to CAC. Some employees helped me juggle the bike through a narrow passageway and down several steps, and we were off. What a day in Hell! Was all this related to the Border Curse? That would deflate my Radio Waves Theory, and disprove my hypothesis. But let's wait and see until the database is complete.

Riding back to town I reflected that the only good thing about having made a trip to the airport three times was that I could now find my way back to the hotel in the dark without getting lost.

In the throes of an uncontrollable burst of performance anxiety I left the hotel before breakfast. It was Thursday, and the week was almost over. I had learned by now what that implied. The spectre of yet another weekend condemned to inactivity was looming ahead, at the border of Venezuela. I had to be at the Venezuelan Consulate in Cúcuta on Friday morning, the next day, to get my visa, or else hang around that border town until Monday. That left exactly one day to cover a distance of 1,150 km.

A look at the map showed that there were two roads to Cúcuta. The one, a narrow brown line, involved crossing the City of Bucaramanga. The other, a bright red ribbon, bypassed Bucaramanga, and showed only small settlements along its way. This was the Pan American Highway. The choice was easy. In order to make time it would be the bright red ribbon that avoids the big city. Big mistake.

This was my first day of riding a motorcycle in Colombia, and I loved it. It was the beginning of my love affair with Colombian highways and Colombian traffic. There were no speed bumps. I was supposed to turn left at the town of Duitama, but did not see a road sign, and by the time I discovered my mistake I had overshot my turn-off by some 10 km. I stopped at a workshop at the side of the road and asked for directions. "To Cúcuta? Don't turn at Duitama. Very bad road. Go back to Tunja, and go via Bucaramanga. Very good road." I should have listened to the man. That was my second big mistake. If Colombians say, "Very bad road," they really mean it. I did not feel like backtracking fifty-odd kilometres to Tunja, and made my turn at Duitama. As I discovered much later, while rereading Ed Culberson's *Obsessions Die Hard* Ed had used the same AAA map as the one I had used, and was also seduced by this broad red ribbon marking the Pan American Highway. But Ed really had no choice in the matter. He had to follow his "obsession," which was to ride the Pan American in its entirety no matter what. I did not share his obsession, and would gladly have settled for the easy road via Bucaramanga had I known what was coming.

At first the road was a dream. In excellent condition, it wound up and down in hairpin turns over mountains, across valleys, with breathtaking scenery, at times hugging a mountain with a sheer drop of hundreds of feet to a river on the other side. And what was most amazing, there was hardly any traffic. That should have opened my eyes. About 300 km north of Duitama the pavement ended. But the road was still good gravel to the town of Malaga. Then it deteriorated rapidly. Potholed and rutted, it continued in the same gorgeous setting as before, except that now it was impossible to take one's eyes off the road even for a second. Part-way up yet another mountain, this one over 4,000 m high, road maintenance had stopped completely, and there were pieces of gravel the size of baseballs scattered about. For us, being Bilstein challenged, this meant first gear most of the time. Once the rear wheel started to bounce this was the only way to regain traction. At six o'clock it was dark, and we continued climbing. One hour later the last human habitation passed by, and we were in no man's land. It was two hours since we met another vehicle. On our way down on the other side of the mountain we hit soft gravel. A truck must have dumped a load, but then spread it only superficially. A big rock threw us off course, and we went down on the left side. Same routine as in Tupper Lake. Crawl out from under the bike, shut off motor and fuel taps, and lift the beast up. I gave it such a good jerk that it came up too fast, and I couldn't hold it. It went over on the other side. Once again, up we go, this time for good. It was pitch dark. A superficial check with the headlights on revealed no visible damage. The motor started immediately, and we reached Pamplona at 10.00 p.m. Stopping at a traffic light I noticed that a hotel, *Residencia San Carlos,* was just closing. They still had a vacancy. I called it quits for the day, and had no problem falling asleep under a mountain of blankets (at an altitude of 2,200 m it gets cold at night in Pamplona), having had nothing to eat or drink since breakfast on the road at 8.00 a.m.

Now there was only one little problem: I was running out of time. This could only be solved by ruthlessly climbing out from under the blankets at six o'clock next morning, and making a run for the Venezuelan Consulate in Cúcuta, still some 80 km away. A more thorough check of the Old Cow revealed that no damage had been inflicted by last night's tumble. We were on the road at 6.30 a.m., without breakfast. This was one way to save money, perhaps not the best way. It certainly saved time.

I loved that Colombian traffic. From Pamplona a beautifully paved road, coming over from Bucaramanga, descends steeply to Cúcuta. This is a main traffic artery of the country, and there was heavy traffic, particularly heavy truck traffic. Colombians are good drivers, predictable, courteous, and sporty. They have one flaw, however. They are reckless in their passing habits, and the truckdrivers are the most reckless. Truckers are passing other truckers no matter where, on hills going up, on hills going down, on curves with visibility, on blind curves, level, up, or down. Coming round a blind curve, I could almost count on there being two giant Kenworth trucks side by side heading straight at me. Just for variety's sake, one of them might be a Mack truck, or a bus. In the last second, when I could already see the whites of the driver's eyes, he would squeeze over just a little bit, and we all lived happily until the next curve. I tried to figure out the Colombian law of the open road. I reached the conclusion that the only law governing traffic in Colombia was that of survival: Don't kill or be killed, if you can help it. In other words, there was a certain degree of   lawlessness on

Colombian roads. I loved it and tried to adjust my riding style accordingly. Whenever I entered a blind curve, I always checked the ditch for an emergency escape route. I never needed it. I loved riding in Colombia. It was never boring. It kept the adrenalin flowing.

Having done most of the passing myself this morning, and having survived, we arrived at the Venezuelan Consulate in Cúcuta at 7.55 a.m. It opened at 8.00 a.m. and there were already over one hundred people waiting to get in. I asked some of them how long they would have to wait to get a visa for Venezuela. "At least eight days," was the reply. Bad news. When I finally reached the wicket, about one hour later, I was told that of course Canadians needed a visa if entering overland, and that I could pick up my visa at 2 p.m. But first I had to fill out an application form in duplicate, leave two photos, and then go to their bank downtown, pay the equivalent of US$30 in Colombian pesos into their account, and bring back the receipt immediately. By the time I had asked my way to the bank, waited in line again, and found my way back to the Consulate, it was 10.30 a.m. Now off to *Hotel Casa Blanca* and to my first food and drink in over twenty-four hours. It felt good to be once again in positive water balance. I congratulated myself for having beaten the inertia of another Latin American weekend. I shouldn't have done that.

The visa was, indeed, ready at 2.00 p.m. They assured me that customs would be open the next day at the border, and I believed them. There was still enough time to take in the sights of Cúcuta.

The whole town seemed to be one open-air market, with a multitude of cheapy stores and money-changers. Thousands of Venezuelans cross the border every day to buy duty-free goods, mostly shoes and textiles, which are much cheaper here than on the other side. Shopping here looked more like work to me than pleasure. The temperature had climbed to the high 80s F already early in the morning, and because there was no appreciable breeze, the air was thick with exhaust fumes. But a bargain is a bargain, and elsewhere in the world people have done more than breathe bad air in order to get a good one.

At six o'clock next morning I was called by the front desk to come down, and bring my *documentas* with me. I was greeted by five policemen, who checked me out. They seemed to like what they saw, wished me a good trip, and left. Was this a good sign, or a bad sign? We were off to the border after breakfast. The Colombian Immigration officer stamped my passport and sent me over to Customs. There I had to wait almost an hour for the officer to arrive with "the Big Book" to clear the bike. He also cleared my *Carnet de passage en douane*. No problem. Now across the bridge to the Venezuelans. "*Señor,*" I was greeted, "Customs does not work during weekends, *lo siento,* sorry. Please come back on Monday."

Will I ever learn? Costa Rica, Panama, and now here. I should have learned that one can never, ever trust an embassy or consulate official. This was demonstrated clearly by the fact that even the Venezuelans themselves didn't trust their own staff, or else I could have paid them in cash for the visa at the consulate, and would not have been asked to go downtown directly to their bank. Well, it was

3:0 in favor of the Latin American Weekend. They won; I lost. But this would be the last time. I swore it. They would never trap me again.

As I approached the outskirts of Cúcuta it occurred to me that in fact I was now in the country illegally. I had my *Salida* stamp in the passport, and the bike was cleared for export by customs. If the cops should come calling on me again at the hotel, I could be in deep shit. So, back again to the border. Immigration cancelled my *Salida* stamp, and the customs officer told me that since Cúcuta was a "Duty-Free Zone," no paperwork was necessary for the bike. "But don't leave the city, *Señor*." I had no intention of doing so. Now I felt better.

If it were not for the intense heat, Cúcuta could be a pleasant place to spent a couple of days. After almost total destruction by an earthquake in 1875, the town was rebuilt on the typical Colombian checkerboard pattern, and a generous number of trees were planted. All of them mature now, they provided enough shade that walking around town almost became comfortable. On this Saturday all the hotels had been booked solid by Venezuelan shoppers. It was amusing to watch whole families carry their purchases back to their hotels in large black garbage bags. After having been approached by countless touts and hustlers, I felt like carrying a black garbage bag myself in order to blend in better. Cúcuta looked a bit like Istanbul after a big cruise ship from Odessa had arrived.

That night beside the hotel pool, the cocktail waitress, Korina, was surprised to see that I was still around. Always in need of a compassionate ear, I poured out to her the story of my bad luck with Latin American weekends. She was just serving my second beer when the lights went out. They were prepared for this. Apparently it happened quite frequently. Candles were lit, and the whole place took on a romantic atmosphere. Like myself most of the guests decided to eat when the lights came back on. Hence, Korina had some time to sit down and tell me her story. She was a divorcee in her early forties with two children, aged thirteen and fifteen. The three of them shared a two-room apartment with her mother. This worked out well, but they had money problems. Although her former husband paid child support, this and her own salary at the hotel was not enough to make ends meet. Her dream was to emigrate to Spain, where all her problems would be solved, she hoped. I did not have the heart to put a damper on her fantasy. I asked her if she wanted to take her two daughters along. "No, no," she replied. "They have their own life; I have mine." When the lights came back on, after about an hour, Korina was again busy. I asked her what people in Cúcuta did for excitement on a Saturday night. "Disco," she said. "Most go dancing to one of the local discos." She liked to dance herself, but had not been out lately. Asked if she would like to be a tourist guide and go with me to one of the discos after she finished work, she readily agreed. She was off at 9.00 p.m.

All discotheques seem to be alike, whether in Hongkong, Moscow, Key West, or Cúcuta, too loud music, too much smoke, too much booze. There are, however, small regional differences, and these are worthy of study. Some segregation of the sexes was the most noticeable aspect of the disco Korina and I visited, located on the second floor of a building across the street from my hotel. The men had established themselves near the bar, and the women were huddled in one corner of the room in animated conversation. Most of them seemed to know one another; many knew Korina. Evidently going to a disco was indeed the thing to do here on a Saturday night. The music was a mix of American pop, and Central and South American salsa, of course too loud for my chronologically challenged eardrums. Fortunately there's no need to talk while you're dancing and hence no need to understand your partner, so I was O.K. Although she had worked since nine o'clock in the morning, Korina was in great form, and she looked gorgeous with her long jet-black hair held back by a red ribbon, her tight black sweater, and her body-hugging jeans. In her case it was certainly true that age was just a number. I noticed that she succeeded in attracting many admiring glances from the male bastion at the bar. Oh — The eternal feminine! A few couples appeared to have come together, like ourselves; the majority, however, had come solo. All were dancing most of the time, and all seemed to have a good time without getting dead drunk. Perhaps we did not stay long enough to find out. Around midnight Korina seemed to be fading fast. She said she had to report to work again at nine o'clock in the morning. It was time for her to get some sleep. No need to get a taxi, since she lived just around the corner. I walked her home. This was a pleasant way to forget my frustrations of the morning. I hoped that her dream of the castle in Spain would come true.

On Sunday I spent most of the day working on the bike. Hence, when we arrived at the border on Monday morning at eight o'clock we looked our best.

It was another hot day, and it was getting hotter by the minute as I ran the gauntlet of Immigration and Customs. Got Colombian *Salida* stamp. Crossed bridge to Venezuela. First stop: Immigration (DIEX). This was in town (San Antonio). Found it. Got *Entrada* stamp. Back to Customs at the border. Filled in application. Went across street to be registered and to get a number. The lady sent me to town to buy Tax Stamps for twenty-five cents. Found them for sale near DIEX. Back to border. The lady glued them on the application, signed, and gave me a number. Back across the street. They wanted photocopies of everything. Again across the street, 300 feet up, got copies, and back to Customs. Oh, shit! Forgot helmet at copy shop. Back across the street 300 feet up, retrieved helmet, and back to Customs. Sweat was pouring off me. But file not good enough. Needed copies of visa and entry stamp as well. Once more across the street, 300 feet up, got copies, and back to Customs. Lady nodded her approval. Chief signed, she initialled. Was I done? Not quite. Run over to *Transito,* the transit police, to get my driver's permit certified. Where? Near DIEX, for the third time. The police looked at my passport, driver's licence, and bike, and endorsed my *Autorization* on the back. I was done. It was 11.00 a.m. Borders were never easy. And borders with a Curse in effect were the pits.

Now I needed more money. There were a number of banks in the centre of San Antonio. Unfortunately they had just closed for siesta. Venezuela was one hour ahead of Colombia: it was past twelve o'clock. Although the automatic teller machines outside advertised CIRRUS and MC, they refused to cough up money for me. Instead of waiting an hour and a half, I decided to ride over to San Cristóbal, 55 km away.

Out of San Antonio the highway rose sharply to cross a high mountain, and the cooler temperature made travel much more pleasant . The pavement was excellent. However, the centres of both lanes were one continuous oil slick. Fortunately it wasn't raining, or riding here would have been like riding on ice. This section of road was the most slippery I had encountered anywhere. It was even more slippery than in downtown San José after the parade of pie-making oxen had passed.

The bank in San Cristóbal opened at two o'clock. They refused to accept cash dollars, nor did they take VISA, or Mastercard. The only foreign currency they accepted were Amex Travellers Cheques in US dollars. No problem. But I had to lower my pants to get at my stash. As I was trying to do so discreetly behind a pillar, I was approached by an employee, who looked at me reproachfully, and said, "*Señor, por favor,* not here. Please go to the washroom back there." I had no objection to that, not being a flasher by nature. I left the bank with a big pile of money, 160,000 bolívares for 300 dollars.

A social history of the world could be written in which each ethnic group, or nation, could be distinguished from their neighbours by the way they drive. The Venezuelans are, for example, a great deal more pusillanimous in their driving habits than the Colombians. In general they drive more slowly, are careful passers, and never, ever pass on blind curves. And yet, although the highway to Caracas was excellent, winding its way with gentle curves through a beautiful countryside, there were speed bumps at regular intervals, at times without warning signs. I was so happy to be on the roll again that I got seduced into continuing to ride after sunset. This I was to regret immediately. I could not see the speed bumps with my headlight on, and went flying on several occasions. Furthermore, I witnessed two serious accidents in quick succession, in both cases with passenger cars upside down in the ditch, and the injured passengers laid out along the road until the ambulance arrived. That was the last straw. The next hotel I came to was the chosen one.

It was called *Motel El Bosque* a name that was a dead giveaway of its function, another variation of the "in Paradise" theme, a paradise with trees; perhaps apple trees? There were no plastic curtains on the carports, however. The rooms featured king-size beds, beautifully appointed bathrooms, and air conditioning. The restaurant was for take-out only. Food and drink could be ordered by telephone, and was delivered through a small hatch at the rear of the room. Hence, one could receive one's order in a state of *déshabillé*. They did not rent by the hour. This was saying a lot about Venezuelan loving habits.

The drive to Caracas made up for the stresses of border crossing and night driving. Just as well, for a few unpleasant surprises were waiting for us in the big city. It seems to be my destiny to arrive in a big city during rush hour. My arrival at 5.00 p.m. cancelled everything I had learned so far about Venezuelan driving habits. In Caracas, traffic was chaotic, and the motto seemed to be "everyone for him- or herself." But we muddled through. Then the real fun began, finding a hotel that wanted us. The hotel in my price range that I had picked from the travel guide had no parking, and therefore, was not acceptable. The next one strangely declared that they had safe parking for cars only, not for motorcycles. The third one claimed it had no vacancy, or was it no vacancy for bikers? The fourth one, *Hotel President*, when they saw us park in front, quickly hustled us over to the side, obviously to avoid arousing the suspicion that they welcomed bikers. From the way I was treated by reception and by the various flunkies showing me to my room, I got the distinct impression that we were not wanted there. The nicest person of the whole staff was the parking attendant, a motorcycle-owner himelf. This was by far the most unwelcoming place I encountered during the whole trip, and for US$150.00 a night a real rip-off.

What had happened in Caracas, I wondered, that had made this city so biker-unfriendly? I put this question to Mario, the parking attendant, adding that when I was here five years ago, the city seemed to me a biker's paradise. At every stoplight there were always a dozen or so bikes in the front row doing power take-offs when the light changed. Now there were only a few bikes visible in downtown traffic, mostly small models, ridden by delivery men, at times on the sidewalk. Mario believed that this state of affairs had been brought on mostly by the bikers themselves. Motorcycles had become the getaway vehicles of choice of the bad guys. Bank robbers used them, purse snatchers used them, even drive-by, or should one say ride-by, hit men used them. The city had had to pass some stringent laws to curb this sort of motorcycle crime. In front of every bank there was now a no-parking zone, no-parking for both cars and motorcycles. Motorcycles could not be ridden between 11.00 p.m. and 5.00 a.m. The rider had to wear a helmet, but only open-face helmets were allowed. And finally, it was forbidden for same sex-couples to ride two up. This I found hilarious. What did these same-sex couples do on motorcycles that made doing it so offensive? Mario said that this law was only a face-saving way for not appearing sexist. Women don't ride motorcycles in Caracas, at least not in front. They may be passengers on the pillion seat, which was O.K. The law was obviously passed to prevent two men on a bike robbing a bank, snatching a purse, or shooting someone on the run. Because of these problems in the past, motorcyclists had received a bad reputation in Caracas, and were not welcome in better establishments. The whole story sounded somewhat familiar in light of the ambivalent attitude toward bikers back home. But I didn't have to like it. I still thought that I had received shabby treatment at *Hotel President*.

At least the area surrounding the hotel, near the Plaza Venezuela pedestrian zone, made my stay in Caracas a pleasant one. There was a great choice of restaurants for dinner, as well as for breakfast.

My first order of business was to get a visa for Brazil. But when I arrived at the Brazilian Embassy, only four subway stops away, I was told that a visa would take twenty-four hours. No way was I going to stay another night in this expensive, snooty dump called *President*. The next item on my agenda, then, was the

BMW dealer, Oscar Amantini, whose shop was in El Hatillo, a suburb on one of the mountains surrounding the city, half an hour away by taxi.

Although I had the correct address the place was still difficult to find. It would have taken me hours if I had gone on my own. With the help of the taxi driver, who had to ask repeatedly, we finally arrived. Señor Amantini had **not** received word from Costa Rica about a shock absorber. Nor had he received the object itself. Of couse he did not stock exotic parts like a Bilstein, or its equivalent. "Sorry!" In all honesty this is what I had expected. There was no chance that the part would have arrived from the United States in this short time, even if Herbert Von Breymann in San José had placed the order on the day I left. It would have been a miracle. And I had my doubts if the higher powers in charge of miracles were kindly disposed toward bikers, especially in Caracas. At least I tried. It appeared that I was destined to finish the trip on an Old Cow with a Bilstein Bedspring up its rear end.

Riding in Venezuela continued to be pure pleasure. The roads were excellent. And gasoline was dirt cheap. It was roughly half as expensive as in the U.S., one third as in Canada. Proceeding east out of Caracas, Highway #9 descends for some 15 km and follows the coastline, passing through banana and palm groves affording glimpses of the blue Caribbean. At Barcelona we turned south on #16 bound for Ciudad Bolívar, where we spent the night.

Another weekend was approaching fast, and so was the Brazilian border. The super-modern toll road they had just built was so new that they had not yet finished the toll booths, a fact greatly appreciated by the Retired Biker. We arrived at the Brazilian Consulate in Ciudad Guyana at 9.30 on Thursday morning. It was supposed to be located near the CANTV Station. Having parked the bike I asked an older gentleman for directions. He simply approached a young guy sitting in a car, and asked him to take me there. The latter seemed genuinely pleased to help the gringo from the cold north. The consulate was just around the corner. Once more I had to follow a routine that had become familiar, a routine dictated by governments that distrusted their own civil servants.

I needed an application form to be completed in duplicate and two photos, but first the equivalent of US$54 had to be paid into their account at a bank downtown. The queue was long, as usual, but I made it back to the consulate at 11.30, just before they closed for siesta. The visa would be ready in the afternoon at 3.30. This allowed plenty of time for lunch at the "Grandfather's Beard" next door, and an oil change at a local oil slick, a familiar sight since Mexico. We were back at the consulate at three o'clock, hoping to get a head start in the race to the border to beat the approaching weekend. But true to the stereotype the civil servants took their time, and delivered as promised a half-hour later.

The road south, Highway #10, had just been repaved. There were no markings on the pavement and no road signs yet. There was, however, heavy truck traffic, mostly overloaded lumber trucks heading north, toward us, and not wasting any time. We got as far as Guasipati when darkness fell, and it was getting too dangerous to continue.

Another Friday had dawned, and I was determined to beat the buggers to their weekend. They would not trap us this time. I left the hotel at 6.30 under brilliant skies, which, I was convinced, this augured well. El Dorado, where Papillon, the famous escapee from Devil's Island, had spent some time in the local prison, seemed to be a good place for breakfast. South of the little town the road climbed steadily through the rolling hills of *La Gran Sabana,* the Guyana Highlands. The jungle of the lowlands soon gave way to subtropical vegetation, which in turn disappeared almost completely in an almost desert-like landscape as we gained altitude. It was gradually getting colder and it began to drizzle. At the peak, at 1,300 meters, the rain gear was perfect for keeping me dry as well as warm. We made good time, since the road continued in perfect condition into Santa Elena, the last town before the border. It was 1.00 p.m. when we arrived.

I remembered from my visit in 1992 that Customs and Immigration had to be cleared in town, rather than at the border. The building, however, was deserted, and I was told by the lonely guard to come back at 2.30. No problem. This gave me some time to have lunch, as well as to get some Brazilian money in town. When I came back at two o'clock, there was still no one to be seen. Instead I heard loud voices coming from behind the building, where everyone seemed to be having a good time. Empty beer bottles littered the lawn, and the contents of several full cases were waiting their turn to join the others on the ground. The boys from DIEX, the border guard, most of them in undershirts and suspenders, were getting a headstart on the weekend. I asked one of them when the office would reopen. He gave me a sheepish grin and said, *"Mas tarde,"* later. I had heard that term before, and didn't like to hear it at all in this context. *Mas tarde* in this latitude could mean in a half-hour, or tomorrow, or next week, or never in this life. I was getting worried. What else could I do but wait? At 2.45 I overheard by chance a policeman telling one of his colleagues that DIEX was at the border today, because it was Friday. Bastards! Why didn't they tell me? Off to the border, some 5 km south of town.

It was true. I got my exit stamp from Immigration. Customs took my *Autorization* for the bike, and we were rid of Venezuela in the record time of five minutes. Again this appeared to augur well. Now off to the Brazilians.

12. *Brazil*

"Welcome to Brazil," said the Immigration Officer, while he stamped my passport. "You have thirty days." All that was done in less than five minutes. I thought that I had beaten them this time. Now only Customs remained to be cleared, my last hurdle. The Customs Officer asked me for all my papers and disappeared into a back office. While I was waiting, a motorist arrived in a beat-up VW bus with New Zealand licence plates. He introduced himself as William, on a trip around the world. As we were exchanging tales of the road, the officer came back to the counter, and said something to the effect that he could not issue the document I needed. Due to my limited Portuguese I did not quite understand the reason. Now William intervened and tried to interpret for me, while at the same time handing over his *Carnet de passage* asking that it be cleared. This gave the impression that we were travelling together. For the next half-hour the officer tried to explain that Brazil did not accept the *Carnet* for customs purposes, and that he could not give me my document, for whatever reason. We were getting nowhere, and I was feeling my temperature rise. Something had to be done fast. First I asked William to shut up and butt out. Then I explained to the officer that we were not travelling together; that I was going south, the other fellow, north. Would he please go over my case again, slowly—. This he did, and to his credit with the utmost patience. He explained that all he was empowered to give to me at the border was a temporary document allowing me to proceed to Boa Vista. There I would have to go to the *Ministerio da Fazenda,* the Customs Office, to get the correct papers to continue. "Welcome to Brazil" had taken on a rather ironic meaning.

They had beaten me again. The Latin American Weekend had again emerged the triumphant winner in the contest. Boa Vista was 200 km down the road. Customs there was open to the public only from 8.00 a.m. until noon, Monday to Friday. It was now four o'clock on a Friday afternoon. All I could say at this moment was an emphatic "Shit! Shit! Shit!" This was the fourth time a weekend had done me in. First, in Costa Rica, waiting for the shock absorber to cross the border and to clear customs. Second, in Panama, waiting for customs clearance. Third, in Cúcuta, waiting to cross the border. Now for the fourth time, in Boa Vista, waiting for customs to open. This kind of thing was not supposed to happen four times in a row. In literature things like that happened to the hero only three times at the most. After that he was either dead, or had learned his lesson and was married to a princess. In my case I was neither dead nor had I learned my lesson, and there was no princess. Why this discrepancy between fact and fiction? The only answer that came to my mind was "The Curse," the power of "The Border Curse." In fairy-tale literature the evil stepmothers seem to be the most accomplished cursers. It appears now that in real life this talent has been preempted by wives. In fairy tales there is always some way to break the spell, by means of a magic kiss, for instance. But what was my spell-breaker? Pondering this question I fired up the Old Cow and tried to make it to Boa Vista at a decent hour.

Boa Vista, capital of the State of Roraima, is a hell-hole. With a population of some 75,000 it might be expected to have some sights, some things to do, some beauty. But there is only heat and disappointment. The town has been laid out in a typical Brazilian megalomaniacal manner, with city streets wide enough to accommodate traffic until the year 2100, and with distances that can be covered only by motorized transport. Furthermore, it is immoderately expensive, because of gold-mining activities nearby. There is also a large industrial sector in the southern part of town. As the result of an unstable economy and high unemployment, the town has a reputation for muggings. In 1992, on the bus from the border, a Venezuelan shopper told me that the last time he had been in Boa Vista he was robbed at gun point in broad daylight thirty minutes after he had stepped off the bus. He was forced to hand over his money, his watch, and his jewellery. Downtown was not a safe place to walk, not even during daylight hours.

If one thinks of the worst that can happen, reality can only be better. The first pleasant surprise came as soon as we had left the border. The road was excellent. It had been paved all the way only recently. In 1992 there were dust and potholes, or quagmire and potholes, depending on the weather, with rickety bridges to add to the excitement. Five years later at least half of the bridges had been replaced with modern structures. The few of the original ones that remained, however, were hair-raising, held up by spindly posts, half rotten, with two sets of three narrow planks for the wheels. Soon to be replaced, they were at the brink of collapse, with many planks no longer held down by spikes, and even more dangerous, with spikes up to two inches in length sticking out of the sub-structure. During daylight these could be seen and avoided. But after dark crossing these structures was like playing Russian Roulette. We arrived in Boa Vista an hour and a half hours after sunset. With a bit of luck it did not take long to find the hotel I had stayed in in 1992, *Tres Nações*, very basic, but safe.

The second pleasant surprise came next morning, during my walk to the centre of town, some 3 km away. Already at seven o'clock the thermometer was well on its way to the high eighties. Looking for a place to have breakfast I noticed that the town seemed to have cleaned up its act. There were only a few shady characters hanging out near the giant statue of the gold panner, the *garimpeiro* in front of Government House, and these seemed to be non-violent. On this Saturday morning the downtown area was almost deserted, although the shops were open. A shopkeeper told me later that the government had made an effort to curb the wildest excesses of the *garimpeiros,* perhaps to appease the native Indians, who had threatened to take violent action against these trespassers on their land. Hence, economically Boa Vista had suffered from the decline in gold prospecting. By the same token it had become a relatively peaceful backwater. That suited me very well.

Since I had to spend two more days in this godforsaken place I had to find a better hotel, or else I would have gone nuts. The rooms in *Tres Nações* were a little better than holes in the wall with wooden shutters for windows. Shut them and you felt you were in a dungeon; open them and in came the mosquitoes, potential carriers of malaria. I was looking for the hotel *Praya Palace,* which I remembered from my last visit. I couldn't find it, so I asked some people sitting on the sidewalk. They sent me down the street, but without success. When I returned and confronted them with this they said that I was standing right in front of "the former"*Praya Palace* which had in the meantime been converted into a private school. I can never understand the Latin mind. Why couldn't, or wouldn't, they tell me this immediately? Perhaps in order not to disappoint me? I'll never know. When I asked them for the name of a hotel similar to the closed one, they suggested hotel *Aipana Plaza.* I decided to pay them a visit for breakfast.

The dining room of the hotel *Aipana Plaza* seemed to cater to a full house. All tables were decked with white linen and matching napkins, a full set of cutlery, crystal glasses, cups, and plates, with a colorful floral arrangement in the centre. A head table took up the whole of one wall. On the wall adjoining a buffet breakfast was laid out the like I had not seen in a long time: mountains of fresh fruit, flanked by freshly baked rolls, cold cuts, cheeses, juices, yogurt, and milk to go with the various cold cereals. But this was only leading up to the main dishes: boiled, fried, or scrambled eggs, ham, bacon, sausages, pancakes, and for dessert assorted pastries. I was the only guest there at this early hour, and began with a giant helping of fresh fruit. I also filled my coffee cup with delicious Brazilian coffee; it seems that they keep some of the good stuff for local consumption. After my third trip to this Table of Earthly Delights, the room started to fill up with elegantly dressed ladies and gentlemen, most of them carrying books that looked like hymnals. They all chose seats either at the little tables or the head table, and tried to disregard the lavish buffet. I was just finishing my second cup of coffee, when a gentleman at the head table called the meeting to order. They all rose for prayer, and began to sing a hymn from their hymnals. One of them shoved a copy under my nose, urging me to sing along with them, which I did with the same voice I had used the last time to scare away grizzlies in the Yukon. They didn't seem to mind, not having any preconceived ideas about the singing ability of gringos. Soon I learned that I had crashed the Saturday morning prayer meeting of the representatives of various evangelical churches of the state of Roraima. Since I had partaken of their food, it was only fair that I should also partake of their song and prayer, at least for a while, for, of course, I had not understood a word of what I was singing or praying. But, coming to think of it, neither had the Roman Catholics for centuries, before they changed the text of the Holy Mass from Latin to the vernaculars, and they, it seems, had gotten away with it without suffering any ill-effects. I could only hope that this would also apply in my case. I found it rather strange, however, that I had gotten my reward in terms of food and drink before praying and singing, whereas at Salvation Army luncheons in Canada, and for the other folks in the room, it was the other way around. Before the sermon began I tried to make a hasty but discreet escape, thanking the good brethren and sistren for their hospitality.

In light of their efforts at breakfast I concluded that *Aipana Plaza* deserved my business. My room featured air conditioning, satellite TV, and a frigo-bar. It overlooked a palm-fringed swimming pool. The Old Cow was parked securely right under my window in the shade of a palm tree beside the pool. The room cost only half as much as the one I had at *Hotel President* in Caracas, and was twice as nice. Although it was an extravagance that was not good for my travel budget, I looked at it as a therapeutic measure necessary to assuage some of the pain inflicted by a merciless Latin American bureaucracy. And I continued this therapy through the whole of Sunday, with a replay of the same lavish breakfast, charged to my account this time, and several tall cool ones to be served beside the emerald swimming pool.

My visit to the *Ministerio da Fazenda* on Monday morning had many similarities with K.'s visit to Franz Kafka's *Castle*. Having informed the gatekeeper of my problem I was ushered into an office, whose inmate did not know what to do with me. So he transferred me to the office next door, whose inmate found himself in a similar position. In the last office on the corridor they were stuck with me, since they had run out of offices. Something had to be done. But what? To find a clue the official in charge started to study manuals of biblical proportions about procedures, e.g. how to deal with motorcyclists in transit. After he had been searching fruitlessly for about an hour, a lady passing through his office suggested that this would perhaps be the job for a *despachante*. This was the clue he was looking for, the light at the end of the tunnel for this poor overworked civil servant. A telephone call was placed to the office of *Despachante Mazinha, Serviços Aduaneros* downtown. They promised to come to my rescue immediately, releasing me from the confines of Boa Vista *Castle*.

"Immediately" in this context meant in thirty minutes. A boy on a bicycle guided me to the *despachante's* office, where three people in a room the size of a broom closet on the second floor of a dilapidated building were busy typing out documents on elderly typewriters. It seems that a *despachante* in Brazil fulfills a similar function for the government as a paralegal secretary does for a lawyer in the US. They typed out the required customs document in three copies, which took forty-five minutes, at a cost of US$50. Back at the *Ministerio* the official signed all three copies, kept one, gave me the second one to be handed in when leaving the country, and the third one for me to keep as a souvenir. We were now free to go anywhere in Brazil, legally. Back on the road again by 11.30.

In retrospect Boa Vista was not as bad as I had anticipated. Perhaps I should reconsider my judgment in light of my most recent experience, and forget 1992. Instead of "hell-hole" let's upgrade it to "purgatory."

Since there were no road signs to point the way to Manaus, I had to ask several times in order to avoid the mistake of Dave Barr and friends *Riding the Edge,* who, when passing through in 1992, had taken a wrong turn and ended up at the Guyanese border. Road conditions permitting, I had planned on this day to get as far as the Equator Monument, a distance of 411 km. The remaining 359 km to Manaus could perhaps be covered the next day. The highway continued in the same excellent condition as it had been since the border. Even the ferry over the *Rio Branco* at Caracaraí had been modernized. The many dilapidated bridges

9) Brazil: equator monument

waiting to be replaced were the only obstacles that spoiled an otherwise great riding experience. Pavement ended 395 km south of Boa Vista, a great improvement over 1992, when it had extended only 80 km south of town. We arrived at the Equator at quarter to six, with only fifteen minutes of daylight remaining for picture-taking. Now covered with loose gravel, the road was being prepared for paving and was difficult to negotiate, particularly in the dark. It was with relief, therefore, that one hour later we arrived at the *Restaurant e Fazenda Santa Clara*, 333 km north of Manaus, which offered to prepare a full course meal, and also one of their hammocks to spend the night, the latter free of charge.

I had made it half-way through a small mountain of rice with two kinds of beans, and corn, topped with a fried egg and a chicken leg, when a big rig, coming from the south, pulled up. The driver and his young lady companion seemed to be well-known by management. Since there was only one table for guests, I was introduced to Jorge and his wife, or daughter, or both; I could not figure out what applied, and did not have the courage to ask. After they had ordered the same meal I was working on, question period started. In keeping with their usual routine every Monday, they had left Manaus in the morning with a full load of shoes and textiles, bound for Boa Vista. They had just managed to cross the Indian Reservation before sunset, as required by law, and were determined to continue to Boa Vista after their meal. This was the plan. But there was a snag. Jorge was very thirsty. The dust of the unpaved road must have dried him out.

The *South American Handbook* issues the following warning concerning truck drivers on this road: "They drive for too long, haul too much, and drink." I was about to find out. Before his meal arrived Jorge needed some liquid to clean his whistle. He disparaged beer for this purpose, and instead ordered a round of the local sugar cane brew, called *cachaça*, which he downed quickly while chewing on a slice of lime. I tried to keep up with him, but failed miserably. The burning sensation in my mouth and throat caused by this devilish concoction, probably also used undiluted as fuel for their cars, was so intense that I had to quench the fire with several gulps of beer. Nevertheless, even a gringo has his pride. I insisted it was my turn to order the next round. By the time our plates were empty, we barely remembered whose turn it was. This state of affairs did not sit well with Jorge's lady love. After every round she insisted that this was the last one, and that they should be leaving, while he insisted that this was the penultimate one, and that driving could wait. When the generator was stopped at midnight, and the lights grew dark, Jorge had his last one and staggered back into the cab of his truck, not for driving, I hoped. He could not have made it without the assistance of his lady. I had an easier time of it, since my hammock was strung right next to the dining table. If I had been bitten by mosquitoes during the night, I'm certain that they would have died of alcohol poisoning. I awoke with a heavy head next morning just as Jorge was pulling out, a Brazilian trucker by the book.

I was privileged to watch my first sunrise in the Amazon from my hammock. It was an experience not to be forgotten. As the fireball emerged over the treetops, gaining in size and intensity, the songs of cicadas and birds of the night abated and were replaced by the crowing of roosters and the barking of dogs of the *fazenda,* which was surrounded by almost impenetrable jungle. What is a headache compared with this miracle of nature? A small nuisance soon to be forgotten. Breakfast was interesting, consisting of two fried eggs, no bread, no rice, no potatoes, *"Desculpe Senhor!"* and coffee with milk. Hardly a gourmet affair. There was no need to linger.

For the following 150 km the road was as I remembered it from 1992, packed clay, rutted, with potholes, at times covered with a thick layer of dust, on both sides impenetrable jungle. Fortunately we were in the dry season. At first we made good progress, but after about an hour the trucks appeared, one after another, coming toward us at a good clip, hiding us in a desert storm with zero visibility. Why all of a sudden? And why so many travelling in convoy, as it were? Now I remembered what Jorge had told me yesterday. Traffic (with the exception of buses) was forbidden to cross the Indian Reservation during the night. These trucks had accumulated last night at the other side of the Reservation, and had started off at sunrise. This explained why there were so many of them bunched together. But the answer to this puzzle did not make my life any easier. By the time asphalt returned we were covered with a thick layer of uniform Amazonas Red, which had penetrated the farthest recesses of man and machine. For the next three weeks my white undershorts had taken on a pinkish hue, which came out only gradually in the wash. Nothing had changed in this respect since 1992.

The last 180 km to Manaus were again full riding pleasure. In 1992 the whole area had been a sad example of slash and burn, with charred trees pointing accusing fingers skyward. While some of these reminders of the past were still standing, the pasture appeared to have recovered somewhat from the scorched earth. The sparse grasses seemed to support large herds of cattle, and little else. The soil was too poor to support large-scale, or even small-scale, farming. The Brazilians will have to learn from their own mistakes. It would be arrogant for us to tell them what (not) to do, since we ourselves are the worst offenders in the clearcutting of first-growth forests. The dwellers around the Mediterranean had not learned their lesson, and had clearcut their forests, with dire results. We have not learned our lesson, and are doing the very same thing. Can the Brazilians be expected to act any differently?

With the bike safely parked in the yard of *Pension Sulista* in downtown Manaus, and after a hasty shower, I walked over to the floating dock to book passage on a ship that would take us down the Amazon to Belém. I made sure this time that the ship would indeed go all the way to Belém, and not go only as far as Santarém, where one would have to change ships. In 1992 I had been caught in this trap, and the same thing had happened earlier in the same year to Dave Barr and friends. There was no choice. The only ship going all the way during the next three days was the *Clivia* slated to sail the next day, the third of December, at 16.00 hours. We paid the equivalent of US$70 each for passage, including meals. Embarcation time was to be after 8.00 a.m. on the day of departure. I made sure that my tickets spelled out "From Manaus To Belém." Now back to a night on the town, and indeed a night it was, literally.

There are two compulsory sights in Manaus. One is the large floating dock, built to accommodate the annual 14 meter rise of the *Rio Negro,* and connected to the city by a floating ramp 150 metres in length. The other is the *Teatro Amazonas,* the famous opera house, where Caruso once sang, built in 1896. I had made my booking on the floating dock earlier, and had made a return visit to the *Teatro* to ascertain that it was still as beautiful as it had been in 1992. All sweaty from the excessive heat, the high humidity, and the climb up the hill, I had just settled down to a tall cool bottle of *Antárctica,* the delicious beer brewed locally, when the overhead fan stopped turning, the lights went out, and the TV went dead. The waiter just shrugged his shoulders when asked what had happened—blackout. It happened every day. Since it was close to six o'clock, darkness was falling fast, and they lit candles, which lay ready to use beside the cash register. This would have been romantic under other circumstances. But since there was not a breath of air stirring, I was bathed in sweat almost immediately, not having quite recovered from my trip up to the *Teatro.* I had to leave to get a breath of fresh air, and to look for a place to eat. Just around the corner there was a restaurant and bar that had its own generator, and hence at least a working fan, where I could get more of that delicious *Antárctica* to replenish my body fluids, and a bite to eat. The whole setting was great for conversation with the local bar-flies. They told me that Manaus had such blackouts at least twice a day, once in the morning, and once in the late afternoon. I found it almost unbelievable that a city with close to one and one half million inhabitants would put up with this. But all they could do was buy their own generators, which most commercial establishments had to do in order to survive. Since it was comfortable here under the fan, I stayed until the lights came back on, shortly after 8.00 p.m. I would have melted in my little room in the *Pension* without the fan. Like Boa Vista, Manaus had cleaned up its act. Walking back to the *Pension* through the narrow pedestrian streets surrounding the Post Office I felt quite safe, unlike in 1992. Perhaps they had been doing something right.

The fan stopped turning as predicted at 5.00 a.m. In no time I was bathed in sweat and left my cubicle to take a shower. Even this did not help to cool me down, for the water was tepid. The other guests had also been driven from their rooms, and were sitting around the courtyard, where I proceeded to restore the bike to its original color, from Amazon red to BMW *marakeschrot* and *alpinweiß.* My onlookers proved to be great connoisseurs of large-bore motorcycles. Some even helped me wipe the bike in order to get a closer look at this marvel of German engineering. I didn't tell them about the Bilstein flop, so as not to spoil their illusion. Time passed quickly. When I checked out at eight o'clock electricity had not yet returned.

In spite of the intense heat and the early morning hour the floating dock area was chaotic. Ships were being unloaded, or loaded. Trucks were hauling off large loads of bananas, live chicken, and goats, and thousands of empty beer bottles in large cases. Others were bringing in load upon load of electric or electronic gadgets, refrigerators, microwave ovens, computers, stereos, and television sets, and

10) *On board the "Clivia"*

of course thousands of full bottles of beer in large cases, all going down into the holds. When we rode up, carefully slaloming around the trucks, there were a number of sturdy helpers offering their services to wrestle the Old Cow down to the Lower Deck of the *Clivia,* and of course double the number of calloused hands expecting payment.

The crew parked the bike immediately beside the engine hatch. I secured it to a rising steel pipe with my kryptonite bike lock to keep it from toppling over in rough weather. Then I strung my hammock, which I had bought in San Salvator, next to the bike, and I thought we were ready for the four-day voyage. It wasn't as easy as that.

During the morning hours the *Clivia* was filling up with passengers only slowly. It was not too difficult to defend my turf beside the bike against intruders. After twelve noon, however, passengers began to board in large numbers. There were three decks. On the top deck were the cabins of first class passengers, reserved, so there was no need for them to hurry. One level down was the second class. Here the early bird gets the best perch for his or her hammock. The next level down, and just above the engine room, was the cheapy class, where the Old Cow had to go, because she was considered cargo, and where I ended up by choice, because of my feeling of solidarity with the beast. Again, the early bird gets the best perch, the best space to string the hammock. By four o'clock both hammock classes had become incredibly crowded, and I lost out in the fight to keep a bit of breathing space around me. I gave up fighting, not wanting to be the selfish gringo. The ship was rated for 300 passengers. I was sure that there must have been at least 400 on board. Then I was told that departure time had been moved down one hour to five o'clock, and they were still streaming on board. By the time we left there were so many hammocks strung across the width of the ship that the Old Cow looked like a little insect caught in a spider's web. It was difficult to move about, since the area under the hammocks was piled high with commercial goods belonging to the person whose hammock was strung above. There was no place to sit in the hammock classes except in one's own hammock. There was an open-air section with tables and chairs on the top deck adjoining the bar, but this section was fully exposed to the sun, and became unbearable after 9.00 a.m. The *Clivia*   appeared to be well-maintained. In case of accident, however, there would have been a Titanic-like situation or worse: no life preservers, no lifeboats, no safety drill. Fortunately there are no icebergs on the Amazon, and human life is cheap in Brazil, hence we didn't need all those things.

I was surprised to note that the two great cities of the Amazon basin are not really on the *Rio Amazonas.* Manaus lies on the *Rio Negro,* ten miles upstream of the latter's confluence with the *Rio Solimões.* Belém lies on the *Rio Pará,* flowing into the Amazon delta. One of the great experiences when leaving Manaus by ship, having sailed past the giant *Antárctica*   brewery, is the "Meeting of the Waters," the place where the black waters of the *Rio Negro* join the muddy brown flow of the *Rio Solimões,* the birthplace proper of the *Rio Amazonas.* For the following twenty miles both rivers flow side by side, before the different coloured waters mix. This process is repeated at Santarém, where the turquoise-colored *Rio Tapajos* mixes only gradually with the muddy brown *Amazonas*. Some of the native travellers took great delight in pointing out this phenomenon to the big-eyed gringo.

One of them, Pedro by name, liked to talk, and after a couple of *Antárcticas* had kicked in, he stopped only briefly now and then to take a breath. Pedro was on his way home to Salvador after having spent several months playing soccer for semi-professional farm teams in Boa Vista and Manaus. He was twenty-six years old, unmarried, and the father of two children, aged three and five, whom he supported, and who stayed with their mother in Salvador. Although he smoked incessantly he claimed that this did not impede his performance on the soccer field. He could still run as fast as he could at the age of fifteen. His dream was to be discovered some day to play in the big league. Pelé was his hero. We drank to each other's health and good luck, he to my trip, and I to his future as a Brazilian soccer star. When we called it a day, at around 11.00 p.m., my troubles were just beginning.

It was dark on the lower deck, and I was having difficulty crawling over the baggage on the floor, and between the tightly packed hammocks containing human bodies, to get to the bike and to my own hammock. Once safely tucked in I found it impossible to fall asleep. The heat coming up from the engine room was unbearable, but what was worse was the noise of the engines, now running at high revs. Ear-plugs did not help. I had to move if I wanted to retain any degree of sanity. But where to? All of the available space had been taken. In every possible nook and cranny was hanging a human cocoon, slowly swaying with the roll of the ship. The only place that offered itself was a narrow spot toward the bow, parallel to the starboard railing, and directly above it. The advantage of this spot was that I had nice fresh air to breathe and relatively little noise from the engines. But if the ropes of my hammock should give, I would be in the river, as fishfood. I hoped that the El Salvadoreans knew what they were doing when they knotted my hammock.

Sleep during the night was intermittent. When the ship stopped briefly at Itacoatiara to disembark and board passengers, I had to get out of my hammock, because I was hanging precisely over that section of the railing that had to be removed for boarding. Since I could not fall asleep thereafter, I went to have a shower, thinking that with only two showers and toilets for each sex, there would be long lineups later on, which proved to be true. At seven o'clock the first shift took their seats for breakfast.

In 1992 I had taken the suggestion of the travel guide to heart and had brought my own food, in order not to tempt the local bacteria to wreak havoc in my gut. It worked, but I had walked away feeling like a wimp. This time I was ready to brave the wrath of the gods of the Amazon, and was going to eat with the rest of the passengers. During off-meal hours the two dining tables hung suspended on the ceiling of the upper hammock deck; the benches, one on each side of the tables, lay collapsed on the floor. At breakfast, lunch, and dinner the tables were lowered, their legs were extended, and the benches were unfolded. The crew was hardly finished with this task when the mob charged to get a seat. First come, first served. Each one of the tables seated sixteen. I usually managed to get a seat during the sixth or seventh sitting. By this time the rush was less intense, but the tables were in a shape not conducive to a great appetite. For breakfast we were served coffee with milk and a bun, which could be buttered from a large tub of half liquid butter standing in the middle of the table. It was perhaps not the most hygienic affair, but it was great fun, and great fellowship. One got to meet many fellow passengers during these sittings, and conversation flowed easily. I was wondering why I was always surrounded by so many women, until I discovered the next day that the single men usually ate on the table on one side of the ship, the solitary women and families on the other. Since the latter were in the minority it was only natural that I, not knowing the rules, should end up on the less numerous side. But they all took it in stride. They did not expect a gringo to know these things. Nice people, these Brazilians. Lunch began at noon; dinner at 5.00 p.m. Both meals consisted of rice, spaghetti, beans in a liquid, some unidentifiable dry crunchy stuff, and a huge pile of beef stew. Plates, plastic drinking cups, and cutlery were provided. There was enough food to feed everyone. Water was the drink of choice, water with plenty of chlorine added. During the following four days only the order in which the food was served was changed; the items remained the same. This was definitely not a gourmet cruise.

What was left on the plates was simply thrown overboard, a feast for the piranhas. What was also thrown overboard were plastic cups, non-returnable bottles, wrapping material of various kinds, and anything else that needed disposal. This is not to say that there were no garbage cans on the *Clivia*. When they were full they were emptied regularly, but overboard as well. I had seen this in 1992 and was saddened by this flagrant abuse of the environment. They were still doing the same thing without any qualms. The Amazon must be the world's largest garbage dump and sewer. How long can it last?

At 9.30 p.m. we pulled into a floating police station, where we were given a once-over by six officers of the *Policia federal*. One of them immediately spotted the bike. Having been informed about the identity of its owner, he was having his day in court going over my documents, while dozens of onlookers were having a great time watching me being grilled. After he had found the stamp in my passport matching the one on my landing card, he gave me his nod of approval, and didn't bother with the vehicle documents. While this was going on on the deck of the great unwashed, another officer had found a shotgun in one of the first-class cabins. This model must have been a leftover from the Seven Years War. It was a single-barrel ten-gauge flintlock affair, and quite rusty. It was a weapon, however, and it was the duty of this defender of life, liberty, and the Brazilian way to confiscate it and to write a report "To Whom It May Concern" in triplicate, while the whole ship had to wait until he had located the p's and q's on his antique typewriter. We were finally released at 11.00 p.m.

Barely having shut my eyes, I had to untie my hammock again half an hour later for a brief stop at a little town called Juruti. Back to sleep just after midnight. This lack of sleep was threatening to age me beyond my years. I needed to find another place for my hammock at the earliest opportunity.

My chance came during our stop at Santarem, the half-way mark, where we arrived at six in the morning. Many passengers had disembarked, and there was enough space available that I was able to be selective. I thought that I had found the perfect spot, when I noticed that some women around me gave me rather peculiar looks. This was the moment that I discovered that I had again trespassed on the section reserved for solitary women and families. "Oops!" Over to the other side of the boat and try again.

Although many passengers had left the ship in Santarem, an even greater number boarded. When we left port at three in the afternoon the hammock classes were packed tightly. For a long time the Brazilians had left some private space around my hammock, but the moment arrived when this was no longer possible. Since the women's and families' side could not squeeze in another person, some of the overflow had to trespass on the men's side. My breathing space was invaded by a mother with six children, the latter like organ pipes, ranging from an infant of barely six months to the tallest, who was about six years old. The mother looked at me questioningly before she strung her four hammocks. When I smiled at her invitingly she proceeded to do it in a strategic manner, which I had learned to appreciate back in 1992. Stringing the hammocks exactly side by side invited disaster later on. With every roll of the ship they all started to swing. Soon, however, those containing fatsos once in motion continued swinging in the same rhythm, like a pendulum, whereas those containing lightweights slowed down quickly, with the result that they would all bump into each other's neigbours on both sides, and no one could sleep. This mother and seasoned Amazon traveller strung her hammocks in a staggered pattern, always alternating between high and low, so that all, heavyweights as well as lightweights, could swing without impeding the motion of their neighbours. My respect for her grew by the minute, and I gave her a closer look. In her late thirties, with a wild jet-black mane, dark complexion, sensuous mouth, narrow aquiline nose, and big dangling gold earrings, she looked like a Romanian gypsy. Noticing her voluptuous body, wrapped in a colourful dress accentuating all of her womanly charms, I thought of an "Earth Mother" surrounded by her children. Jean-Jacques Rousseau would probably have seen in her an embodiment of the "noble savage."

Because of the overcrowding on the two lower decks, the bar on the upper deck had to absorb much of the overflow, particularly after sunset. Once *Antárctica* started to flow there was music and singing, even some dancing by the younger set. No one was eager to squeeze into his or her hammock until at least partially sedated. It was a great party.

If I hadn't taken my shower at 3.00 a.m. I would have missed out during the day. The rush for the showers and toilets was incredible. Similarly for the meals. On this Saturday they served sweet buns for breakfast, for the other meals the same fare as usual.

In the afternoon we entered the first narrows, and we were close enough to the shore to see something. Just before sunset we passed through a narrow channel with little tin-covered shacks on stilts lining the shore on both sides. The ship was surrounded by numerous *piroques* paddled by women or children, who held out their hands soliciting gifts. One of the little boys was wearing a T-shirt with a large red maple leaf on the chest and the word "Canada" printed on the back, a reminder of the homeland, probably spirited over by my wife (How did she do it?—Women!!). Some passengers were throwing in little gifts wrapped in plastic, T-shirts, junk food, money. "*Pobre gente*" (poor people), said the fellow beside me, throwing down a chocolate bar. This beats picking bananas or gathering coconuts, I thought. If they get as much from each passing ship as they were getting from us, they were doing very well. It was fun to watch the little boats negotiating the high wake of the *Clivia*. It must have been rather tricky.

On Sunday, the last day on board, I went back to my hammock after breakfast for a second wink, and as I woke up again I witnessed a strange sight. The "Earth Mother" was combing her beautiful mane with the help of her six-year old, and the four-year old in the other hammock held the head of the two-year old cradled in her lap. What was she doing? She was grooming the little one, picking nits off her head, cracking them between thumb and index finger, and eating them. The last time I had seen this done was in the London Zoo by a family of baboons. At first I was rather amused by the spectacle, but then I got to thinking that the hammock of this little nit-picker and her victim was hanging right above mine. What if some of the relatives of the pickees had jumped their host during the night and landed on me? I was getting itchy. That was the end of hammock time for me this morning. I had to go up on deck for fresh air and fresh thoughts.

*   *   *

She was sitting in the bow of the ship on the forward windlass like a figurehead on a pirate ship. She appeared to be paying homage to the rising sun. What a body! Slim waist, a well-rounded *derrière* squeezed tightly into a pair of black spandex shorts, long shapely legs, an ample bosom barely contained in a low-cut red sweater, and skin like cinnamon-coloured velvet. Many years of politically-correct thinking went down the drain in an instant as I contemplated this picture of female perfection, a perfect 10, an A+, without a doubt. She must have seen me watching her, but didn't blink an eye. I thought she was the haughty type, ignoring everybody around her. To my satisfaction I noticed that her face was rather ordinary, her nose a bit too long, her mouth a bit too large, and her hair could be thicker. Her head deserved no more than a B+. But this would still give her an overall straight A average. Not bad. The elderly professor was glad nobody could read his thoughts. But grading this beauty was better than thinking of nit-pickers.

The ship was entering another narrow channel, and many passengers had come on deck to watch the occupants of the little *piroques* doing their soliciting.

A plastic bag barely cleared my right ear. It had been dispatched by Perfect 10 pitching for charity. *"Pobre gente,"* I said, mimicking the best Brazilian accent I could command. *"Oh,"* she replied, *"o Senhor fala brasileiro."* "No, no, not at all," I said, "That is why I need a good teacher." This marked the beginning of a number of lessons in Brazilian Portuguese, *brasileiro,* not soon to be forgotten.

Having been on the giving end of language lessons most of my life, I knew that on this elementary level of human communication the medium indeed is the message. In an attempt to learn the medium, the content, or message, assumed only secondary importance. Hence, in the context of language learning one could ask rather embarrassing questions for the sake of learning structure and terminology, questions that one would not dare to ask under ordinary circumstances.

Her name was Luci, a short form for Lucider. She said she was twenty-five years old (I found out later that she was thirty—Oh, the eternal feminine!!—). She was from Belém and had taken a week off from work to visit her aunt in Santarem. She had to be back at her job after the long weekend, on Tuesday. She was working with computers. Whether she was programming them, or just typing in information, as for instance into a computerized cash register, I couldn't figure out with my linguistic handicap. She was still unmarried, because Mr. Right had not shown up yet. She believed that this was because she was too skinny for the taste of the average Brazilian man. She admitted candidly that at this stage in her life she was too old to have many chances, since Brazilian men went for younger and younger women the older they got. This gave me a chance to ask her why there were so many unattached women on board, some with children. Luci said that many of them had been left by their husbands, and were forced to support themselves. Even though some of them received child support, this was not enough to support the mother as well. One relatively easy way to earn a lifelihood was to take the ship up to Manaus, a duty-free zone, to buy as many consumer goods as they could take with them, and to sell their purchases at a profit in Belém. Sometimes even that was not enough to make ends meet. Some women were forced to have "boyfriends" to supplement their incomes. Asked what she thought about this state of affairs, Luci said that it was hard on women, but nothing could be done about it. That's life in Brazil! That was the reason she was working with computers and living with her parents and unmarried brothers and sisters.

This conversation, interspersed with observations about what we saw on the shore and about our fellow passengers, made the time fly. We decided to skip our gourmet lunch in favor of conjugating more regular and irregular verbs in the past and the present tense, active and passive, attempting imperatives and interrogatives, even drawing upon the odd subjunctive and conditional. Luci corrected my mistakes with the patience of a Job. To show off my accomplishments in spoken *brasileiro* and to thank her for her efforts, I invited her for dinner at seven o'clock at the Belém Hilton. She said she would be there. In the meantime the ship had docked, and it was time to disembark.

With two well-muscled stevedores assisting, landing the bike went quickly, much more so than leaving the harbor facilities. The guards at the gate needed a document stating that the vehicle was indeed mine. Back to the ship. The crew informed me that I had to get this document at the Office of the Harbor Commission, several hundred feet up the quay. Oh boy!!! Here we go again! This was a Sunday. This was government. Would there be anyone present? After knocking at several doors, I found one that was open. I received my document. We shook hands, and I was on my way downtown to Hotel Regente.

The Belém Hilton is a seventeen-storey highrise in the centre of the city, next to a lovely park, and to the *Teatro da Paz*. It was within walking distance of my hotel. When I arrived there, Luci was waiting for me outside. The restaurant featured an *à la carte* menu, or a buffet. Since we had skipped lunch, we thought that we were ready to do justice to the buffet. The food was laid out in three sections. In the first section were fruit and desserts. I had never seen so many different kinds of fruit as here, heaped high, some carved in various shapes, all presented beautifully among floral arrangements to tempt the most jaded appetite. Next to the fruit and dessert section were the cold dishes, salads, cheeses, cold cuts of meat and fish, and little eggs, that looked like pigeon eggs, or eggs produced by dwarf chickens. In the hot section was a selection of beef, veal, pork, and fish, all artistically presented by a chef who must have been apprenticed in Paris. We tried to be fair to each section, sampling here, nibbling there, tasting a bit everywhere. By the time we were ready for dessert there were two of the little pigeon eggs left on Luci's plate. She couldn't eat them, and was offering one to me with the encouragement, "You eat it, is good for *masculínidad!*" This may be so, but a man has his pride. Of course I refused, saying there was nothing wrong with my *masculínidad*. No help needed in that department. This sumptuous feast was not only a fitting celebration of a great day, it was also a splendid opportunity to acquire a long list of vocabulary items, particularly relating to food, eating, and drinking. The Hilton had lived up to its reputation, and my travel budget could testify to that.

It was a great evening for walking, with a balmy temperature and low humidity, since the rainy season had only just begun. The itinerant junk merchants in the park were still in business, selling cheap jewellery, leather goods, paintings, and sculptures. This whole area near the neoclassical structure of the *Teatro da Paz* was turned into a living language laboratory, as we belaboured the niceties of *brasileiro*. But we were slowly getting tired from all that walking and talking, and needed a drink in aid of digestion. Not wanting to go back to the Hilton, I remembered that my hotel featured a bar on the ground floor. Why not go there? However, the bar was closed. It was Sunday, and here the motto seemed to be "never on Sunday." So, what now? I remembered that I had a well-stocked frigo-bar in my room, and suggested that we could have our drink there. I was asking for my key, but the receptionist, an elderly gentleman, bluntly refused to hand it over. "Is the lady a registered guest?" he asked. I answered in the negative. Then he said, "Only registered guests are allowed in the rooms." Then Luci got into the act and said, "No problem. I'll register." "All right!" replied the gentleman. "Let me see your identification." Luci did not have it with her. She had left it in her travelling outfit at home. This she tried to explain at length to the gent, but to no avail. After a while I was becoming highly amused by this exchange. There was this guardian of my virtue, the King of the Castle, defending his turf against an aggressive female. The more Luci argued, the more stubborn he became, the more difficulty I had in suppressing my grin. In the end he said, "No identification, no registration. *Basta!*" That was clear enough, even for Luci. She gave up. So I suggested we go back to the Hilton, since they obviously did not want our business here, and the night was young.

As I stepped over a curb, all engrossed in a difficult conjugation, I had not noticed the taxi, which had been waiting there with the door open. "You take taxi now," said Luci. "Where to?" I asked. "We go dancing near my place." So we got into the taxi, Luci gave an address to the driver, and off we went. I had no idea where we were going. Having watched numerous Brazilian soap operas during my stay in Boa Vista, I had noticed that Luci's behaviour was typical for Brazilian women, at least as they were portrayed on television. They let their men make all the decisions all of the time, while they themselves stayed in control all of the time. It had been my duty, therefore, to hire the taxi. It was all right for her to give directions. After all she was in her own hometown.

After a couple of turns the taxi had left the bright lights of downtown behind, and was slowly making its way through the narrow, dimly lit streets of a section of town that did not look very reputable to me. I remembered that in 1992, I had been waiting for a city bus near this area, when a teenager had ripped my wristwatch off my arm in broad daylight, and had run away with it. Even though he was caught by passers-by, and my watch was returned to me, I had been quite shocked by this incident. I was surprised that at this moment I should be thinking of this rip-off. Then all of a sudden it dawned on me: I had been set up. I had been suckered. How stupid! stupid! stupid! And it was so simple: Young woman befriends elderly gentleman. They talk and become acquainted. Then she invites him to see "the real Brazil." They take a taxi. The taxi is stopped in a dark alley by fake policemen. One of them gets in and asks them to show their identification and all of their money. Of course she and the driver, being in cahoots with them, comply; the gentleman follows suit. The next day he is found lying in the gutter, dead. Later in the local newspaper there is a small notice, "Gringo found strangled, robbery the motive." It was happening almost every day in Lima, Peru. There I had heard this scenario repeated again and again by ripped-off travelers, with a few variations. It was a classic case, and could be Lesson #1 in a course entitled Fundamentals of Mugging 101. But here in Belém?

While these thoughts were flashing through my mind, Luci had made herself comfortable against my left shoulder. Then the engine sputtered and stalled. The driver turned the key; it came back to life, but only briefly. Luci said something to him, which I didn't understand. He answered back, got out of the car, and walked away. This is it, I thought, Endsville. This is not happening to me. What have I done to deserve this? If I should get out of this alive, I will not tell a soul about it. If they find out about this stupidity, my children will despise me, my friends will ignore me, and my wife will not speak to me again for six months. As I was waiting for the fake cops to appear, Luci made herself more comfortable against my shoulder.

This was the moment to decide what to do, fight or flight? Under no circumstances would I run away this time. This would be Tapachula all over again. I would have to take a stand and fight like a man, to the death if need be. And I would adamantly refuse to sign my travellers' cheques.— There was a scrape on the rear left side of the car. I would have jumped, if Luci's head had not rested against my shoulder. It was the driver, who was pouring gasoline from a plastic bottle into his fuel tank. He mumbled something as he got in, turned the key, and the engine sputtered back to life. We were on our way once again. For the second time this day I was glad that no one could read my thoughts.

Five minutes later the taxi turned into a well-lit street, which I identified as the main highway leading out of the city. We kept on going for at least thirty minutes. Then the traffic got denser, and we stopped in front of a brightly lit neon sign. I paid the driver, and we got out. The sign read, *GARROTE.* There seemed to be no end of hilarious situations this evening: It was the garrotte for me after all.

The throbbing beat of the music could be heard out in the street. It was an open-air beer garden featuring a large concrete floor in front of the band stand, where several couples were dancing. On the stage were four musicians doing their thing behind an array of microphones, speakers, electronic keyboards, and percussion instruments, one of the musicians doing double duty as disc jockey. Coloured electric lights were strung from tree to tree, bathing the little tables in a romantic glow. I did not want to sit too closely to the band for the sake of my eardrums, and was looking around for a strategic location. "You lead," said Luci, steering me to a table near the bar. Clever woman. I had told her on the ship that I liked dancing. She had taken me up on it, and here we were. But first we needed that drink, which had triggered this whole excursion.

At this relatively early hour in the evening the place was still half empty, and there was plenty of room on the dance floor. Again I had my bout of performance anxiety, and after having quenched the worst thirst invited my date for a spin. Appraising the performance of the other couples I tried to blend in, doing what I thought they were doing, and not doing it too badly, I thought. Thank goodness for modern dancing. Hence, I did not have to draw upon my Fred Astaire routine. The Brazilian beat of the music was perfect for this perfect evening under the stars. We went back to our table frequently, but only to prevent our large bottles of *Antárctica* from getting warm and stale. After four days of inactivity on the ship I needed this workout, if only for cardio-vascular reasons.

I was about to order two more bottles of this delicious brew, when Luci said, "No, wait! You call taxi now!" "Where are we going, Luci?" I asked, "I like it here. I'm having a great time." In the taxi Luci replied, "We are going to my place." What was she up to this time? Was she going to introduce me to her family and friends? That would be good for a laugh, perhaps even more fun than dancing to a Brazilian beat. When the taxi stopped, after having crossed several ditches of open sewer, by now far away from the main highway and down several dark alleys flanked by one-storey houses, Luci said, "You wait in the car." She was back in five minutes, and gave the taxi driver new directions. "Where are we going this time, Luci?" I asked. "Back to more dancing," she said, as we made our way back to the *Garrote*.

In the meantime the place had filled up. There was standing room only. We left our beer at the bar and joined the throbbing throng of steaming humanity on the dance floor. A Fred Astaire routine in this teeming mass of bodies would have been disastrous. We were packed so tightly that only short jerky movements with small body parts were possible. Those dancers who could not find room on the dancefloor were bumping and grinding wildly in the aisles beside their tables, eyes closed as if in a trance. The music was pounding away, the sweat was pouring down their faces and bodies as mountains of flesh barely restrained were heaving in rhythm with the beat. It was pandemonium, a witches' sabbath, Carnival in Rio without the feathers. Now I understood what Luci meant when she said that she was too skinny for the taste of the average Brazilian male. They seemed to like their women on the fleshy side. During one of the short pauses Luci said, "Sorry, I think is very dirty dancing." The music started again, so I could only think of my reply: It may be dirty, but I love it. At home I paid a lot of money just to see this in a movie. Here I can not only see it live, but even do it, and all for the price of a beer.

We were reaching the bottom of yet another *Antárctica,* and I was looking for the bartender to place my order, when Luci said, "You call taxi now. We go!" "What's up, Luci," I asked. "I'm not tired yet. Where are we going?" "Your hotel," she said, "for the drink you promised me."— "Forget it, Luci. Don't you remember what the man at reception said: 'No identification, no registration?'" Luci looked at me, reached into the back pocket of her jeans, pulled out a laminated piece of paper, and said triumphantly, *"Identificação!!"*

In the taxi various thoughts were criss-crossing my mind. So, there is going to be more instruction in oral *brasileiro.* More conjugations, more regular and irregular verbs, more imperatives, interrogatives, and conditionals, more actives and passives. I'll have to ask her if in *brasileiro* there are such things as "dangling participles" and "split infinitives," which are giving endless problems at home— I should not have had that last bottle of *Antárctica—* I should have eaten that pigeon egg at dinner— No, both of them.

*   *   *

Waking up in the morning I realized that this would be another sandpaper-in-the-eyeballs day. It was the Day of the Immaculate Conception, December 8. Some readers of this account might raise an eyebrow at this point in light of the events of the night before. But I swear that the choice of this day for the day after the night before was purely fortuitous. No irony must be read into this, nor any amateurish attempt at oxymoron, hyperbole, or understatement. The fact is I had a king-size hangover, a hangover that only bugs in your eyes and sand in your teeth could cure. We managed to get rolling at eleven o'clock. This proved to be a mistake. We should have stayed a bit longer, if not to smell the roses, then at least to replenish my travelling kitty, for we were quickly approaching a cash-flow problem.

Once we were out on the open road, on Highway #010 S, the fun of riding overrode all other concerns. Not even the numerous speed bumps could dampen our spirit. They were called *Lombadas,* and justly so, for every time we took one of them at speed (because there was no warning sign), the Old Cow, with her Bilstein Bedspring up her rear end, did a credible imitation of a Lambada, becoming airborne like a young heifer. There was still some pep left in the old bovine. Farther down the highway their name had changed to *Obstructos,* which I found very objectionable. Why would anyone deliberately place "Obstructions" into an otherwise perfectly good road? Still later their names had been changed again. They were now called *Ondulaçáos,* undulations, a designation I could live with, since it had a somewhat romantic overtone. Traffic was moderately heavy in this part of the country, and I found my fellow motorists quite courteous. Truckdrivers, for instance, signalled when it was safe to pass; left for no go; right for go. They even pulled over onto the shoulder to let you pass when there was oncoming traffic, and they expected the same courtesy in return.

But unfortunately all was not fun along this road. It traversed the worst area of environmental damage I had seen on the whole trip. A large area south of Belém had been clearcut and torched. The air at times was so thick with acrid smoke from the burning fires that visibility was impaired. The countryside looked like a desert on fire, with charred trees sticking up into the sky as mute reminders that an outrage had been committed. Wrecks of multi-axle trucks and of cars in various stages of dismemberment lined the ditches on either side, a testimonial to the lifestyles of Brazilian drivers ("They drive for too long, haul too much, and drink."). And then there was this private battle going on inside my intestines. The local good guys were fighting pitched battles with a foreign invader. There was ominous gurgling in the nether region. Was it retribution exacted by the gods of the Amazon? or by my wife? Repeated pit stops were called for. At one of these stops, as I swung my right leg over the high top case, I had the feeling that something had gone terribly wrong. Closer inspection in one of the toilets revealed that the invaders had won the last skirmish. It was no fun cleaning up the battlefield.

Having lived somewhat beyond my means in Belém I had made a dent into my travel kitty, which the price of gasoline and oil only exacerbated. Since I had left the city on a holiday, when all the banks and cambios were closed, I had had no chance to cash travellers' cheques anywhere. The travel guide warned about using credit or debit cards in Brazil's ATM's, since some of the machines had been reported to have debited the accounts even though no money had been dispensed. I had not wanted to take the chance. But now I was running low on cash, and was ready, if I could only find a bank to accept them. At every town of reasonable size I tried the banks either for cashing US Dollars, or travellers' cheques, or for a cash advance on one of my credit cards. "Sorry, *Senhor* we do not have a foreign exchange. Try in the next town," was invariably the reply. In regards to VISA or MASTERCARD, yes, they had heard of either one, but did not accept them in this branch. *Desculpe.* The small hotels in the little towns did not accept credit cards either. I had to save on meals, if I did not want to have to push the bike the last few miles into Brasília, the capital. We arrived there at 8.30 on Wednesday evening in streaming rain, with the equivalent of two dollars left in my pocket. Fortunately *Hotel Byblos* accepted plastic, and on the next day all banks and cambios were open.

Although Brasília is a beautiful modern city, it is one the most people-unfriendly cities of the world, even ranking ahead of Los Angeles in this respect. Brazil's capital since 1960, it is laid out on the pattern of a bow and arrow, and in such a megalomaniacal way that one cannot walk anywhere, because of the enormous distances involved. Motorized transport is absolutely essential. Having spent several days here in 1992 I had no intention of redoing the tourist circuit. I patronized one of the local service stations instead and indulged in an oil and filter change, making such a mess that I felt the need to tip the attendant generously to ease the pain of cleaning up. On my way out of town early the next day, I noted with satisfaction that nothing had changed in regard to the city's hatred of pedestrians. A ride via the tip of the arrow confirmed that Congress, the Supreme Court, and the office and residence of the President had not changed since 1992. But there was also a good side to this space-squandering urban megalomania: it was easy to find one's way out of town, and traffic flowed smoothly.

A look at the calendar and the map revealed that there were only thirteen shopping days left until Christmas Eve, and an equal number of riding days to cover a distance of 7,500 km (4,700 miles). If we wanted to be in Ushuaia in time for the party, we had to make a decision about our itinerary. Since I had been in Rio de Janeiro twice, once in the 1970s with my wife, and again in 1992, I decided to give it a miss in favour of getting a taste of São Paulo, which I had by-passed back then.

Although the road continued in the same good to excellent condition I had become accustomed to since Belém, I had to change my assessment of my fellow motorists. In the first place there were a lot more of them around, now that we were approaching large urban centres, and as a result of their being rather crowded on the road, their behaviour had changed. They continued to be courteous, and unlike their Colombian counterparts were neither potential assassins nor kamikazes. But there was something about them that made driving in Southern Brazil very vexing and a continuous challenge. For instance, after passing they would pull right in front of you, clear your front tire only by inches, and this even when it was unnecessary because there was no oncoming traffic. But what was worse was their apparent inability to follow the flow of traffic. They had to pass, no matter what. It meant either pass, or be passed. There was no going in convoy. That seemed to be against their nature. And then there were the exhaust fumes. More than half of Brazilian passenger cars run on alcohol, a high-grade cane-sugar brandy, *cachaça* which costs only half as much as regular gasoline. It tastes awful when swallowed. It smells just as awful when burned in an internal combustion engine. These alcoholic automobiles emit an exhaust that smells like the breath of a bedpartner who had been on a drinking binge before going to sleep. Every time I was passed by one of these boozers my head went into a spin, and my throat tightened. I preferred the relatively inoffensive smell of diesel fumes to this toxic whiff of second-hand brandy. But this, I suppose, cannot be used to judge the driving habits of Brazilian drivers.

The sign marking the Tropic of Capricorn, some 20 km north of the centre of São Paulo, also marked the beginning of the urban jungle. The traffic in this city of over twenty million people, the largest city of South America, three times larger than Paris, is simply mind-boggling, worse than in Caracas, not as bad as in Rome. I wanted to get a taste of São Paulo, and I got a mouthful. Even at two o'clock in the afternoon there was one continuous traffic jam. Being on a motorcycle here allowed at least some degree of mobility. One could slalom between standing or slow-moving vehicles, or even use the sidewalk to get by. I had no intention of staying overnight. I got my taste and got out, keeping a sharp lookout for signs pointing in the direction of Curitiba, Highway #130. And there were plenty of road signs. I did not get lost once. The Mexico City Traffic Department should take a short sabbatical down here. They could certainly learn something.

It had been raining for several hours each day since we left Brasília, and it was raining hard as we rolled into our last overnight stop in Brazil, *Hotel das Cataratas* next to Iguaçu Falls. The hotel is rated five-star, and was a fitting finale to a stay in a country where I would have loved to stay longer, and to which I shall certainly return soon. Being a member of the CAA/AAA I was given a 30 per cent discount, a fact that eased the damage inflicted on my travel budget. We arrived on a Sunday at noon, and the timing was therefore perfect for attempting a border crossing next day.

Iguaçu Falls ranks with the Machu Picchu ruins and the Perito Moreno glacier as one of the three most famous sights in South America. Twenty metres higher and almost twice as wide as Niagara Falls, they are a sight not to be missed. For the visitor from the cold North they have the added attraction of a lush tropical setting, with orchids, ferns, palms, and climbing and creeping plants, providing a habitat for monkeys, sloths, anteaters, and a myriad of birds and butterflies. Even though I had had my share of humidity on the open road, I enjoyed the walk from the hotel to the bottom of the falls down the steep and wet (from above and below) pathway. Since it was Sunday there were many tourists from tourbuses and private cars, making the trail a promenade for citizens from around the world.

Hotel das Cataratas was staffed by the friendliest motorcycle aficionados I had encountered so far in this line of work. There was no end to their questions concerning the bike and the trip. They were helpful without being pushy, and one had the feeling that tipping was not expected. They succeeded in reinforcing my estimation of Brazilians as great people, open, friendly, helpful, and beautiful.

13. *Crime and Punishment.*
From Paraguay to Buenos Aires

It looked like a great day for a border crossing. The rain had stopped during the night; it was overcast with moderate temperatures, and the buffet breakfast at the hotel, reminiscent of the feast in Boa Vista, set the tone for what I thought would be a routine affair. The ride to the Brazilian border post this side of the Friendship Bridge was slow-going, because of the heavy traffic at this early hour. As I expected, the customs officers had no idea what to do with the documents I gave them, documents so carefully prepared at great expense by the *despachante* in Boa Vista. After a few telephone calls they signed my copy and kept the other. I was off the hook. Now across the bridge.

On the Paraguayan side of the Friendship Bridge a surprise was in store for me. "Where is your visa, *Señor?*" said the friendly officer. "Visa, *Señor?*" I asked, "In 1992 I did not need a visa. Are you telling me that I need one now?" "Exactly, *Señor,*" he replied. "This is 1997, and things have changed. But no problem. There is a consulate in *Foz do Iguaçu* across the bridge. They will give you a visa while you wait. *Hasta luego.*" I must confess that I was totally stunned. I had not expected static from this quarter. But what could I do? I rode back past the Brazilian border post, not bothering to report, located the Paraguayan Consulate downtown, filled in my application in duplicate, left two photos, and went for a cup of coffee. The visa would be ready to be picked up in two hours. It was 10.15 a.m.

I was back at 11.45 and saw my passport lying on his desk, ready to go. The official, however, informed me that he had said "in two hours," and that would be at 12.15. I would have to wait. The visa was ready. It was free of charge. What was the point? Obviously nothing but chicanery by a little shit of a civil servant who had been given a bit of power, which had gone to his head. At exactly 12.15 p.m. he pompously had me called into his office, where he pompously handed me my passport, whereupon I pompously thanked him for his great kindness, thinking, you pompous little fool!

Back at the border I didn't stop at the Brazilian side, since I had officially left the country several hours ago. The Paraguayan official across the bridge recognized me, smiled, stamped my passport, and I was off to Customs. Here the receptionist looked at my papers and said, "All you need in Paraguay is your driver's licence and your registration." In my naïveté I took this to mean that no further document was necessary. Great! At the checkpoint, some 300 feet from the border, these same documents secured my onward passage, and again some 20 miles down the road. I thought that this was strange, and did not feel good about it, but pushed this feeling to the back of my mind. I was in Paraguay, and that was all that mattered for the moment.

As soon as we left Ciudad del Este, where we had gone through immigration and customs, traffic grew thinner, and animal traffic across the road grew thicker. The Brazilians had warned me about this road hazard. They had also asserted with a smile that Paraguay was a bit backward. I soon encountered an example to support this assertion in the form of slow-moving traffic: ponderous ox-carts with solid wooden wheels, pulled by rather nondescript oxen in comparison with the prime specimens on display in the parade on Thanksgiving Day in San José. They were pulling heavy loads of manure, or some other bulky substance, and were producing the same kind and amount of slippery road hazards as their jumbo-size brethren had in Costa Rica. Life in general and traffic in particular seemed indeed to be much slower here than in neighbouring Brazil. I stopped at a restaurant called *Arche Noah,* which intrigued me because its name that had a definite German ring to it.

Still in the process of metabolizing my substantial buffet breakfast, I wanted only a sandwich. Explaining this to one of the waiters, I noticed that he looked rather familiar in his white collarless shirt, dark blue pants, and haircut that made him resemble a toadstool. I had seen people wearing this kind of costume in Mennonite Country, South-Eastern Ontario, and in Southern Manitoba. So I asked him outright if he were a Mennonite. He smiled and nodded. Then I told him that I knew many of his brethren in Canada, that I was just coming from there. He smiled some more and called over an older gentleman, who introduced himelf as his father and the owner of the *Arche Noah,* Señor Lorenzo Wiebe. As I was digging into a large roast-beef-on-rye sandwich, Lorenzo told me that his father, Jakob Wiebe, had emigrated from Manitoba in the 1920s, in protest against a government that had reneged on a promise given in the 1870s guaranteeing the Mennonites exemption from military service, an exemption from taking oaths, a guarantee of religious freedom, and non-interference in the schooling of their children. Although they did not have to enlist in the army, and were not forced to take oaths, they had lost the right to run their own parochial schools. Paraguay had promised them all these things, but it looked as though history was about to repeat itself. The Paraguayan government was trying to force Mennonite children into the state-run public school system. Asked what he thought about this, Lorenzo shrugged his shoulders. In the early 1930s his father had sold his farm in the Gran Chaco to land-hungry neighbours and had bought the restaurant. Lorenzo had been born in Paraguay and had learned his German in a Mennonite parochial school. The same was true for his six boys and one girl. They all spoke an accent-free German and, of course, Spanish. If the state took over, German would be relegated to the status of a foreign language, and it would be only a matter of time until it disappeared, and having lost their distinct language, their last defence against "the world," they would very quickly assimilate with the Spanish-speaking majority. This was of course what the Paraguayan government wanted. For sentimental reasons he did not like to see this happen. But for practical reasons he thought that it was inevitable. "And besides," he confided with a smile, "God speaks many languages. He will understand our Spanish." That evening I watched a debate about this very problem on Paraguayan television. Both sides were talking, but neither side was listening and understanding. It was like a rerun of the debates raging in Manitoba during the First World War. The outcome will perhaps be the same. Some of the Mennonites will compromise with "Caesar," and will send their children to the public schools. Others, more conservative, will be looking for another country to which to emigrate.

When I was ready to leave, the whole family saw me off in front of the restaurant. Even mother had come out of the kitchen. I am sure that some of the boys would have liked to come along. Their eyes sparkled as they bade me farewell. I did not envy them their sojourn in the land of the solid-wheeled ox-cart.

Asunción, Paraguay's largest city and its capital, looked as though it had lost its connection to the modern world somewhere. With a population of over one million, most of whom seem to be drivers, there was but a handful of traffic lights, and some of these were not working. Hence, driving in Asunción was very slow and dangerous. Fortunately, Asuncióñis are careful and much less aggressive than Brazilians. If you manage to get through the endless traffic jams, downtown can be very relaxing. There are plenty of green spaces, and some high-rise buildings scattered among a few leftovers of Spanish colonial architecture. But something was missing here, particularly noticeable to someone coming from Brazil. The town had no charm; it lacked the *joie de vivre* that was present in every little town across the border. In other words, Asunción was a rather dull place. It had been dull in 1992, and had not changed since.

To avoid getting caught in the local traffic nightmare on my way out of town, I left the hotel at 6.30 a.m. There was not one road sign to be seen anywhere. I had to ask at every intersection for directions to the bridge to Argentina, which is some 20 km from downtown. Fortunately Paraguayans are not as mixed up about directions as some people were in other countries. They all sent me in the same general direction. When I finally saw a sign for the "Bridge to Argentina" I almost let out a holler of happiness.

The Paraguayan border with Argentina is at Clorinda, some 20 km from the bridge. Clearing immigration was no problem. But then came customs. The fat little inspector went through my papers and asked me for the green paper, the document required for motor vehicles. Of couse I had no such document, and I explained to him that his colleague in Ciudad del Este had told me that I needed only my driver's licence and my registration. He shook his head in dismay, and indicated that this was a serious crime. I had been riding my moto illegally in Paraguay. I knew then that I could be in serious trouble. Yesterday in Asunción I had met a motorcyclist who told me that he had met a German couple who, when they entered Paraguay from Bolivia on a motorcycle, had failed to get an *Entrada* stamp at the border. They were sent back over a distance of more than 600 km to obtain their stamp. I could see myself being sent back to Ciudad del Este to get my green customs document. Some delicate negotiations were called for. I assumed the mien of a penitent and explained to the officer that I was very sorry for the illegal act, which I thought was only partly my fault. Could he not make an exception and issue this document himself on the spot? I would be very grateful. He scratched his head and invited me to step into his private office in the back, where he explained to me that this was highly irregular, that he was breaking the law. But he would do me a favour, which would cost me US$40, cash, no receipt. Well, I knew that substantial "development aid" would have to be paid to get out of this scrape. But this was better than being sent back to Ciudad del Este, a distance of over 400 km. To pass Argentinian Immigration and Customs, on the other hand, took only a little over ten minutes. Here I made sure to get a customs document for the bike. This kind of lawbreaking was getting too expensive.

The road south follows the right bank of the Rio Paraguay, which just north of Corrientes flows into the Rio Paraná. This is the Agentinian Chaco, the northern continuation of the Pampas, the Argentinian equivalent of the North American Prairies, and it's cattle country.

Cattle had been the road hogs of Paraguay. They were still almost monopolizing the road on this side of the border, but here they were doing it in style, riding piggy-back on multi-axle semi-trailers on their way to the stockyards of Buenos Aires. You could see them, you could smell them, and you could hear them coming for miles. At times you could even taste them as the slatted semis pulled in front of you while their passengers were doing what comes natchur'ly.

Cattle-ranching had put Argentina on the world map in the nineteenth century, and had made it into one of the world's richest countries. Even today beef and leather remain the country's main export. Cattle had never played such a dominant role in the American and Canadian West. What both North and South had in common, however, was that conquering the grasslands had been synonymous with taking possession of the country. This had been the job of the early settlers, the cowboys of North America, and the gauchos of Argentina and Uruguay.

Both cowboys and gauchos made their appearance as cultural icons during the Romantic period, after 1825. It did not take long before these free spirits of the wide open spaces became the heroes of creative literature. Cowboy and gaucho literature, as trivial as it may be, still has a large following in both North and South America. In North America, however, it received an even greater boost after Hollywood took over in forming the myth of the Cowboy, glorifying his lifestyle, and his code of honour. Some of the myth-makers, subsidized by Hollywood, made their way into the big time, actors such as Gary Cooper, John Wayne, and Roy Rogers in the United States, to mention but three. Argentina lacked the power of Hollywood, and the gaucho made his chief impact in literature, Gaucho Literature, a literary genre on a much higher level than the trivial cowboy novel of North America. In the United States actors who played the roles of cowboys became role models for many of their fans. In Argentina the role models were characters of literature, such as Juan Facundo Quiroga, a gaucho, main character in one of Sarmiento's novels, and Martín Fierro, a gaucho, hero of a poem by Hernández, to mention but two. Quiroga's author even became President of the Republic.

We crossed the river at Santa Fé on our way to the Uruguayan border, and were now in an area bordered by the Rio Paraná in the West and the Rio Uruguay in the East, called Mesopotamia, between the rivers. It was still grassland as far as the eye could see, flat, marshy in places, and green on green. The only relief from the monotony of seeing thousands of heads of cattle on either side of the road were the sighting of small groups of ostriches grazing among the cattle, and snakes of various sizes, road kill, victims of the cattle trucks. But let us not forget one important phenomenon to relieve boredom, the police control.

Near every little town, usually at an intersection, there stood invariably one of Argentina's finest, impeccably dressed in blue and white, a flower of the country's cop-hood, the policeman to check the validity of every passing motorist. The routine was always the same: one step forward, hand upheld signalling a full stop. Polite request for papers. Questions, where from, where to. Papers handed back with a correct salute; one step backward to allow passage. Always the same routine, except once. This bright young officer looked through my papers, and then looked again, because he had not found what he was looking for. *"Por favor, Señor,"* he asked, "where is your proof of insurance?" This was a very good question, if only for its novelty. No one had ever asked me that. Prior to entering Mexico for the first time, I had bought insurance, and had found it totally useless, a waste of money. I was not going to run down a donkey, a cow, or a Kenworth truck. If there were to be a collision, it would certainly be their fault, and *they* would have to pay *me*. Hence, I did not bother getting insurance for the bike if I could get away with it. And I had gotten away with it so far in every country. Even in Costa Rica, where insurance for motor vehicles is mandatory, I had evaded the collectors. In Argentina I had no idea what the law was for motorcycles. But I had to think of something quickly in order to avoid another possible scam for collecting "development aid." I remembered that I had taken along the insurance certificate of my Canadian insurance company, my pink slip. This I proudly presented to the officer, explaining the date when it had come into effect and the expiration date. Of course I didn't tell him that this was only valid in Canada and the United States. Why should I? He hadn't asked that question. The routine continued: papers handed back with a correct salute; one step backward to allow passage. Justice had been served.

I had learned early in the trip that it was best to move away as quickly as possible from any person of authority, border guard or policeman, in order not to lead them into temptation for further action. I usually took my papers as they were handed back to me, stuffed them into the glove compartment on top of my fuel tank, and left quickly, but then stopped around the next curve to sort them out and put them back in the proper order. This time for safety's sake I had gone off the road, crossing a cattle grill, and was about to do my paper work, when I spotted a horse's tail behind a tree. A second glance revealed the owner of the tail and a four-legged companion nearby. Since both animals carried saddles, it stood to reason that their riders would not be very far. I saw them behind some bushes busy repairing a fence.

They had to be gauchos, Argentinian cowboys. I had learned from watching countless cowboy movies never ever to sneak up on a cowboy from behind. This might also hold true for gauchos. These guys could be armed and dangerous.

They would shoot first, and ask questions later. But I didn't think that this was the right place to do my Yukon anti-grizzly song routine, so I started to talk to the horses as I was walking over slowly in their direction.

If there is truth in the saying, clothes make the man, then these men were gauchos all right. Both wore the billowing pants called *bombachas* tucked into their black, spurred riding boots, trademark of the gaucho. A bright neckerchief, a wide leather belt with knife, and the typical black flat-topped wide-brimmed hat completed their uniform.

My compliment on their good taste in horses was well received. They were curious as to how I had gotten here. When I showed them my horse on two wheels, they said that some of their friends had chosen to ride the fenceline with motorcycles, but they were a bit smaller than mine. They themselves preferred doing it the old-fashioned way. It was slower, but cheaper. Both in their early forties, they were working for a large *estancia* nearby. The spring roundup was over. What was next was a thorough inspection of the fences. They added with a grin that repairing fences was the main occupation of a gaucho nowadays. In their youth they had worked in the *Pampa Seca* in the Far West of the country, where the *estancias* were huge spreads of land some of which took days to cross. Often there were no fences, so that a round-up could take weeks. They preferred their present life in the relatively humid North. Here they could be home with their families every night. And even though they would probably never own their own *estancia*, since the price of land was out of their reach, their employer had embarked on a new system of profit-sharing, which kept them from moving on. What had become of the free spirits of the wide open spaces, the gauchos of tradition? I asked. They understood my question. They had probably watched as many horse operas, including "Bonanza" re-runs, as myself. At their age, with wife and children, the romantic life of the free-roaming gaucho had to take a back seat to security. Still, they believed that their life was preferable to that of the pencil-pushers, the bureaucrats, of the cities. I agreed with them, having been one myself. Then the ball was in their court, and they could ask the questions, which I tried to answer the best I could. Time passed quickly. The broken fence, however, needed to be repaired before sunset. We shook hands. Guillermo and Ernesto returned to their fence, and I headed for the Uruguayan border near Paysandu.

With the gaucho's ill-concealed contempt for pencil-pushers still fresh in my mind, I wondered what surprises were waiting for me on the Uruguayan border. It was Wednesday, the seventeenth of December, exactly one week before Christmas Eve and the "party" in Ushuaia, and I had been debating whether I should go via Uruguay at all. I needed new tires before hitting the gravel roads of Tierra del Fuego, and Buenos Aires was the last chance to get them. If I did not arrive in Buenos Aires on Friday morning at the latest, the shops would be closed, I would have to wait until Monday, and would never make it to the End of the Road in time. So I would have to get as far as Montevideo today, or else forget Uruguay. We arrived at the border at 1.30 p.m.

It seemed they had been waiting for us. There was no line-up, no one was behind us. We had their undivided attention. Argentinian and Uruguayan Immigration and Customs were located in the same building, shared the same office, sat side by side. The stamping of passport and the cancellation of customs document by a friendly Argentinian lady took a matter of minutes. Now on to the Uruguayans. The officer took my passport, leafed through it, looked me straight in the eye, and said, *"Señor,* where is your Uruguayan visa?" I did not want to understand this, so I asked him to repeat it, more slowly, please. He repeated exactly the same words. I could feel myself turning red.*"Señor,"* I replied, trying to keep from shouting. "I did not need a visa for your country in 1992. I inquired at your country's embassy in Canada before leaving and was told that I would not need a visa now. Are you telling me that they did not tell me the truth?" He just shrugged his shoulders. Nothing he could do. He did not make the rules. But, he advised, in the last town on the Argentinian side, Colón, there was a Uruguayan consulate, where I could get a visa. It was two o'clock. Consulates don't work in the afternoon. I would have to wait until tomorrow. Shit! Out of the question. I was furious, and I let him have it. *"Señor,"* I fumed, "all around the world countries are making it easier to cross their borders for the sake of tourism. You are making it more difficult. You obviously do not want my visit or my money. Give me back my passport. I don't want to go to a country where I'm not welcome." Take that, you bureaucratic sonofabitch! He just shrugged his shoulders.

Immediately I felt better, having let off pressure that had been building since Tapachula; having punished these buggers. But then I felt ashamed for having lost my temper. What was it to them anyway, the pencil-pushers, the bureaucrats, probably underpaid and overworked. Why should they care whether I was coming or going. And I thought I was punishing them. What a joke. They were victims as much as I was. What chance did I really have to get through this border unscathed, since I had been predestined from the beginning of the trip to suffer on account of the unexplainable conspiracy of "The Curse." How long must shit happen until I was out of its reach? This had gone too far. This passed all human understanding.

Having regained my composure I politely asked the Argentinian officer to reinstate my *Entrada* stamp, and to give me back the document for the motorcycle. The first item was easy, but where was my document? The lady who had taken it had finished her shift, and had gone home. No one knew where she had "filed" my document. This was a matter that called for the highest intervention, that of the *Jefe* the Boss. He was called, and when he arrived he told me not to worry. He was here, would take the matter into his own hands, and everything would be O.K. He took me in tow as we made the rounds of various offices, looking into nooks and crannies, desks and drawers, until I finally spotted the familiar piece of paper on a book shelf. I was going to hand it to him, but he told me not to touch anything.*"Lo siento, Señor!"* The cancellation stamp at the bottom of the page was blanked out with liquid eraser, and we were on our way to Buenos Aires.

Good highways afford a great opportunity for flights of thought. I could well imagine what had happened regarding the change in visa requirements. With the arrival of the new Liberal government in Canada, which was trying to live up to its election promise of balancing the budget, the Department of Foreign Affairs was threatened by downsizing. Governments do this all the time. First they go into a hiring frenzy in an effort to create jobs in order to get votes. Then a little later they go into a firing frenzy in an effort to put more money into the taxpayers' pockets and to balance the budget in order to get votes. The South American desk was in trouble. Most South American countries had abandoned their visa requirements and Canada had followed suit. Hence, many employees in South American embassies and at headquarters in Ottawa had become redundant. Reading newspapers still occupied half of their working day, which was all right, but the other half was now dedicated to smelling the roses, which could not be justified in light of recent directives from above. Hence, a high-ranking mandarin of the South American desk in Ottawa had decided to turn the tide. He had telephoned the *chargés d'affaires* of various South American embassies in town and had invited them for a power lunch at the Dining Room for Diplomats on the ninth floor of the Lester B. Pearson Building to discuss the present dilemma. During the meal it became apparent that similar problems had developed in the countries that had dropped their visa requirements. Over Cuban cigars and liqueurs it was decided, therefore, that "in the interest of national security" of all countries concerned, visa requirements would have to be reinstated, bilaterally. Face was saved. Jobs were saved. And Canadians could continue to sleep in tranquility for a while longer, since the security of Canada and that of their South American *amigos* was assured, thanks to the initiative of this stalwart Canadian diplomat standing on guard for me and thee.

14. *The Assault on the End of the World.*
From Buenos Aires to Ushuaia

Buenos Aires has many things in common with Paris. Avenida Nueve de Julio reminds one of the Champs Élysées. As in Paris the side streets off the super-avenues are narrow and mostly one-way, with the inevitable traffic congestion. The buildings lining super-avenues and side streets alike look very European. The subway systems of both cities are modern and efficient. Even the local cops bear a striking resemblance to the Parisian flics. Both cities celebrate their heroes and their history with numerous statues and columns. Both cities have beautiful-ly landscaped parks. Their park-like cemeteries rival one another in regard to the fame of their long-term residents, celebrities to whom pilgrims from around the world pay homage. Shopping in the elegant Calle Florída does not lag behind that of the French capital, nor do the prices. Each hotel washroom even the dingiest one, features a bidet. Fresh *media lunas,* croissants, and *café au lait* are available in sidewalk cafés and in pastry shops around the clock. There elegantly dressed ladies and gentlemen can be seen taking their *aperitivos* from the time it becomes socially acceptable until late at night. Like Paris, Buenos Aires radiates elegance, an elegance that comes at a price.

With the bike safely stored in the cavernous garage of the Hotel Waldorf, I was trying to find a motorcycle shop that sold enduro tires. "Do you want good tires, or cheap tires?" replied the delivery man, whom I had asked where he had bought his motorcycle tires. When I indicated that I was interested in quality, he said that on Avenida Pueyrredón there were a number of motorcycle shops side by side. I would be sure to find what I was looking for in one of them. A double check in the Yellow Pages of the Buenos Aires Telephone Directory confirmed this. It was worth a try.

The first shop I visited next morning had a beautiful pair of Dunlop Trailmax tires in stock in the exact sizes to fit the Old Cow. At eleven o'clock we rolled out of the shop with our new tires expertly mounted, and with a reasonable debit on one of my credit cards. I still had time to enjoy the sights, sounds, and smells of the big city before our assault on Ushuaia, *el Fin del Mundo,* the End of the World, as it likes to be known.

But first I had to pay a courtesy call on the wife of a late colleague from the University. Rodolfo, Professor of Spanish, had been one of the world's foremost authorities on Gaucho literature, having spent a large part of his academic life researching and writing about this phenomenon of Argentinian literature. He had been with the University of Ottawa for many years, and had taken his retirement one year before me. Unfortunately retirement had not been kind to Rodolfo. Shortly after retiring he was called to the Great Pampa in the Sky where we all must go some day. He had been a good colleague and friend, and I was sorry to see him go so young. I had seen his wife Alicia in Ottawa before I left. She had also been on her way south, and had suggested I give her a call when I was in town. Rodolfo's name and number was in the Buenos Aires Telephone Directory. I reached Alicia on the first try, and she invited me for tea. Her apartment was located only one block from the motorcycle shop I had visited earlier in the day.

To me Rodolfo and his *Señora* had always exemplified the typical Argentinian couple: he, tall, dark, and handsome, with an easy, winning smile, and a charm only South American caballeros can put on and retain credibility; she, tall, slim, with a classical beauty that time cannot erase, proud without being haughty, with a smile that makes caballeros click their heels. I had pictured them in my imagination on the dancefloor of a large ballroom swaying to the hot rhythms of a tango. Now I was curious to see how their apartment in Buenos Aires would fit this image. It fit perfectly. The living room was of generous proportions, elegant without being ostentatious, beautifully appointed with a few fine pieces of undoubtedly hand-crafted furniture. These and the paintings on the walls suggested class. Indeed, Rodolfo and Alicia always personified class.

Alicia seemed happy to see me, a reminder of the other half of her life. She divided her time between Canada and Argentina, and had children and grandchildren in both countries. She appeared to be quite content with her Argentinian life. The apartment, almost in the centre of town, was secure, and in an area that had all the services, from supermarket to delicatessen to boutiques; even motorcycle shops, should she ever decide to take up that hobby, she added with a smile, referring my experience this morning. She played the role of the perfect hostess, as I expected. Over coffee, delicious sandwiches, and pastry, time passed quickly, as we discussed our plans for Christmas, which for Alicia included family, while as for me, it would be my first Christmas in many years in my own company. As I left I reflected that I had been right: Alicia had class. She was a great lady.

Lacking the guidance of a Beatrice, who had steered Dante through the delights of Paradise, lacking the guidance of a Luci, who had steered me through the less exalted delights of Belém, I was reduced to the suggestions offered by my travel guide as to how to spend my last evening in the Argentinian capital. I knew what I did not want to do: to be part of a group of tourists who were treated to a package tour of the city, dinner, one free drink, a tango show, with one tango lesson thrown in, all at an affordable price. I thought I had nothing against the tango on principle, in practice I considered myself too young for this kind of exercise. Tango and golf I had relegated to the declining years of my life. But what else was there to do? Salsa! I loved salsa. Salsa was the answer; salsa at *El Club* according to the *South American Handbook* "friendly, for all ages, not trendy, all welcome." This sounded like my kind of place.

At eleven o'clock that evening *El Club* looked as though it had just opened its doors. There was hardly anyone there. Although the band played diligently and with dedication, nobody was dancing. After ordering a bottle of the local brew I asked the waiter where everybody was. "Much too early for action, *Señor*," he replied. "We don't really get going until after midnight." This was a Thursday. Do the people that come here actually work the next day, or are they all retirees, or government employees? No matter. The music was great, the beer was excellent, and there was at least a handful of people present to watch, and they didn't look like tango tourists.

The waiter was right. After midnight the place started to fill up, and by one o'clock it had almost reached capacity. The music had become louder, to the chagrin of my eardrums, and the small area in front of the stage was replete with couples of all ages stomping to the hot salsa beat. With the impressions of Belém still vividly in my mind, I could not help doing an impromptu study of comparative cultures. I asked myself what the most striking difference was between this place and the *Garrote*. Sophistication! Everyone here tried his or her best to appear sophisticated. Smartly dressed in designer this and designer that, they tried their best to achieve sex appeal, something that came naturally to the Brazilians, who did not need designer-aid to look sexy. To my relatively untrained and admittedly biased eyes, the crowd here was trying a little too hard becoming almost frantic in the process. To sum it up, I concluded that *El Club* and *Garrote* were good examples of the eternal opposition between art and nature, artificial and natural. The Porteños (the citizens of Buenos Aires) represented the former, the Brazilians the latter. I was glad that I did not have to make a choice.

Leaving the hotel early in the morning I was reminded by *El Niño* that he was still a force to be reckoned with. It rained so hard that the water was rushing in torrents down the streets, a replay of Tapachula. Fortunately there were no open sewers in Buenos Aires, and fortunately this time I was dressed for the occasion. Armed with the doorman's directions, I had no problem finding my way out of town. My only problem was digging into my waterproofs for money at the many toll booths. After two hours the suburbs and the exurbs were behind us, and so was *El Niño*. He had done his duty by reminding us that we were now riding through the *Pampa Húmida*. From now on it was straight down the road on Highway #3, all the way to road's end, a distance of 3,063 km (1,914 miles), measured from downtown Buenos Aires.

This was again cattle country as far as the eye could see, miles and miles of fences, *estancias* seemingly in the middle of nowhere, cattle by the thousands on both sides of the highway, and of course coming toward us on the highway in giant cattle trucks on their way to the stockyards in Buenos Aires. Who is going to eat all that beef? With his somewhat rash off-the-cuff remark that he did not like broccoli, U.S. President Bush had survived in office in spite of the veggie growers' and health nuts' outrage. Here in Argentina, on the other hand, I was certain that if any politician as much as breathed the word "vegetarian," his or her career would be over in an instant.

The town of Pedro Luro, where we spent the night, lies on the Rio Colorado. Having crossed the bridge next morning we were greeted by a large sign, a bit rusty, but still legible, *Aqui Comienza 'La Patagonia,'* Here begins 'Patagonia.' It did not take us long to realize that we had arrived. The wind had picked up in speed. It was coming at us from the South-West, fluctuating between one and two o'clock, and it was getting uncomfortably cold. Traffic was moderate and the road was good, but I had to find a way to deal with this wind, which forced us to lean into it at an uncomfortable angle. At times it was so strong that the headlight fairing was bent out of alignment. The sixty horses at our disposal did not develop enough torque to propel us in fifth gear. I had to shift down into fourth, and at the slightest hill even into third. Ducking behind the little windshield and leaning at this crazy angle was very tiresome. There was only one way affording a little relief. It required attaching ourselves to one of the big cattle trucks.

Following directly in the airstream of the big trucks did not help. There was still the crosswind, and turbulence as well. The solution lay in following the truck in the oncoming traffic lane as closely to its left rear wheel as possible. In this position the crosswind was blocked by the truck and there was no turbulence, although there was still a considerable amount of drag. Here I could ride in an upright position and in fifth gear. Unfortunately there were disadvantages. For one, if there was oncoming traffic I had to slow down rapidly and move over behind the truck. Secondly, the truck drivers were less than enthusiastic about having a crazy biker attached to their rear wheel. After a while they tried to shake us by slowing down, and signalling for us to pass. When I thought I had taken them to the limits of their tolerance, I simply slowed down and waited for the next truck to catch up with us so that I could play the game over again. Often I could see their faces clearly in their rear-view mirrors, and could virtually read their lips, which seemed to be forming choice expletives not fit for family consumption, but (as rumour has it) notoriously at the ready disposal of truck drivers everywhere.

Apart from the strong crosswind, riding through Patagonia is relatively unremarkable for the normal motorist. But some of us (this rider included) are unfortunately a little less than normal at times. The countryside had begun to change almost imperceptibly. Trees had given way to low shrubs. The lush pampa had merged into sparse grassland, and the large cattle ranches had given way to sheep stations. Villages and service stations were gradually moving farther apart. Passing one of these I checked my odometer, and figured out that I still had fuel for at least 150 km before having to switch to reserve, enough to get us to the next station, which was supposed to be 125 km down the road. When I stopped there and opened the fuel cap, the attendant informed me that he had just sold the last drop of gasoline to the motorist in front of me. He still had diesel fuel, he added with a grin. Nice guy! The next station was about 100 km away. I was hardly back on the tarmac when I had to switch to reserve. I had never tried to find out how many miles I could go on reserve, and was hoping for the best. But now another scary thought occurred to me. What if the next station had also run out of gasoline? Luckily they had not. I resolved on that day never again to let my fuel level go down so low, a resolution that unfortunately went the way of most resolutions.

Pavement ended south of Rio Gallegos. We had arrived there on Sunday evening, and had difficulties finding a restaurant open for dinner. I would fill the almost empty gas tank next morning. But next morning no service station was visible. By the time we reached the Chilean border, some 55 km out of town, we

11) *Entering Patagonia*

12) *Tierra del Fuego: end of the road. The author, Andreas, Jo, and Birgit*

were on reserve. There was good news in store for us and bad news. The good news was that we were through on both sides in ten minutes flat. Had distance finally weakened the power of "The Curse"? The bad news was that there was no gasoline available for at least another 50 km. Not trusting their estimate I stopped at a restaurant and asked if they could sell me five litres. The proprietor, a motor-cyclist himself, looked at my 35-litre tank, smiled (I could guess what he was thinking!), and measured in the requested amount. Fifty kilometres later, at the *Primera Angostura* ferry across the Strait of Magellan to Tierra del Fuego there was still no sign of a service station. I was getting nervous. On the ferry I met Kurt, a German bicyclist, who groaned that in this wind he was getting only five to seven kilometres per hour. I could only guess how much we were getting per litre of fuel, certainly not much, not having any trucks to latch on to (I would have suffocated in the dust). Finally, 45 km down the road from the ferry landing, lo! a filling-station. We took on 34.5 litres of gasoline. Too close for comfort. I didn't bother with another resolution.

Now with the fuel problem under control, I could unleash all my displeasure on the road. Ten years ago Garry Sowerby and Tim Cahill, *Road Fever*, in their attempt to establish a new *(Guiness Book)* world record for driving from Ushuaia to Prudhoe Bay (in 23.5 days), inflicted serious damage on their brand new GMC SIERRA truck on this stretch of highway, the worst they encountered on their whole journey of some 15,000 miles. Five years ago Dave Barr, *Riding the Edge* had damaged his Harley-Davidson motorcycle and himself on this excuse of a road. It seemed that the Chileans had not made any improvements since. The road surface consisted of a close succession of deep potholes, held together by small bands of loose gravel. There was road kill by the hundreds on both sides of the road: tattered truck tires. The curves were steeply banked, which was fine if one could negotiate them at a speed of at least 70 km/h. However, the fastest we dared to go on this surface, with the Old Cow's rear wheel wildly bouncing because of the Bilstein bedspring handicap, was 50 km/h. If we took the curves at this low speed the camber was too steep, and we started to slide down to the bottom, which was no problem when turning right. When turning left, however, we often had to struggle not to end up on the wrong side of the road. Fortunately, the Fuegan sheep stayed on their side of the fence, and traffic was very sparse. Hence, there was little chance of meeting oncoming traffic in a curve. This road deserved to get a straight F, an irredeemable failure as a road.

At the Chilean-Argentinian border at San Sebastian, some 300 km south of Rio Gallegos, only good news awaited us. Crossing both sides of the border took again a grand total of ten minutes (Woman—eat your heart out!!), and the next 80 km of road into Rio Grande was beautiful pavement. The last time my wrists had been as sore as this was after that infamous stretch of the Pan American Highway back in Colombia.

Nowadays riding to the end of the road on Tierra del Fuego takes no great skill. However, it takes planning, for timing is of the essence. The first motorcy-clist to ride down here, Danny Liska *Two Wheels to Adventure* discovered this back

13) *Ushuaia: "End of the World"*

in 1961. He had tried to reach Ushuaia in late August, but had to give up 40 km short of his goal, stuck in deep snowdrifts. He finally reached the town after having been dug out by a snowplow. Dave Barr and his mount *Riding the Edge* at the end of May, 1992 reached town and the end of the road hitching a ride in a pickup truck. Jim Rogers and his lady friend *Investment Biker* at the end of June, 1991 did not even attempt a bike crossing of Tierra del Fuego. They had left their motorcycles in Rio Gallegos. Having done my homework I was convinced that arriving at The End of the World before the beginning of the southern summer, December 21, would be foolhardy. Would I attempt to ride up to Prudhoe Bay on a motorcycle during the Arctic winter? If I had continued my trip after the débâcle of Tapachula as planned, I would have spent the two months of the "Interlude" riding through the Guyanas or in Brazil. It was Tuesday, December 23, the third day of summer, and we were ready for the final assault.

We left Rio Grande under a bright blue sky on excellent pavement. As the road climbed steadily, the lush Fuegan pastures gave way to low bushes, and finally to forests. After about 100 km of biker's heaven a gravel road, very dusty, but well-maintained, took us up into the snow-covered mountains around Lake Fagnano, and through Garibaldi Pass. It started to rain, and continued for the rest of the day. Dust turned into mud as we descended on the other side, and going was slow for a while, also partly because of road construction. Culverts were being laid and fresh gravel was dumped, in an attempt to upgrade this last rough section of the road. The last 20 km into town had already been paved. We had reached Ushuaia, the southernmost town, the self-proclaimed *Fin del Mundo*, End of the World, but not yet the end of the road.

Highway #3 from Buenos Aires ends 26 km west of Ushuaia in a National Park, Bahia Lapataia, near the Chilean half of Tierra del Fuego. A wooden sign marks the end of *La Ruta Nacional N°3* and gives the distances to Buenos Aires (3,063 km) and to Alaska (17,848 km). It is, of course, *de rigueur* for anyone having made it that far to have his or her picture taken under this sign. Having paid my entrance fee to the park, and having safely negotiated the rather slippery trail to the sign, I was surprised to be received not only by one other live person, but by a whole committee. Next to the sign were parked three motorcycles with the familiar ugly oversized German licence plates on their rear ends, and nearby, flashing big welcoming smiles, were their riders.

They introduced themselves as Birgit and Jo from Köln, and Andreas from Bönen, Germany. They had shipped their bikes to Buenos Aires, and had ridden down Route #3, to be here for Christmas. Cameras clicked incessantly for several minutes amidst questions and answers. This friendly impromptu get-together had taken the sting out of the somehow depressing thought, that this was *IT*. I had actually reached the "end of the line." The bike's odometer indicated that we had travelled 22,202 km (13,876 miles) since leaving Ottawa on October 21.

15. *Christmas at the End of the World*

For most Germans the celebration of Christmas peaks on the twenty-fourth of December, *am heiligen Abend* on Christmas Eve. All preparations lead up to this evening when the *Christkind* is expected to descend from Heaven and secretly place the presents under the Christmas Tree, whose branches have been beautifully decorated with sparkling, colourful glass spheres, tinsel, and bright lights. After an especially delicious meal, the presents are opened, and a little later the whole family gathers under the tree to sing Christmas carols, whether they can sing or not. Some go to church, and the "once-a-year-Christians" try to make their appearance there on this evening. The next day, Christmas Day, while also celebrated often with a special meal, is but an anticlimax. For most Germans living abroad, after almost all cultural baggage has gone down the assimilation drain along with their mother tongue, this manner of celebrating Christmas is the last item to go, often hanging on tenaciously for several generations. On Christmas Eve their hearts reach out to the homeland. *Heimweh,* homesickness, strikes like an epidemic, and flights to the fatherland have been booked out a year in advance. For most German motorcyclists away from home base, then, it is *de rigueur* to make arrangements with kindred souls if at all possible to celebrate this extremely sentimental occasion in style.

This was the day before Christmas Eve, and there was a lot of work to be done before any celebration could take place. The first item of business was to find out what was going on. Was there a "rally" planned, or what else, and who was the organizer if there was one at all. Birgit, Jo, and Andreas, and two others not belonging to their group, were camping on the Río Pipo campsite in the National Park, and planned to spend Christmas Eve there. They invited me to join them for a barbecue, but since I was not camping on this trip I did not relish the idea of huddling in one of their little tents in freezing temperature and perhaps snow and rain. But I kept their invitation in mind as I made my way back to Ushuaia, to register in the Hotel Canal Beagle, near the harbour, facing the Beagle Channel, named in honour of the ship that had carried Charles Darwin through this passage in 1832.

The small size of Ushuaia, about 30,000 inhabitants, guarantees that any motorcyclist arriving in town will be spotted sooner or later. On this first day I met five bikers in town, all from Germany. They in turn had met others, one Canadian couple, two Frenchmen, and one American. However, no one knew who was in charge, so one could assume that no one was in charge. I left my name and local address with anyone I met and indicated that I would join any group for Christmas Eve dinner, if such an event were to take place.

The next day things were beginning to take shape. Most of the bikers, with the exception of the five camped on Río Pipo, stayed at Club Andino. During the winter Club Andino serves as the local ski resort. It is located on the outskirts, high in the mountains on a south slope, facing the town and the Beagle Channel.

In summer campsites are available at the base of the ski lift. However, for a minimum surcharge bunk beds can be rented in one of the three woodframe bunkhouses, each sleeping six. Since it was cold and rainy, with snow in the forecast, no one was camping out at Club Andino.

Having spread my name around I spent the rest of the morning washing the Old Cow, and giving her an oil and filter change in the garage of the hotel, trying hard not to make a mess. After all, we wanted to look our best for this occasion. In the afternoon word reached me that a buffet dinner was planned for eight o'clock that evening in the dining room up at Club Andino. I must confess that for the rest of the afternoon I felt like a child who could hardly wait until it was time for the *Christkind* or Santa Claus to come.

We were seated on two sides of two long tables running the whole length of one of the bunkhouses, which had been converted into a dining room. On one end of the room was the bar with a door leading into the kitchen, on the other end a stairway leading upstairs. The wall opposite the entrance consisted of one large picture window looking down on the town of Ushuaia, and out over the Beagle Channel as far as the snow-covered mountain ranges on the other side, and to the East and West. There were some twenty-five of us lining the two tables, about half of them motorcyclists, the others locals associated with the management of Club Andino. On my left sat Susan Johnson next to her husband Grant, both of them Canadians, who had been on the road with their Beemer for the past ten years, mostly in South Africa. On my right sat Andreas, a motorcyclist from München, whose almost new BMW R1100 was in the shop for repairs, and who hoped to be able to limp up to Santiago to repair things properly. Andreas, then, was not exactly in a upbeat frame of mind. On the other side of the table, opposite me, sat Gregory, our only representative from the United States. Dinner was being served at eight-thirty.

The people who run Club Andino had created a multi-course meal fit for the occasion. Platter after platter was arriving from the kitchen, to be returned almost licked clean. We were an appreciative dinner party, and did full justice to the artists at work in the kitchen. We were not sparing with compliments to the chef and to the organizers. But it must be said that during the meal the food received only half of our attention. The other half was given to tales of the road. Those riders who had come down the east coast wanted to know what the west coast was like, and vice versa. Susan and Grant offered many a tale about their experiences in South Africa, and hinted that they had started to write their memoirs. When I told Gregory that I had been up to Prudhoe Bay last July, he replied that he had been up in Alaska with his BMW motorcycle more than twenty times, alone or with groups of motorcyclists. One look at Gregory immediately revealed where to place him in the American mosaic. He was tall, lean, muscular, with a bronze complexion, and long black hair hanging loosely down his back. He said he was from Montana. Of course, without a doubt, Gregory was a full-blooded American Indian. This should have rung a bell. But being a notoriously slow learner I felt no such sensation, and we kept on exchanging experiences of the road. Gregory had come down on the west coast, and was planning to ride up to Venezuela, and perhaps sell his BMW motorcycle in Caracas. I promised to leave him the address of the BMW dealer there, which I had in my address book back at the hotel. By this time Gregory was busy collecting names and addresses and vital statistics of all those present, writing it all down in a thick notebook. Asked why he was doing this, he replied, "Because I am a writer." He was trying to do South America on $30.00 a day, perhaps planning to write a how-to book about it. Again this should have rung a bell, or at least caused a quiet tinkle. But again nothing. Perhaps all that delicious food had dulled my senses. It could not have been the wine, because when I am riding, it is zero alcohol for me. The whole evening I had been on Coke, as in Coca-Cola.

Platter after platter had come and gone. Desert and coffee had been taken care of, and it was time to stretch our legs. What better place to do this than in front of the large picture window looking down on Ushuaia and the Beagle Channel. Darkness was slow in coming at this high (or is it low?) latitude. At first only a few lights were sparkling up to us from the little town. Then there were more and more, until the whole town had disappeared in a sea of lights. In the distance the snow-covered mountains provided a frame for this idyll for a while, but soon they also disappeared from view in the darkness of Christmas night. As usual at moments like this, I was asking myself the crucial question, "Where else would I rather be today than here?" The answer came quickly: "Nowhere else. Happiness is being here, right now at this moment, alive and well to enjoy it." Neither the *Christkind* nor Santa Claus could have brought a nicer present than this.

Shortly after midnight I took my leave, grudgingly though, shaking hands all around. It had been a great party, and I complimented the host for a job well done. Gregory gave me his business card, an elaborate laminated work of art, which I could not read in the dim light. The ride down the mountain was cold, and I was glad to be back in my heated room at the hotel. Unwinding, while playing back in my mind the last few hours, I remembered Gregory's card. On the front side was printed,

DR. GREGORY W. FRAZIER
Professional Motorcycle
Adventurer

Roaming Racing and Repairing

Then a veritable *Glockenspiel* went off in my mind. I knew this guy. I had read his book, *Alaska by Motorcycle* several times as part of my homework before setting out. As an academic I wouldn't dream of embarking on any project before doing my research. Gregory's book had answered many questions, and had allayed apprehension and fear of the unknown. I had also read his opus, *Motorcycle Sex* though not as part of my homework, considering myself to be past the age of kinkiness. Nevertheless, it had been hilarious, and a great reading pleasure. I had missed my chance to compliment him personally. The least I could do was to add a few complimentary lines to the address of the Caracas BMW-dealer, which I had promised him. One does not meet a "professional motorcycle adventurer and writer" every day, and hardly ever one who is a genuine North American Crow Indian, who rides and repairs BMW and Indian motorcycles in addition to being one of the world's outstanding Post-Freudian experts on motorcycle sex.

16. *From Christmas to New Year.*
Ushuaia to Bariloche

Being one of those Germans whose celebration of Christmas peaks on Christmas Eve, I had no difficulty in deciding what I wanted to do on Christmas Day. I could have stayed another day in Ushuaia to swap more tales of the road, to indulge myself with another buffet dinner, or perhaps even to find out who had started the rumor of a "rally," but I knew from experience that replays of such occasions have the tendency to be but a pale repetition of the première performance. So I decided to treat myself to what I loved doing most, riding my motorcycle.

When we left the hotel at 8.00 a.m. there was a light drizzle falling, and the temperature was just above freezing. It had snowed in the mountains during the night, perhaps even up at Club Andino, but not in the lower part of town. At the outskirts of town the road starts its climb up to Paso Garibaldi, and after about 10 km the drizzle turned into light snow. Soon after, as we reached a higher altitude, we found ourselves in the midst of a snowstorm that could have competed with Canada's best. The world around us had changed from green on green into white on white, and snow was sliding off the branches of the pine trees lining both sides of the road. And we in turn were sliding and slithering in two inches of slush on the pavement, which was soon replaced by mud, slushy mud. I was tempted to break into song (since no one was listening) with that famous Bing Crosby tune about a "White Christmas," if I had not been too busy wiping my face shield every few seconds in order to see where we were going. But song or no song, it was great, and I enjoyed every minute of riding through this winter wonderland, a special present from the higher powers. What would Christmas be for a German and a Canadian without snow!

On the other side of the pass the snow stopped, and soon we found ourselves on the same dusty gravel we had learned to dislike on our way in. Back on pavement for the next 100 km into Rio Grande we were also back in the rain, cold rain. By the time we reached town, I was so cold that my hands and feet had turned numb, a sure reminder to call it quits. It was Hotel Atlantida's turn to treat me to a Christmas dinner, and the Old Cow to a wash to get rid of some of the Fuegan goo. After all it was still Christmas for man and machine.

*   *   *

I have always had a healthy respect, bordering on hatred, for watercraft of any size, since I have no sea legs to stand on. Usually after about an hour or so at sea my knees buckle, my stomach protests violently, and the fish are treated to a gourmet dinner. Knowing this, I had taken a motion sickness pill after breakfast, for I also knew that the crossing of the widest part of the Strait of Magellan, from Porvenir on Tierra del Fuego to Punta Arenas on the mainland, would be rough.

The border at San Sebastian had again reconfirmed its reputation as the fastest border-crossing south of the U.S.A., and the gravel road to Porvenir had been in excellent condition, so that we arrived at the point of embarkation two hours before departure, scheduled to be at 2.00 p.m. I had taken the same ferry five years ago, the *Melinka* and noted that this ancient vessel still looked as decrepit as it had then. It was a smallish affair, and could accommodate about four big trucks, or their equivalent. This ship had obviously been designed for basic transportation, not for pleasure cruising.

The vehicle deck took up two-thirds of the forward section; it was open to the elements. Sea water would be pouring in over the gunwale by the gallons whenever the ship ploughed through a wave, and that would be most of the way. Asking politely for a good place to park the bike, I was ushered to the rear near the bulkhead of the engine room. There I was left to my own devices. I tried to secure the bike to the wall with a rope, sideways to the direction of travel, and had detached the left saddle bag in order to use the carrier as a point of attachment. A high three-axle truck was parked about six feet away, with rear wheels blocked, acting as a perfect shield for the worst breakers. On the wall was a sign reminding motorists that the crew did not accept any responsibility for damages. Passengers were required to clear the vehicle deck before departure, and had to proceed over a narrow unprotected catwalk on the gunwale to the lounge on the upper deck, the door of which was screwed tight against the elements. Hence, there was no possibility of checking on the Old Cow now and then, to see how my tie-down was holding. Both of us were on our own. But at least I had medication to fortify my landlubber's legs, and to cheat the fish out of a Christmas dinner.

The two-and-a-half-hour crossing took three hours. The waves were worse than expected. I was the first over the catwalk on my way down to the vehicle deck. What a sight! The whole area was under six inches of water, and only passable over a wooden crate, which was very slippery. The Old Cow was lying in the water on her right side, barely propped up by its crash bar in front and by its rear saddle bag. The rope was hanging loosely on its attachments. The detached left saddle bag was standing in six inches of seawater, and horror of horrors—the three-axle truck had rolled backward in spite of its blocked wheels, and had come to a stop within inches of the prostrate machine. A quick inspection revealed that nothing appeared to be damaged that could not be bent straight again. Fortunately I had closed the fuel tabs, or else the tank would have been empty, drained through the carburetors. But what about the battery? The bike started on the first try, so it could not have been drained. A check that evening revealed that its breather pipe had come to rest on top. What luck! I hated ships, with the exception, perhaps, of the small ones on the Amazon.

I could hardly wait to get to the hotel to check the contents of my left saddle bag, from which water was spurting as I attached it to the bike. However, it was my luck on our way from the harbour into Punta Arenas to be caught in a political rally, which had brought traffic to a halt. The pavement was littered with

14) *Ferry across the Strait of Magellan to Punta Arenas*

leaflets, the marchers were shouting in chorus, and the police had come out in their riot gear to prevent vandalism. It did not take me long to learn that the object of the protest was the marcher's former leader, General Augusto Pinochet Ugarte, who was making his bid for a seat in the country's Senate. The marchers, mostly young people in their late teens or early twenties, were calling him a dictator and butcher, and expressing their disgust at his impudence of even thinking of such a thing as running for public office. They felt that Pinochet's gaining a seat in the Chilean Senate would legitimize what he and his military junta had done during the purges of the 70s and 80s, when hundreds of people were murdered. It would make a mockery of democracy; it would make the country the laughing stock of the world; it would be a supreme embarrassment. I sympathized with their cause, but was eager to inspect the contents of my saddle bag. I was glad, then, when the marchers dispersed and I could make my way to the hotel of my choice.

Most of the evening I spent in the bathroom doing laundry. Fortunately my water-sensitive electronic spare parts, the voltage regulator and the diode board, had been packed high in the saddle bag. They were damp, but at least they did not get immersed. All the other items had to be washed, or rinsed carefully. This interval of manual labour offered a good opportunity to plan tomorrow's itinerary.

Going north from Punta Arenas one has two choices. The one would be to follow the Strait of Magellan and join Argentina's Route #3 into Río Gallegos and points north. The alternative would be to proceed north to Puerto Natales. Not wishing to backtrack on Route #3, I decided on the second choice. Puerto Natales is the gateway to the Torres del Paine National Park, famous for its bizarre rock formations, its wildlife, and its hiking trails. But having tasted all these pleasures five years ago, I was not keen on a repeat visit this time. Instead, since I had brought my own transportation I was in a perfect position to visit a site that then had been difficult to access by public transport, the Perito Moreno glacier, near the town of El Calafate in Argentina. Hence, near the entrance of the park we turned right to cross the border into Argentina at Cerro Castillo, again an unproblematic crossing. The spell appeared to be broken.

The tourist season had already started in El Calafate. The little town was full of private cars and tour buses, and it was difficult to find accommodation. The third try, Hotel Kapenke (Welsh for Flamingo), finally had a vacancy, but only because there had been a cancellation. Since the town was well-prepared for the tourist rush, there was no shortage of restaurants catering to all tastes, but not to low budgets.

Perito Moreno lived up to expectations. As one of thirteen glaciers coming down from the Great Patagonian Icefield it is moving at a speed of two metres per day. In the past the advancing glacier would gradually block off part of Lago Argentino, the Brazo Rico, from the Canal de los Témpanos. The water level would rise until the pressure would be great enough to break the ice dam, sending a tidal wave through the Canal to the eastern part of the lake. Lately, however, the advancing iceflow is melting at the same rate as it advances, so that no damming up of the lake occurs. But it is still spectacular to watch great chunks of ice break off the ice wall at the lip of the glacier some sixty to eighty metres high and several hundred metres wide, and plunge into the lake with a roar of thunder. It is well worth braving the mediocre gravel road wending its way over from El Calafate to the vantage point across from the glacier, a distance of some 80 km, for the sake of witnessing this spectacle.

Back in El Calafate for dinner at *El Rancho* I met a German couple riding two up on a Beemer on their way to spend New Year's Eve at the End of the World. Kurt and Monika had started their travels in South America in Buenos Aires and had come down via Bariloche. They had been impressed by the sophistication of this town, which they compared with Swiss watering places of the European rich and famous. Asked if they thought it worthwhile to celebrate the arrival of the New Year there, they waxed enthusiastic, and said that it certainly would be their choice if they were proceeding north. Since it fitted into my schedule, I let their enthusiasm be my guide.

We arrived in Bariloche on New Year's Eve at two in the afternoon. The road from El Calafate as far as Río Mayo had been a mixed bag, mostly B-grade gravel, but well-maintained. The surrounding countryside had been the usual Patagonian monotone, yellowish-brown pastures dotted with sheep, and the usual South-West wind, this time pushing us from the left rear. This was pleasant as long as the road allowed a good speed. If I had to slow down for any reason, however, I ran the risk of suffocating in our own dust, which threatened to overtake us due to the strong tailwind. At Río Mayo we reached asphalt, and had smooth sailing via the towns of Esquel and El Bolsón all the way to Bariloche.

Kurt and Monika's enthusiasm about Bariloche seemed to be shared by others. This became apparent the moment I started to look for accommodation. All the major hotels downtown were full, booked solid by a multitude of students in town to usher in the New Year. Bariloche looked like Fort Lauderdale during March Break. Tour buses from faraway places were cruising up and down the downtown streets, their occupants, flag-waving high-school, university, or college students, slouched in the seats or hanging out of the windows, shouting to people they knew or thought they knew. Private cars tried to keep their places in the parade, their occupants looking like carbon copies of those in the buses. Students were lounging in the many sidewalk cafes, sauntering down the streets, or lying on their backpacks in the local parks on benches or on the ground. They were blocking the entrances and lobbies of the hotels. They were hanging out of hotel windows, and were greeting each newcomer with a ceremonial swig from their beer bottles. It was obvious that Bariloche was ready for a great party. But I still needed a place to stay. After several referrals I finally lucked in at a little hotel next to the cathedral, Hosteria Sur, with safe parking. I took the proximity of the cathedral as a good omen. One never knows! There is a whole new year coming up. One ought to call on all the help one can get.

Having been to one of the annual Rites of Spring in Fort Lauderdale, I imagined that similar laws would apply here, namely that the groups booked into the various hotels would be more or less homogeneous and would have parties among themselves at which outsiders, particularly elderly professor types, would not be welcome. So where was the action in town for non-aligned individuals? If anyone present were to know this, it would be the taxi drivers. Taxi drivers, as a rule, know everything there is to know about "action." About certain types of "action" they are more knowledgeable than tourist information. A couple of cabbies near my hotel told me that the big party in town tonight would be at the Hotel Panamericano, a twenty-minute walk from my hotel.

Reception said that my ticket to the festivities that evening was all-inclusive. This meant that it was not cheap, and I would have to live on bread and water for the next few days to balance the budget. But what the hell! I deserved it. This had been a good year, and it needed to be ushered out in style.

The Dining Room at Hotel Panamericano brought back memories of the Belém Hilton. However, it was a little smaller, and a little more intimate. Arriving there at nine o'clock in the evening, I was seated among some twenty guests from around the world, it seemed. Particularly noticeable were the Japanese couples and the Americans. The others, both couples and solitary diners, were speaking Spanish, so I assumed that they were Argentinians or Chileans. As in Belém the food was laid out on several large tables for appetizers, salads, and desserts. But one had to order the main dish from the waiters, who almost outnumbered the guests. My order of a modest small bottle of wine was disregarded in favor of a big bottle. My enquiry elicited the response that they were out of small bottles. But this should not matter, since everything, food and drink, was included in the price of the ticket. Hmmm—I hated that. This was sure to bring out the worst in me.

At the table across the aisle, between the Japanese and the American couples, sat a lady of a certain age, blond hair hanging losely down to her shoulders, meticulously made up, dressed in a fashionable dark robe, a study of understated elegance. I knew at first sight that she must be a school teacher, or a professor. She had that look, part martyr, part missionary, and part nurse, that many dedicated female teachers acquire after a number of years in the classroom. I had to find out.

After the main course and after the bottle of drinkable Chilean *Sangre de Torro*, I happened to find myself "by chance" beside her at the table of desserts, fishing for the same piece of chocolate cake. I apologized and offered her first choice, with the added remark, since Bariloche was full of students, I guessed that she also must be a student. This comment seemed to amuse her, for she laughed out loud and replied that I was almost correct, only a few years off the mark. She was a teacher now, but force of habit had been bringing her here every year for the past several years. When I told her that we were practically colleagues, and that I would be interested about the profession in Argentina, she invited me to join her at her table to continue our conversation.

Eva had studied Spanish literature at a university in Buenos Aires, and after graduation had taken up a teaching position at a high school in Rosario. She had started to celebrate the New Year in Bariloche as an undergraduate, and since then had made the trip every year, with the exception of two, the year she had married, and the year she had divorced. Asked if the pressure of the job had anything to do with the breakup of her marriage, she grew pensive, and said that it wasn't really the job. The problem was that she was promoted faster than her husband, who was also a teacher at her school. He found this hard to take, and the relationship started to deteriorate rapidly. At the end of the academic year he resigned from the school, and left town and her. He had lost face, and reconciliation was impossible. This sounded familiar. If the students don't get you, administration will, and professional rivalry between husband and wife is sure to cause problems, especially in a country like Argentina, where the code of machismo requires that a real man not be outclassed by his lady in earning power and in intellectual pursuits.

Time flew as we exchanged notes on the pleasures of teaching and the pains of administration, between repeated trips to the Table of Earthly Delights, i.e. sinful desserts. Liqueurs and a cognac added finishing touches, and it was time for champagne, for the obligatory midnight toast. A countdown by the headwaiter ushered in the magic moment, twelve o'clock midnight. The glasses were emptied, and most of the guests shook hands all around, wishing one another a happy New Year in several languages. The ones who knew each other kissed, and the party in the dining room adjourned to the Grand Ballroom upstairs.

Four musicians, surrounded by the standard electronic paraphernalia, overlooked the large dance floor, where about a hundred people were dancing already as we joined the fun. Eva was a great dancer, and was determined not to miss a single number. I didn't dare to tell her about my attitude toward the tango, and tried to fake it as best I could. It was fun, but it was way past my bedtime, and it had been a long day. What spelled my doom, however, was the "all-inclusive" ticket. The wine, the liqueurs, the cognac and the champagne had done what I was afraid they would do, they were making me sleepy. I was wilting fast, had a hard time keeping my eyes open, and was beginning to stumble. Around two o'clock I couldn't take it any longer, excused myself from Eva, saying that I had a long way to go the next day. I had to leave. The music was just getting warmed up, Eva was in great shape, and I was out of commission. Blast those "all-inclusive" tickets. Never again.

The walk back to my hotel was refreshing. Bariloche was still very much alive. Groups of students were circulating around the centre of town, holding hands, forming long queues, clapping rhythmically, and singing. This went on until daybreak, and even though I was dead tired I couldn't fall asleep. Tossing and turning in my bed I thought that this was the proper moment to make a delayed New Year's Resolution: from now on there would be less alcohol in my life, and more of those little pigeon eggs, as recommended by Luci.

17. *From Bariloche to Santiago*

New Year's Day of Year #1998 on the road was a struggle between the dark forces represented by a giant hangover caused by the debauch the night before, and the forces of light as yet only latent, wishful thinking triggered by the Resolution. It was a Thursday, and another Latin American weekend was approaching fast. I had to visit the BMW dealership in Santiago in order to buy two more oil filters. Hence, I could take my time if I wanted to be there on Monday. How nice to be able to dawdle along this well-maintained stretch of highway around Lago Nahuel Huapí with vistas of Bariloche on the other side against a magnificent backdrop of snow-covered mountains. Pavement ended at the Argentinian border. The road over Puyehue Pass was gravel, but passable. Pavement returned some 55 km later at the Chilean border. These were just two more routine border crossings. At Osorno we turned left, south, to Puerto Montt, embarcation point for ferries to Puerto Natales.

At Puerto Montt the Old Cow rewarded me with a New Year's present, a leak of transmission oil at the seal of the gearshift lever shaft. This came as a surprise. I had always thought that only Harleys, "Hogs," as their owners call them, leaked oil. Does this Old Cow have ambitions to become a Hog? Would I have to park her in a bathtub from now on, like some of my Hog-riding friends? Depressing thought! The oil drip was fairly heavy when the bike was parked on its side-stand. It was much slower when parked on the centre-stand. So, centre-stand parking from now on. Well, we had 102,000 km on the clock by now. Perhaps at the ripe old age of almost seven the machine could be excused for a bit of incontinence. We would have to keep this a secret, though, or else lose face.

The oil leak and the merry bounce from the non-functional shock absorber as we rode along Chile's Route #5 North toward Santiago did not dampen my spirits. We were passing through Chile's bread basket. Fertile fields, orchards, and pastures with well-fed cattle, against a backdrop of snow-covered mountains, reminded me of the foothills of Upper Bavaria. The countryside looked very European, the people were friendly, the highway was excellent, and the drivers courteous and predictable. Of all the countries I had seen in Central and South America Chile would be my first choice if I had to live down here.

As these thoughts were going through my mind, I found myself stuck behind a long column of cars blocked by a heavy soot-belching truck labouring up a hill in low gear. The law-abiding Chilean drivers did not dare to pass, and had slowed down to a crawl. The mad Northern motorcyclist, however, still in Colombian and Brazilian driving mode, flicked his wrist and zoomed ahead, past the cars, and, at the crest of the hill past the truck. Another victory for man and machine. But wait! At the bottom of the hill were waiting two of Chile's finest in immaculate green, undoubtedly policemen, who had immediately spotted the transgressor, and pulled us over. *"Buenos dias, Señor. Documentas, por favor!"* Returning their greeting with my most winning smile, and wishing them a

Happy New Year, I handed over my papers with a flair, and remarked on what a great day it was. They looked at my passport, and said, "A Canadian! Welcome to Chile. How do you like our country? You have snow in Canada, yes?" "Do we have snow in Canada!" I said, "Mountains of snow and ice. It is very dangerous to drive in Canada at this time of the year. But it is a pleasure to drive here. Chile is a great country, *Numero Uno* in South America." The policeman returned my papers, took a ballpoint pen from his pocket, and drew a double line in the palm of his hand, saying, "*Señor,* if you see a solid double line painted on the highway in Chile, this means, no passing." "Oh," I replied naïvely, "no passing?" He continued, drawing a broken line, "This broken line means that you may pass if there is no oncoming traffic." "I see," I answered hesitatingly, "solid line, no passing, broken line passing, in Chile. I understand." They saluted smartly and sent me on my way, both of them officers and gentlemen. I could only guess what they were thinking: with all that snow and ice on Canadian roads it was probably impossible to put line markings on the pavement. Or were they just being friendly? I didn't want to find out. I liked Chile and the Chilenos.

On Saturday afternoon at five o'clock we arrived in Santiago, and immediately felt at home. South America's fifth largest city, with a population of over five million, has as much excitement to offer the visitor as cities such as Caracas, Rio de Janeiro, or Buenos Aires, without their problems. For instance, traffic is less hectic and more civilized than in Caracas. Set against the backdrop of the snow-covered high Andes, Santiago is as magnificently located as Rio de Janeiro, but does not have the latter's security problems. But most of all, since its inhabitants are much more laid back than the Porteños of Buenos Aires, they don't try as hard to appear sophisticated, and are much more fun to be with. What could possibly go wrong in a city that is blessed around the clock by a statue of the Virgin Mary of colossal proportions looking down from San Cristóbal hill? I could live the rest of my life in Santiago, or anywhere in Chile for that matter.

At the BMW dealership at opening time Monday morning I felt that I had not left my hometown. Williamson Balfour Motors S.A. was located in the far eastern outskirts of Santiago, and was the distributor for both BMW cars and BMW motorcycles. I had brought with me my last oil filter still in its original package, and was going to ask the parts man for two of the same. I was under the illusion that all he had to do was to go to the stock room, to fetch two filters, and take my money; I would be out of there in five minutes, maximum. But that was too easy. That's how it was done in the olden days. Enthroned behind a counter in the midst of a showroom featuring the latest in BMW four-wheel fashion, this gentleman, dressed in a blue suit, immaculately white shirt and matching tie, showed little interest in a motorcyclist who was not even riding one of their latest creations. He indicated that motorcycles were only a sideline, and not even sold on the premises. They were sold several blocks away. But they did motorcycle repairs and sold spare parts here in the automobile department. For this reason he wanted to know the year, type, and serial number of my mount. After he had this information he got down to business by booting up the three computers surrounding his throne. He fed the data into the BMW computer, which was linked directly to BMW headquarters. As a result, he was eventually able to acknowledge that he had identified the part, and was now looking for it by means of his parts computer. Several minutes later he confirmed that they had the requested oil filters in stock. Could he get me two, please? That was not his job. That was the job of the stock man, whom he proceeded to call on the phone. Thirty minutes later the two oil filters were lying on the counter, and I was pulling out my wallet to pay for them. But not so fast! First, all the relevant information, name, type of bike, year, serial number, and description of the parts had to be fed into computer #3, linked to the Accounting Department. Forty-five minutes after entering the store I had my two oil filters and two attractively printed out copies of my bill. Then I made a big mistake. I asked him if by chance they had a replacement for my broken shock absorber. This started the whole process over again, with the difference that some thirty minutes later I was informed that, yes, he had located the part on his BMW computer, but the parts computer had drawn a blank, and that the part could be ordered, but would take about ten days to arrive. By this time all I could think of was to get out of this place. Under no circumstances would I mention my oil leak. Computer idiots such as this one, both here and at home, always succeeded in driving me to the brink of insanity. I paid my bill and asked one of the mechanics if he could refer me to a machine shop that knew how to weld aluminum. He wrote down an address, and I breathed a sigh of relief as I left Williamson Balfour Motors S.A. behind for good, never to visit again, ever. Joint dealerships for BMW cars and motorcycles are bad news, and so are computer-assisted parts departments.

At the machine shop I detached the rear shock absorber from the bike in order to have the bushing through the bottom loop repositioned. The continuous pounding of the bouncing rear wheel had once again worn out the aluminum loop, which was on the brink of breaking open. The shop foreman behind the greasy counter, wearing dirty overalls and a friendly welcoming smile, took the Bilstein, listened to my request, and disappeared into the back. Some twenty minutes later he reappeared with the repaired shock, still hot from the welding. He handed it to me and said, "No charge." I thought that I had missed something, and asked him again for the price. Again he repeated with a grin, no charge. No way! This guy deserved a generous tip, which he accepted only reluctantly. Then he helped me to reinstall the shock. The whole operation had taken thirty-five minutes, and the part had been restored to the condition it had been in Costa Rica. It would hold until it could be replaced in North America. Riding off I thought, if only one could manage to stay away from large dealerships, life would be simple.

18. *El Niño Strikes Again. Chile and Peru*

My original plan had been to turn east on the Pan-American Highway in the direction of Mendoza, Argentina, thence north to Bolivia via Tucumán and Salta. The latest development along this route, however, made me reconsider. The weather channel on Santiago television had shown pictures of heavy flooding in Southern Bolivia. The towns of Sucre and Potosí had been cut off from the rest of the country. The pictures of washed-out roads and fallen bridges were strong incentives to pick an alternate route. The commentators blamed it all on *El Niño* obviously the scapegoat of choice of the season in progress.

The alternative route at hand was to continue on Chile's Route #5 North, the Pan-American Highway, as far as Arica near the Peruvian border, and then turn right in the direction of La Paz, Bolivia. Leaving town just before noon, I was aiming to get as far as La Serena, a distance of some 500 km. La Serena, however, turned out to be a strange sort of place. Located on the Pacific Ocean at the southern edge of the Atacama Desert, it seemed to be in season as a holiday retreat for beach- and sun-loving Chilenos and Argentinians. Dozens of locals lined the highway holding up signs advertising bungalows for rent. There were a few hotels, but these were booked out. Since I did not find anything in my category, I decided to move on in spite of the late hour. There had to be something farther down the road.

One hour later, and quite far down the road, it was getting dark, and I had difficulty seeing the pavement. I had made it a habit to ride with the high beam of my headlights on at all times, and had not noticed that it had burned out. In anticipation of this happening I had kept the low beam in reserve. Somewhere along the line, however, the filament of the low beam had burned out as well, and I was riding with the parking lights only. I should have stopped right then and there and changed the light bulb while there was still some daylight left. Instead I asked at a restaurant how far it was to the next hotel. Not far, I was told, about half an hour. This would be enough time to get me there before it was completely dark, or so I thought. However, I had not taken into account the locals' peculiar relationship to time. A half hour could mean anything between thirty and fifty-nine minutes. In another thirty minutes it was pitch dark, and I had to put on my four-way flashers to see anything at all. But one problem often seems to arrive in tandem with another. A flash flood thundering down from the High Andes had washed out a bridge, and a detour had been hastily cut that serpentined up and across a steep mountain. This was the last straw. Not being able to see the deep potholes in the rough gravel road was one thing, but not being visible to passing traffic was more serious. I had to stop in the dust by the roadside and try to change my lightbulb. This proved to be the scariest time of the whole trip. The passing trucks happened to see me at the last moment, invariably giving me a blast with their horn, and covering me with dust as they laboured past on the steep grade. My flashlight did not give enough light for me to see how to get the clip in place that holds the new lightbulb. After fiddling for some thirty minutes, I simply stuck the bulb into the hole and rode on. At least I had some light. Back on the main highway at the end of the detour some forty-five minutes later I reached the hotel near the little town of Incahuasi. Beer never tasted so refreshing, and a shower never felt so good as after this harrowing experience.

Going north from Santiago I felt that the change from a Mediterranean climate with cherry orchards and vineyards to a desert climate without any plant life at all was painfully abrupt. Endless miles of sand gave way at times to rugged fields of lava rocks, veritable Devil's playgrounds. But whenever just a hint of moisture happened to touch the soil, perhaps as the result of coastal fog, a riot of little pink flowers erupted over the desert floor as far as the eye could see. Just north of Antofagasta we again crossed the Tropic of Capricorn, duly marked, and I remembered our crossing on the way down less than four weeks earlier just north of São Paulo. On the east coast we had ridden through stretches of lush rain forest, the most fertile region of Brazil. On the west coast, on the other hand, we found ourselves in one of the driest regions of the continent. Relief came only now and then when a river, or canal, run-off from the High Andes to the east, crossed the desert and formed an oasis, invariably providing life to a little settlement. Climatic tables list Arica as the driest city in South America, with "the average number of wet days encountered in each month" given as "0." It is said that it rains in Arica only once every hundred years. On the day we arrived light rain was falling. What a coincidence.

Or was it? Next morning over breakfast at the Hotel King I remarked to the waitress that I had been under the impression that it never rained in Arica. As a reply she shrugged her shoulders in resignation and mumbled, "El Niño." Turning off the Pan-Am some 12 km north of Arica onto Chile Route #11 East on a 16,000 foot climb up to the Altiplano, I had plenty of time to think about this phenomenon called *El Niño* "The Little Boy," the season's fall guy and bogeyman for everything that was wrong with the weather. Formerly we would have declared that God was punishing us for our sins, or that the Devil had received the green light to play tricks on us. But with the death of God in Nietzschean terms, the Devil also appears to have received a mortal blow, so that all he seems to be able to do these days is to impregnate unsuspecting ladies, and this only in Hollywood. Lately it is more fashionable to blame our bad weather on the greenhouse effect, global warming, and a depletion of the ozone layer, a result of too many hydrocarbons or other unfriendly gases in the atmosphere. But in human terms gas of any kind is not a satisfactory enemy. It is too abstract. Humanity being what it is likes to follow tradition and prefers to see the enemy personified. We prefer a "he" or a "she" to a mere "it." And *El Niño* sounds somehow cute. It is devoid of metaphysical implications. It absolves us from guilt and makes us all feel better. So let's pile it on. So far my thinking. There was, however, still one nagging doubt in my mind about this episode of rain in Arica that came out of nowhere as it were, a sheer coincidence, just at the moment when we were passing through. I would have to think about this problem a little later on. At the moment the road took all my attention, and a dream road it turned out to be.

Starting at sea level, Chile Route #11 follows the Río Lluta for some 20 km, and traverses one of the many Chilean riverside oases, lush plantations producing fruit and vegetables in abundance. As the valley narrows into a canyon with 1,000- metres vertical walls on either side, the road begins to climb, hugging the right-hand canyon wall. It continues to climb for several hours, twisting and turning, and climbing some more, affording vistas unlike anywhere in the world. It is a mountainscape in the desert, with snow-capped mountains in the distance and sheer drops to bone-dry valleys below. After about two hours it was getting unbearably cold. It was time to stop to put on long underwear. Just putting the bike on the centre stand and struggling with zippers and buttons had me winded, and I realized that I had entered the first stage of altitude sickness: shortness of breath and a slight headache. Noticeable as well was the fact that the Old Cow was no longer her former self: she lost some power when accelerating, and tended to stall in idle, obvious signs that, because of the high altitude, the mixture was too rich. But it was not bad enough to start fiddling with the carburetors. Headache and light-headedness were easily forgotten as we passed through the *Parque Nacional Lauca,* and a little later the *Reserva Nacional las Vicuñas.* Road signs warning of danger from crossing wildlife had to be taken seriously here, since large herds of llama-like vicuñas were grazing along both sides of the road, and could cross at a whim. The road was still climbing until we reached the Bolivian frontier at Tambo Quemado. Within three hours we had climbed to an altitude of 5,000 metres (over 16,000 feet), higher than the highest mountain in Europe, and my head was throbbing.

Fortunately, frontier officials on both sides of the border could not do enough to be helpful. The Chilenos had me out in five minutes. It took a little longer on the Bolivian side. Bolivian Customs was just in the process of becoming computerized, and the officers were busy with their brand new toys learning the transactions. On their menu for vehicles they found an entry for BMW automobiles, but BMW motorcycles were not listed. What to do? Back to the manual. After they finally muddled through, the operator told me that everything had been taken care of and I was free to go. This brought back memories of Paraguay, where I had crossed the country without the proper piece of paper, at considerable expense later on. I, therefore, tried to explain to the gentleman that without *documentas* there was no life in this world; without *documentas* we do not exist as persons, and neither does a motorcycle. Would he, please, give me a piece of paper to show that the motorcycle had been duly imported into the country. He smiled and readily agreed with me on the importance of *documentas,* typed up the required paper, and I was on my way. It had taken no more than thirty minutes and had cost nothing. But meanwhile the hammers in my head were still pounding away.

The road continued to be in excellent condition. It had descended a bit and had levelled out, and was thus much less demanding than it had been on the way up. The sun was shining brightly, and there was little traffic. This was one of those times when one could go on automatic pilot and let the mind wander. Looking back at our border crossings during the past several weeks I remembered that the last problematic crossing had been my aborted attempt to get into Uruguay. After this disastrous affair border crossings had been a piece of cake. The "Border Curse" had obviously become history; it was over, defused. What if the ineffectiveness of the Border Curse had something to do with the onset of *El Niño*. What if "The Little Boy" and my wife were indeed in conspiracy to make my travelling life miserable? Literature provides a wealth of examples of women demonstrating a certain control over higher powers to gain their ends. Sibyls at Delphi could predict the future; the Furies could easily use their magic powers to destroy a man. On his way home from Troy, Odysseus, the archetypal traveller, encountered problems with obstinate females: gorgeous Circe, for example, had turned some of his men into swine (who could blame them, after they'd been at sea for months?), and ungainly Scylla had devoured six of his companions (which shows that even the homely ones succeed in getting a tasty morsel now and then). Moreover, Nemesis, a goddess of righteous revenge who pursues wrongdoers, had been powerful enough to be invoked again and again by both Greeks and Romans in aid of supposedly just causes. Given this vast literary corpus of similar situations it was not unthinkable that *El Niño* had been called into action by a modern day Nemesis, had become my nemesis, justice bringing deserved punishment for the wayward traveller. But these were thoughts emanating from a brain wracked by a splitting headache. These were thoughts befitting the rather desolate semi-desert landscape of the sparsely settled Bolivian Altiplano through which we passed. As we approached La Paz, other problems began to occupy the oxygen-starved mind.

A short time after we had joined Bolivia Route #1, some 50 km south of La Paz, all hell broke loose. Mountains of black clouds that had gathered ahead could hold it no longer and let go with a deluge that made it almost impossible to see. Nevertheless, since traffic was still rather light I continued in second gear, snug and dry in my rain suit. Some 20 km later a yellow sign appeared warning of a road hazard ahead, a sign I had begun to detest from many previous experiences since entering Central America. The sign read *Desvio*, Detour. And there it was. A barricade blocked the main road, and the detour led right into a brownish mud puddle whose depth and expanse could only be guessed. Not wanting to become a submarine, I waited for another vehicle to lead the way. A minibus approached, shifted into first gear, and slowly plowed through some twelve inches of murky water, with us following closely behind on its left wheel. From now on for the next 15 km it was alternately plowing through deep puddles and slithering through some twenty centimetres of gumbo mud. I tried to stay close behind the minibus, which sometimes turned left, sometimes right at approaching crossroads. I was hoping that it was also bound for La Paz, for as hard as I tried, I could not see another sign indicating that we were still on the right track. I had gone through this experience several times in some Central American countries, and every time it had been a navigation nightmare. "Detours" in these latitudes are as badly posted as other road signs. Locals know the right way, and foreigners are left to their own devices. Fortunately all nightmares come to an end sooner or later. This one ended later, much later, when we reached the edge of the Altiplano at the new city of El Alto, just before descending into the canyon in which lies La Paz.

The descent into the city on the new toll road is breathtaking. From the road one gets a bird's eye view of the urban jungle below, spreading from Plaza Murillo, the city centre some 400 metres below the Altiplano, up to the rim of the canyon at an altitude of some 4,000 metres (12,000 feet). The houses, decreasing in size with the increase in altitude, are jammed together with little room to spare for greenery. La Paz, the highest capital in the world, is synonymous with a headache, a splitting headache, at least for the first day.

The Old Cow, running rich because of the high altitude and stalling repeatedly in city traffic, succeeded in prolonging the headache into the second day. Before enjoying the sights, sounds, and smells of the city I considered it my first duty to look after the bike. The cylinder heads needed to be retorqued to specifications and the valve clearance checked. I was curious to see what high-altitude riding had wrought "in there." As I expected, the spark plug electrodes were covered with black oily soot, a sure sign of an overly rich mixture. It was time to renew the plugs anyway, and to alleviate this situation I had brought along a set of high-altitude jets, which I installed into the carburetors. After retorquing the head bolts with my torque wrench and checking the valve clearance it was time to put the valve covers back on. Trying to tighten the centre bolt of the left cover, I received yet another "present" from the Old Cow: the bolt could be turned endlessly; its thread had been stripped in the soft aluminum head. This had happened before on Black Beauty, the 1972 R 60/5. But now I was having the same problem on this modern state-of-the-art marvel of German engineering. Had those boys in BMW Sparte Motorrad learned anything during the past decades? Everyone knew about this recurring ailment of the Boxers. Could they not have taken some remedial action? It would have been so simple. Now I would have to find a machine shop, have them put in a larger bolt, and retap the hole in the cylinder head. Or I would have to find out if anyone sold Helicoils in this neck of the woods. This was an added headache I didn't need. I decided to wait to see how much oil would leak from the valve cover before I dropped in at a machine shop to get the work done, preferably in a smaller town. La Paz would pose too much of a hassle. Besides, it was Friday afternoon, and I did not want to spend the weekend and the coming Monday hanging around, exciting as this town might be.

Indeed, La Paz is an exciting city, with about a million and a half inhabitants, the majority of them Indians, most of whom, both men and women, wear their long black hair down their backs in a thick queue, the women topping it with a quaint bowler hat. The city is colourful, full of life, with many beautiful colonial buildings, outstanding among them the magnificent Church and Monastery of San Francisco, dating from the sixteenth century. And most of the street people

15) *Bolivia: La Paz*

were friendly, especially to gringo *turistas*. Since the bike was parked in a guard-ed car park across the street from Hotel Copacabana, where I was staying, every time I walked over to work on the bike I was approached by about two dozen street urchins to have my shoes shined. And every time I told them *mas tarde*, later, until they finally teased me when they saw me coming, yelling after me *mas tarde, mas tarde!* Having finished work on the bike I thought that it was time to own up. I had to submit to that shoeshine that I had promised them so often ear-lier. But which one of the two dozen shoe sanitation experts should I hire? The one who had asked me first, Enrique, a boy of about ten or twelve, claimed that he should be the chosen one, because he had been the first one to ask me. An older boy of about sixteen, Carlos, denied this vehemently, claiming that the youngster was not much good at his trade, in fact he had been his student, his apprentice. He himself was a recognized master and an expert in the field. He could do a much better job. All that teasing and haggling had been done in good humour, and I had the feeling that they didn't really care who got the job, as long as one of them got it. In order to come to a just decision I asked both of them for bids. He who offered the lowest bid would get the contract. But now all of a sudden there was solidarity between the two. Each one offered to do the work for about fifty cents, not more, not less. Since I had liked the approach of the apprentice, but did not want the older boy to lose face, I hired Enrique to do my left boot, and Carlos to work on my right. They immediately set to work under the appreciative stares of twenty sets of eyes. Each one of them did a great job. My riding boots looked like new, jet black, with a sparkling shine they did not even have in the store. Both deserved their reward, which I proceeded to give them. But now, to add to the fun I asked the onlookers to examine critically the quality of the work, and to vote on the best shine, left or right. This led to much discussion amidst great hilarity. The young members of the gang tended to vote for their peer, Enrique, whereas the older boys, and those probably sucking up to the master, voted for Carlos, who won by a narrow margin. I tipped him another quarter, and was happy that he did not have to lose face in front of a mere "apprentice." A nice bunch of kids these shoeshine boys of La Paz. They had succeeded in making my headache disappear.

On the way up to the Altiplano next morning I was still thinking about the good laughs we had in that shoeshine competition in front of the hotel, when I realized that the shine on my boots would not last very long this day, alas. Light rain was falling and the water rushing down the road covered bike and rider with a uniform brown film, which increased in thickness in the mud of the road con-struction through El Alto. The plan was to get as far as Puno, Peru, on the west bank of Lake Titicaca. Another border crossing was looming ahead, and it was Saturday. Good timing did not seem to be my forte on this trip.

Once we were out in the open country past the suburbs of La Paz, the sun came out, and the whole situation looked a little better. I would probably have to be cleared by Peruvian customs in Puno, which would, of course, be closed dur-ing the weekend. But since I wanted to stay there over Sunday anyway, this would cause no undue delay. Maybe this time my timing had not been that bad after all.

Even the countryside looked better in this part of the country than it had looked on the way over from Chile. The farms looked more prosperous, with bigger buildings, some still thatch-covered, but many others with roofs of corrugated metal. Most farmers had at least a dozen cows and a number of goats and sheep, and their fields looked well watered. This, it seemed, was the secret of their prosperity. They were getting more rain than the area next to the Chilean border.

Even the Old Cow seemed to be in good humour. The smaller jets made her run leaner and had restored some of the lost power on acceleration. A minor adjustment of the idle jets made for a smooth idle. The oil drip at the transmission was not bad enough to cause undue worries, and the stripped bolt holding the valve cover in place held enough to allow just a light film of oil to appear around the gasket. Even the Bilstein Bedspring in the rear did not act up for the moment, for the road was in excellent condition, and continued to be so right into Guaqui. The last 25 km, however, to the border at Desaguadero were back to jungle riding, deep slippery mud and almost bottomless puddles. Fortunately *El Niño* was still on hold this morning, so that we arrived at the border just before noon, covered in uniform Bolivian ochre.

Every border crossing south of the forty-ninth parallel is an adventure, for at every border there seems to be a surprise in store. This was to be my twentieth border crossing on this trip, and I was curious to learn what the surprise for us was to be this time. It started out to be just one of those routine affairs we had become accustomed to since Argentina. All of the officials on both sides of the border were friendly and professional. The Peruvians informed me, as I had expected, that they could only give me a temporary customs certificate valid from the border to Puno, where I would have to get the regular certificate on Monday, when the office would reopen. So far, so good. But here came the surprise. The officer informed me that he would ask his colleague to ride pillion with me to the customs compound in Puno. I didn't quite see the reason for this, and pointed out that because of my relatively large top case, the bike actually seated only one rider. To this he replied that his colleague was rather small and could easily squeeze in between me and the top case. What could I say. He was the boss. So I fired up the Old Cow, he hopped on, and we were on our way. Fortunately from the border on the road was paved. I was not sure if I could have managed to ride two up if the road had continued in the condition it had been for the previous 25 km.

In retrospect my pillion rider and guide saved me a lot of hassles finding the Customs office, which happened to be in the higher section of town in a back alley around several corners. But I still didn't know why we had to go there, since I had my temporary certificate and the office was closed. I was soon to find out. Upon arrival my guide spoke to the armed guard behind the iron front gate. The gate swung open; we entered the yard; the gate snapped shut behind us and was chained and bolted. Tricked!! Were we now prisoners of Peruvian Customs? Not both of us, only the Old Cow. The bike would have to stay under lock and key in the compound until Monday. What an indignity! Poor Old Cow was now a jailbird. They obviously didn't trust us. But at least the beast was safe here. The officer in charge asked me if I had a hotel to go to. When told no, he offered to make a reservation for me at a hotel downtown. Then he called a taxi. Arriving at the designated hotel, I learned to my surprise that it was Hotel Italia, the same hotel I had stayed at five years ago. This was also the very hotel I had planned to use this time, since I knew it was excellent, with safe parking (of course no longer necessary) and within my budget. Not all surprises turn out to be negative.

In spite of the ignominious treatment meted out to my trusty mount, I resolved not to let my stay in Puno be spoiled. Passing through town in 1992 I had arrived late at night, and had had to catch the train to Cuzco and Machu Picchu early the next morning, so that there had been no time for sightseeing. From the train window I had seen Lake Titicaca fishermen spearfishing from their peculiar rafts made of the *totora* reed, which grows abundantly in the shallow water of the lake. I had also learned from the guide book that most of them lived on floating islands constructed of the same material. Now with a whole day at my disposal, I wanted to pay a visit to one or two of the islands, so I booked a seat on an excursion boat, which left Puno harbour at eight o'clock next morning.

Welcoming his motley group of passengers on board ship, the captain proudly announced that Puno, with a population of some 80,000 souls, was the gateway to Lake Titicaca, the largest lake in South America. If we were wondering about the strange name of the lake, he assured us that Peru lays claim to the first two syllables: it claims to have the titi, obviously the superior part. Bolivia, he added, is allowed to keep what is left. (Polite laughter all around.) But as we pulled away from shore I chose to differ with our skipper. To me it looked the other way around, as the boat ploughed through a thick porridge-like layer of sickeningly yellowish-green algae extending as far as the eye could see, totally obscuring the otherwise brilliantly azure surface of the lake. It would have been a perfect likeness of caca had it not been for the colour, which made it look more like vomit. In the interest of good international relations, however, I kept these thoughts to myself. As soon as we reached deeper water (and had left behind us the area of effluence of Puno sewers) the scum disappeared. Fortunately it did not reach out as far as the floating islands.

Stepping ashore on one of the straw islands of the Uros people of Lake Titicaca (about 300 are living on the islands, but no pure Uros exist anymore) is a balancing act. Everything is bouncing up and down, the boat, the island, and the straw huts on it. It brought to mind the story of the Three Little Pigs. If a big bad wolf were to come by and huff and puff just a little bit, there would be instant disaster. As we stepped off the boat the male residents immediately offered us short rides around the island in their delicately constructed reed boats. The women and children in their colourful costumes, wearing the traditional bowler hats, tried to sell knitted goods and trinkets made of the local building material, and were posing for pictures. For the privilege of taking a photo one was supposed to buy something. Being an intruder in this strange culture one could not help but feel a bit like a voyeur, a bit embarrassed. On the other hand, one could ease one's feelings of delicacy by considering the fact that without the tourist dollars their life of fishing, hunting, and gathering on the lake would be rather grim. We were told that in winter temperatures could drop as low as -25°C. Then, at least, the islands would be safe from sinking. At other times the living area has to be continuously replenished with new dried reeds as fast as the bottom rots away. This gave rise to many hilarious incidents. Occasionally an unsuspecting visitor would step into a well-camouflaged soft spot that needed redoing and end up standing in water up to the ankles. As shutters clicked to record the strange, colourful sights, as money changed hands, everyone seemed to breathe a sigh of relief at not having to live in a house of straw, as picturesque as it may be.

On the way back to Puno the captain took time out from his running commentary on the microphone. This gave us passengers a chance to do the cocktail circuit; to engage in chitchat with one another to find out where from and where to. One of the passengers turned out to be of particular interest to me, for he was a Canadian motorcyclist traveling incognito, as it were. While I was wearing my black leather jacket to keep warm, immediately identifying myself as a biker, he was fashionably attired in an alpaca sweater of local workmanship. Stephen was from Vancouver, British Columbia, and had developed what I thought was a neat and unique method of doing long-distance motorcycling without having the required time. He was "doing" South America on a Yamaha 500cc, but on an instalment plan. He had left Vancouver four years ago on a four-week holiday. This had been the maximum time he had been able to wheedle out of his boss. It was either this or quit. He liked his job, but he embarked on his dream journey around South America anyway. In his first year he got as far as Southern Mexico, where he left the bike with friends, and returned to his job in Vancouver. The next year he got as far as Panama, where he had a friend in the Canal Zone, who was willing to store the bike for him until his return. Two years ago he shipped the bike across the Darién gap to Colombia, continued south, and left it at yet another friend's place in Ecuador. Last year he had reached Lima, and had left the bike with the friend of a friend. This year he was planning to leave the bike in Santiago. He was not sure as yet where in Santiago, but he had some addresses and was sure that something would turn up. Stephen's story became even more interesting to me when I found out that he had come up via Peru Route #26, from Nasca via Puquio and Cuzco. He told me that he had had to give up his plan to ride Route #3, the High Road via Ayacucho, Abancay, and Cuzco, since there had reportedly been numerous mudslides and washed-out bridges. It would have taken an indeterminable length of time, which he just could not afford. Even the road via Puquio had been a disaster. It had taken him five days of falling and rising to cover the 650 km from Nasca to Cuzco. He said that he had gotten through only because his bike was relatively light. On the way he had met three Swiss bikers on heavier equipment who had found the going almost impossible. If he were

16) *Lake Titicaca: floating island of the Uros*

in my place, he added, he would forget taking this road, as well as the High Road. It had been raining heavily every day along the way, and there was no hope that things would improve in the near future. This was food for thought. There was one more possibility left, Route #30 to Arequipa. But Stephen had no information on this road. He suggested that I talk to the bus drivers in Puno, who would surely be well informed about what to them would be a routine run. I reciprocated by filling him in on road conditions to La Paz and to the Chilean border. At least my report was much more upbeat than his. By this time we had plowed our way through the sickening green vegetable soup, and had reached the harbour. I wished him good luck for the completion of his fifth instalment, and for the many others that were planned to follow. What an interesting and unique way to spend one's annual holidays.

Acting on Stephen's advice I walked over to the bus terminal to find a driver who was doing the Arequipa run. A mud-covered bus was easing its way out of the yard through several deep puddles. "Puno-Arequipa" was written on a sign-board behind the windshield. The driver was a young man who looked rather friendly, so after flagging him down I introduced myself, and we shook hands. His name was Juan. "Do you know the condition of the road to Arequipa, *Señor?*" I asked him after some small talk. "Do I know it? Like the back of my hand," he replied. "I have to do the trip twice a week. Ordinarily it takes 12 hours. Today it took 18 hours; the last time more than 20 hours. This all depends on how badly we get stuck. At times the passengers have to get out and push. The first third of the road past Vilque is quite good. The second third is passable. But the last third is very bad, axle-deep mud. Lately we have had heavy rain every day. It is the rainy season, *Señor.*" He shrugged his shoulders and mumbled, "El Niño!" This was more food for thought.

On my way back to the hotel, pondering all of these bits of information as I planned tomorrow's itinerary, another factor entered the equation. In the early afternoon, clouds had started to pile up from the West, getting darker, until by about four o'clock the black thunder-head standing over Puno let go. It started to rain in heavy drops, then it poured, then the drops solidified. Marble-size hail was hammering the cars, sounding like machine-gun fire. Only a quick dash into a coffee shop prevented a headache. Within twenty minutes some two inches of roller bearing-like ice pellets had covered the streets. It was dangerous to walk. Traffic had come to a standstill. What would happen, I wondered, if there were a repeat performance of this tomorrow somewhere on this "very bad road" far away from human habitation? A decision was easy.

*   *   *

Two days later, again back in Peru, this time 10 km north of Arica, I congratulated myself for having made the right decision. Getting the bike out of the customs compound on Monday morning had taken less than an hour. With the proper documents in hand we felt rather righteous, and chose a different route back to Bolivia, via Yunguyo and the idyllic little town of Copacabana. It had hailed again during the night, and foot-high piles of ice pellets were melting in the fields on both sides of the road. At the border we were again welcomed into Bolivia on a road reminiscent of the one leading into Desaguadero, very bad. But after Copacabana and the ferry crossing of the Strait of Tiquina pavement returned for good. The only other unpleasant section was the construction site through El Alto. From there on it was like riding in the European Alps, a roller coaster with twisties and hairpin turns set in superb scenery, a motorcyclist's fantasy, a perfect 10, an A+, a descent from an altitude of some 16,000 feet all the way down to Arica at sea level in less than two hours. We had crossed two borders in one day, both without hassles. Riding this road both ways proved to be one of the highlights of the trip.

But just to dampen our spirits a little, El Niño reminded us that he was still a force to be reckoned with, even though he had declared a moratorium for the previous two days. As we were approaching Tacna, Peru, located in the middle of the Atacama Desert, with a recorded "0 days" of precipitation in each of the twelve months of the year, heavy rain forced us to seek refuge at the first hotel that appeared. Gran Hotel Tacna was an excellent choice. We deserved a little celebration. On that day near La Paz the Old Cow had clocked 30,000 km (18,750 miles) since leaving Canada last October.

Another great day of riding was ahead of us on our way to Arequipa. While not as dramatic as the climb and descent to and from the Altiplano, it offered enough variable terrain that we were able to avoid monotony. With new engine oil and a new filter, the Old Cow was hard to hold back on this excellent road. At one point going up a hill we passed a Jeep with two passengers, who turned out to be policemen. We had been riding way over the speed limit, and I think we had passed in a "no passing" zone. They flagged us down. After the initial greeting and document check one of the officers said, "*Señor* do you realize that you were going too fast, and that you were passing illegally?" I shook my head, trying to appear serious. Then he continued, "But you are a tourist, and we don't bother tourists. Ride safely! *Addios!*" We shook hands and I took off. This was a new experience. What a nice place, this Peru. Policemen don't bother foreign tourists. Radar traps don't bother with speeding motorcyclists. Most of the main highways are toll roads, but at every toll booth a toll-free channel reserved for bicycles and motorcycles bypasses the booth. Great sports these Peruvians!

On the boat ride to the Uros islands in Lake Titicaca I had asked a young couple from Arequipa about the highlights of their city, to which they replied spontanously, "We have a convent." I had seen dozens of monasteries and convents in Europe and was only mildly curious about the Arequipa version. But what a surprise. The Santa Catalina Convent turned out to be a miniature walled medieval town in the centre of the city, with cloisters and period houses in white, brown, and blue facing the cobbled streets. For four centuries the home of some 450 nuns living in strict seclusion, it had been restored to its original grandeur and opened to the public in 1970. Here time had stood still. This was a piece of late medieval Spanish real estate transplanted across the Atlantic.

In keeping with its showpiece, Arequipa itself, founded in 1540, has retained the atmosphere of a Spanish colonial city until this day. It is a city for walking. At an altitude of 2,380 m, with a spring-like climate the year round, it boasts 360 sunny days a year. If rain falls, however, as it did when I was there, the whole central square, the *Plaza de Armas,* bordered on three sides by arcaded buildings housing elegant shops and restaurants, and on the fourth side by the cathedral, offers refuge until the sun reappears. To spend only one night in this delightful city seemed unforgivable. I had to remind myself that on this trip I was not a tourist, but a motorcycle traveller.

On the way out of the city the next morning under a brilliant blue sky, I was grateful that *El Niño* seemed to restrain himself until the late afternoon. Peru Highway #1, the Pan Am, would have been a dreary and dangerous ride in the rain. On this day, however, it offered unmitigated riding pleasure. As the road follows the rugged Pacific coastline it clings precariously to steep rock faces, not unlike stretches of the Karakoram Highway in Northern Pakistan. Given that in some places the steep rock face is composed of conglomerate rock subject to landslides and washouts riding in the rain here would be almost like playing Russian Roulette. There were many stretches where the highway was down to one lane, and giant graders were continuously at work keeping at least that one open. In one stretch, where the coastal mountains receded, giant sand dunes had taken over. It was their turn now to swallow up the road. Signs were posted that warned of sandstorms. No sign warned of rainstorms. The daily downpour came at five in the afternoon, as we entered the town of Nasca.

Looking for a place to duck into to wait out the worst part of the downpour, I saw two BMW motorcycles with Illinois licence plates parked in front of a hotel. This required an immediate stop. The two Beemers belonged to Dave and Sharon Thompson from the Chicago area, who were on their way to Ushuaia. Over dinner at Hotel Lineas, I learned that Dave and Sharon had met Dr. Gregory Frazier, the motorcycle sex expert, when they were picking up their bikes at the cargo terminal in Bogotá. They had all shipped their mounts from Panama with the same carrier. The Pan Am seems to function like a funnel, where all South American bikers sooner or later inevitably meet one another. There were many travel stories to exchange, while outside *El Niño* went through his daily routine.

Two things I wanted to do in Nasca. One was to repair the stripped threat of the bolt holding the valve cover; the other was to see the Nasca Lines.

I thought that the little town of Nasca, with a population of some 30,000, where everyone ought to know everyone else, would be the ideal place to find a machine shop in which to tackle the problem. The shop the hotel had suggested was not open yet. The place next door showed activity, but it worked with heavy equipment only. The mechanic on duty referred me to a specialist in motorcycle repairs two blocks away. His yard, cluttered with motorcycle carcasses in various stages of disassembly, immediately inspired confidence. Anybody who could

17) Peru: Atacama desert

take them apart the way it was done here ought to be able to put them back together. The owner of the shop took one look at the Old Cow and immediately understood her ailment, and our case was laid in the capable hands of his machine shop operator. The latter cut off the end of the bolt that had stripped the hole, welded on a larger piece of rod, cut a thread into it and drilled out and tapped the hole in the aluminum cylinder head; one hour and ten dollars later we were on our way, "better than new." They hadn't heard of Helicoils down here. But who cares?

Since it was still early in the morning I made my way out to the airport to book a ride in a little Cessna 172 four-seater to get a bird's eye view of the famous Nasca Lines. These consist of geometrical figures, stylized representations of a spider, a giant monkey with a long tail curled like a spiral, birds, one with a wing span of over 100 metres, a lizard, hands, and a tree, and several other images. They were carved into the desert floor in stages, the oldest dating back to 900 B.C. Since each of the etchings is of an enormous size, they can be appreciated at their best from the air. It was a rather bumpy ride in the little puddle jumper of an airplane, but an unforgettable experience.

Once the initial astonishment has worn off, the question why? invites the spectator to do a little research on the subject, only to discover that there are as many theories about the purpose of the Lines as there are experts offering their learned opinions. Maria Reiche, who dedicated her life's work to the preservation of the Lines (she died in June, 1998, in her mid-nineties), believed that they represent the signs of a pre-Inca zodiacal calendar. Another theory holds that these signs served as an aid to air navigation, since there is evidence that the ancient Nascas knew how to fly in hot-air balloons. Another scholar, taking a closer look at the execution of the lines, claims that the camber of the curves indicates that these were tracks to be used for foot races. Then there is the theory that the whole area was a giant map representing the Tiahuanaco Empire. And finally, to round things off, another scholar claims that the Lines allude to fertility rites (There are birds, but where are the bees?). In the evening back at the hotel I was to learn yet another theory regarding the purpose of the Nasca Lines.

*   *   *

When he made his entrance in the dining room of Hotel Lineas that evening all heads turned in his direction. He was a striking figure, tall, gaunt, and dressed in immaculate white, in the Indian style made world famous by the late Mahatma Gandhi. His piercing black eyes gave him the air of a fanatic, a holy man, a fakir, and his aquiline nose barely protruded past a thick untrimmed black beard with strands of grey. His shoulder-length hair was held together loosely with a ribbon. His presence took over the room. All eyes were riveted on him, particularly those of the ladies. This Rasputin-like character radiated charisma. Since he seemed to be at a loss as to where to sit, I invited him to join me at my table. He accepted the invitation and introduced himself. His name was Vapu, Yogi Vapu. He was a Punjabi by birth, but had been living in Germany for many years. Since his English was rather poor, we continued our conversation in German, in which he showed native-like competence. To my question as to how he had ended up in Germany, he replied that he practised natural medicine there, and taught privately. The waiter interrupted our conversation. Yogi Vapu, who spoke no Spanish, asked me to tell the waiter that he had made a special arrangement with management for his room and for a special vegetarian meal, which he would like to have served now. He proceeded to partake of his veggies daintily with the fingers of his right hand.

Travel for him, he confided, was the only way to escape for a time from the many followers he had in Germany. He had come to Nasca to study the Lines, the last gap in his studies of similar phenomena, studies that had taken him to all of the continents. He was almost ready now to publish his insights into the phenomena of which the Nasca Lines are a part. This publication will be the compendium of his life's work and of the insights that he had acquired during his many years of travelling all over the world, and a legacy to his six sons, all living in Germany. He did not say anything about their mother, or mothers.

Yogi Vapu was convinced that the Lines represent the Zodiac of ancient travellers. He believes that they served as navigational guidelines for cosmic travellers, who had mastered the art of beaming themselves throughout the cosmos at many times the speed of light. When I looked at him somewhat incredulously, he added that he himself had experimented with this type of travel. In fact, last night the magnetic lines had been right for him, and he had "touched the moon." When I suggested that this must have been a kind of out-of-body experience, he denied this vehemently. He had been there in-body. That is the reason why I had not seen him last night at dinner. He continued to add that every once in a while when the magnetic lines are right, he can leave reality as if through a window and become dematerialized, but can always return if he still stays in touch with reality. Yes, he had heard of Stephen King, but had never read any of his books. What could I say? He had taken me in. For the time of our conversation at least I tried to suspend my inherent disbelief. Was Yogi Vapu perhaps a Trekkie in disguise? I probed no further.

Next morning at breakfast Yogi Vapu was nowhere to be seen. Who knows what moon he was touching at this very moment?

*   *   *

On my arrival in Lima the morning papers alternated between two different headlines: this weekend the city was celebrating the 463rd anniversary of its founding by Francisco Pizarro, and there was heavy flooding in the north of the country as a result of *El Niño* activity. The town of Piura and the surrounding area had been turned into a giant lake; lives had been lost, and bridges had been washed out. President Alberto Fujimori had visited the town and had declared it a disaster area. I was looking forward to the promised festivities in connection with the anniversary celebration, but I was a bit uneasy about the disaster unfolding in the north, since I was heading exactly in this direction. There was no way of by-passing Piura. But first things first. First we celebrate.

In 1992 I had stayed in the centre of Lima, and for security reasons had found it impossible to walk about after sunset. On this my second visit I decided to stay in the suburb of Miraflores, some five miles south of the centre. Miraflores was in a festive mood this weekend. Flags were flying, and the whole centre had been turned into a picture gallery and artisan market, with jugglers and musicians to entertain the large crowd of strollers. With the bike safely tucked away in nearby Hotel Esperanza, it was a pleasure to spend the evening walking about and enjoying the amenities the Big City had to offer. As I strolled down *Avenida José Larco* on the lookout for a nice restaurant, I felt a tug on my right sleeve. A lady of a certain age, immaculately put together, asked me in Spanish for the time. To my reply in Spanish she added with the pretense of surprise, "Oh, the *Señor* speaks Spanish? Are you a tourist? What is your country? I work at a place not far from here. I would like to show you my place of work." I may have been naïve and trusting in Belém, but this was Lima. I was not at all curious to see this lady's "place of work," so I told her that I was meeting a friend for dinner at a restaurant nearby, and hurried on. Dinner at the first restaurant that looked inviting was excellent. After-dinner entertainment was supplied free of charge by the many street musicians in *Parque Central.*

Next morning, Sunday, in downtown Lima the anniversary celebration continued in style. During a concert in front of City Hall, given by the brass band of the City Police, I asked a gentleman for directions to the Monastery of San Francisco, whose catacombs reputedly contain one of the world's largest collections of femurs, tibias, and skulls, some 25,000 of each, all nicely stacked in several compartments. He said that since he had nothing else to do this Sunday morning, he would consider it an honour to take me there. After our tour I told my friend and guide, Eduardo, that this exhibit had succeeded in satisfying my morbid curiosity for years to come. Eduardo offered to show me other important sights, assuredly not as morbid, "not too far from here," and he would be honoured to take me there in his car. My gut-feeling told me that this guy was not out to rob me. But this was Lima. I had noticed that security had improved greatly since 1992. This was apparent especially near the *Palacio de Gobierno,* where civilians were outnumbered by army and police. Downtown Lima was probably no worse now than downtown New York. But I had heard too many stories of rip-offs during my last visit. So I thanked my guide and would-be driver, making my escape with the excuse that I had to meet my wife in an hour in Miraflores for lunch, and hopped on the next city bus in that direction.

Parque Central in Miraflores was even livelier this evening than it had been the day before. Dozens of local artists were exhibiting their paintings. Musicians, singers, and dancers were displaying their artistry, and thousands of elegantly

18) *El Niño activity*

clad pedestrians were enjoying themselves on this balmy evening under the stars. Strolling along the row of paintings, I felt a now familiar tug on my right sleeve. "Remember me, *Señor?*" said a lady of a certain age, immaculately put together. "We met yesterday. My name is Esmeralda. I would like to show you the place where I live." Never letting pass an opportunity to practise my Spanish, I introduced myself, and we went through the required ritual of introductions, except for the *besos* and *abrazos*. Esmeralda said she lived not very far from here, and that we should go there immediately. "Let's go for a drink first, then I can practise my Spanish while we talk about life in Lima," I suggested. Esmeralda shook her head, saying, "No, not good. We must go to my place now." "Why now, and not later?" I wanted to know. "Because at ten o'clock my mother will come home, and we will have to leave," was her answer. "But what shall we do at your place, Esmeralda?" I asked. "Fucky, fucky, thirty dollars," came the prompt reply. I had suspected that Esmeralda's place of work and place of residence were one and the same, but her reply left nothing to the imagination. So I said, "But I'm afraid when I am at your place someone will come and take everything I have away from me. What then?" To this I expected a vehement denial on the part of my "date." But nothing of the kind was forthcoming. I was convinced that thoughts like that had at least crossed this lady's mind. "I'm sorry, Esmeralda," I added with a shrug. "I am a married man, and my wife in Canada might find my going to your place 'totally unacceptable.' I can't go with you." "Then give me one dollar for a drink," was her quick reply. This I did, sucker that I am. As Esmeralda was walking away, I saw a young fellow nearby, who had undoubtedly overheard our conversation, giving me the thumbs up sign. What did he mean by that? I'll never know. But I suspected strongly that Esmeralda in her job-specific training had advanced beyond the level of Fundamentals of Mugging 101. She may even have been a graduate with an advanced degree. This was Lima.

*   *   *

The first signs of trouble appeared some 20 miles south of Trujillo. Coming around a bend we found ourselves on the shore of a lake that covered the highway as far as I could see. There seemed to be two options. I could take off my boots, roll up my jeans, and explore the submerged road on foot to rule out any deep potholes or other submerged surprises. The other and much more appealing option was to let one of the natives do the exploring for me, and I would follow in his or her wake. A few minutes later a mini-bus pulled up, shifted into low gear and proceeded to cross the lake, with us glued to his left rear wheel. This was an ideal test run for things to come. The water was about a foot deep at the most. There were no hidden traps and no surprises, so that we emerged on the other side, about one mile later, wet up to the knees, but otherwise not any the worse for wear. If this was all there was, let it come.

Next morning on the outskirts of Piura I had just enough time to slip into my rain gear when yet another deluge descended from the steel-grey sky. As far as I could see, Piura was still a disaster area. The whole downtown area was under water, black water, two feet deep in some places. Again I relied on locals to do the exploring for me. I remembered that even in dry cities in these latitudes it was not uncommon for a manhole to be missing its cover. If we were to hit one of these hidden under a foot of water, it would be worse than the dousing we had received in Tapachula. The local variety of tricycle rickshaws were safe to follow. Where they could go, we could follow, even at times on the sidewalk. After all, this was a disaster area. The President had said so himself. But the fun had just begun.

North of Piura the flooding was the worst I had seen. What was once an area of rolling hills and valleys had turned into a giant lake, with farm houses isolated on hilltops that were now islands. Several times the road was submerged, and each time we relied on pace cars to show the way. Here I saw the first traffic casualties of the flood: cars and trucks on their sides in deep water. They had gotten off the road, perhaps at night. North of Sullana a bridge was washed out, but there was a detour. At the next washed-out bridge there was none.

Torrential rain was falling again as we approached a long column of cars. Easing my way to the front I saw the cause, and did not like it at all. The bridge had been washed out several days earlier, and a road had been graded down to the river's edge, where the water, at least four feet deep, was rushing over loose rocks. Further downstream heavily loaded trucks were making the crossing with apparent ease in five feet of water. One of the drivers of a 4X4 told me there was a good chance that the water level might drop in the next thirty minutes, provided the rain stopped, or at least slowed down. Some twenty minutes later another driver had shed his shoes, rolled up his pants, and was wading into the middle of the river. The water almost touched his crotch, but was slowly receding. Some 4X4 pick-up trucks took a run and made it. The level was still too high for ordinary sedans. One tried, stalled on the way up the opposite bank, and had to be pulled out by a truck. It was still raining. I had been standing around with my helmet on in order to keep dry, trying to make up my mind whether to go now, or take a chance of being stuck here all night if the rain should pick up again. Perhaps there was some saint up there responsible for safe transport to whom I could appeal. St. Christopher was out. He had been deactivated years ago as a fake. Who else was responsible for transportation? Of course, the Good Lord Himself. He had entered Jerusalem riding on an ass. He surely would have chosen a Beemer if BMW Sparte Motorrad had made one available. "Dear Lord," I prayed, "please give me this one, and I'll never make fun of Harley riders again!" At this moment a large bus pulled up beside us, with passengers hanging out the windows, appraising the situation. One smart-ass guy, spotting me with helmet on but not going anywhere, made a remark on my behalf of which I caught enough to get the drift. He was pointing out a motorcyclist who had no *cojones*, no balls. This comment was followed by peals of laughter from an easily amused bus audience both male and female. A man has his pride, particularly a man of a certain age in matters relating to that department. That was all the incentive I needed. I'll show these sons of bitches who has *cojones*. The Old Cow came to life at the first try. Here we go! Oops! Wait, almost forgot to open the fuel taps. Here we go again! The man in the middle of the river, some twenty feet from shore, pointed at the path I should follow, about three feet in front of him. Although I was aiming for this spot, a large rock must have deflected my front wheel and I was heading straight for him. He jumped back. We narrowly missed him and reached the other bank amid cheers from the peanut gallery in the bus, adrenalin (and perhaps even some testosterone) pumping. There was no time to look back, because there was no knowing what lay in store ahead of us. We wanted to reach Tumbes in good time.

The next obstacle seemed insurmountable. The highway ended at the shore of the biggest lake I had seen so far. Dozens of cars were waiting on the side, their drivers in doubt whether or not they should dare a crossing. Having just barely made it across that river, I was not going to go back there, no matter what. Advance! was the motto. A five-axle empty pipe-truck was slowly easing its way forward. We attached ourselves to his left rear wheel, keeping a close eye on it in case it should disappear from view entirely. There were several dips in the road, but at least there was a road under all that water. The foot pegs disappeared, then the two cylinders. The water must have been at least two feet deep in places. Stopping here would mean water over the top of the boots. Steam was rising. The air-head Beemer was now running with a water-cooled engine. I was wondering how deep we could go before the motor drowned. Fortunately I did not have to find out. After about twenty-five minutes of playing submarine, we emerged on the other side of the lake, a bit shaken, but not stirred. The remaining stretch to Tumbes alternated between washouts, landslides, and flooding, the works. What a mess!

At six o'clock it was dark. We still had one hour to go to reach Tumbes. Driving in Peru in daylight was not without danger, and I could only imagine what it would be like in the dark. Peruvian motorists are not aggressive, but they are sloppy drivers. Most of their cars are vintage Japanese imports. Many of them have no lights. They don't signal, ever. They pull out in front of you, or stop without warning. It appears that they know where they are going or what they are planning to do, and they seem to expect that everyone else around them should be able to read their thoughts. We arrived in Tumbes one hour after dark, and I think I must have aged in that one hour beyond my years. Yet—

A gentleman on a mid-size Kawasaki pulled up beside us at a red light and asked me which hotel I was going to. I yelled back, "Hotel Costa del Sol." He replied, "Follow me!" In ten minutes he had guided me to the hotel of my choice and took off without further ado. What did I just say about Peruvian motorists? I owe them an apology, some of them.

As I rode over the curb on the way to Hotel Parking I felt the rear suspension bottoming out. Had the Bilstein Bedspring given up completely? I couldn't tell in the dark. It would have to wait until morning.

Hotel Costa del Sol was great; the room and the food were excellent; but it was somewhat of a misnomer. There was no *costa* as far as the eye could see, and the *sol* was hidden behind layers of dark clouds that were suffering from a serious case of incontinence. Eyeballing the Old Cow I could see nothing wrong with the rear suspension beyond what had been wrong since El Salvador. However, the pressure gauge on the rear tire told a different story. I had a flat tire, the first in my motorcycling career, and the only one on this trip. This was excellent timing, considering we had a covered parking spot, a rainy day, and a hotel that served superb Pisco Sours. On my way into town I had seen a place specializing in tire repairs. They could have my business.

Upon arrival there in one of the ubiquitous tricycle taxis, I was treated to the spectacle of a giant brute of a man swinging a fifteen-pound sledgehammer to drive a truck tire into its bed to facilitate dismounting it. He told me I would have to wait, but he would look after me. True to his word, after about half an hour he took my wheel, placed it on the ground, took the valve out, and started to hit it with his fifteen-pounder to break the bead of the tire. I could feel every blow of this monster hammer hitting me physically. How can you tell an expert, and one who is built like the proverbial brick shithouse, how to do his job? Timidly I tucked at his sleeve. "*Señor por favor* this rim is made of aluminum. If you miss only once, I'll have to walk all the way back to Canada." This seemed to amuse him enormously, and he answered with a big laugh, "I never miss." But he laid aside his lethal weapon, took two three-foot long tire irons, and had the tire off in a few seconds. The tube had a tiny puncture on one of the seams left from the mould. He vulcanized the tube, which I kept as a spare, and I gave him a brand new one to install. But first I powdered it and the inside of the tire with baby powder to prevent its being pinched during installation. This tickled my expert's funny bone once again. He called over his colleague to show him what this wimpy gringo was doing to his tire, something he had seen his wife do to his baby son's bottom. Both of them had a good laugh at my expense. I was out of there in thirty minutes, somewhat red-faced. It had cost me $1.20. The two dollars I gave him were meant to raise myself a bit in his estimation. Nice guys these Peruvians, some of them.

Tumbes and Peru had given me a souvenir. The cook at the Hotel Costa del Sol had shown himself an expert in salad-making. I couldn't resist the temptation to start each meal with a giant salad of his creation, and I should have known better. Northern Peru has been notorious for years for being a hotbed of cholera and typhoid fever, sometimes reaching epidemic proportions. I managed to avoid the worst. But the battle that started to rage within after leaving Peru did not lag behind that waged against the Amazonian invaders a couple of months earlier.

19. *Closing the Bottom Loop.*
Ecuador and Colombia

Huaquillas, the Ecuadorian border town, is known for its abundance of *contra-bandistas,* and of swarthy little men carrying thick bundles of money and calculators. Only frequent avowals of *mas tarde, mas tarde* opened a pathway. Customs at the border informed me that first I would have to clear Immigration, four miles out of town, then return to clear Customs. Why not? The Mexicans in Tapachula had a similar screwy set-up, except that there it had been the other way around. This is just to show the rest of the world that they can do in their country whatever they damn well please. At first the gentleman manning Customs was not overly enthusiastic about my case so early in the morning. But as soon as he heard that I carried a *Carnet de passage en douane* his face lit up, his stamping arm was activated, and I was out of there in ten minutes. Now my previous *mas tardes* were held against me, and I had to exchange some money, whether I wanted to or not.

During the previous few weeks I had almost forgotten what bad roads were like. The Pan American Highway in Peru had been excellent. It may have been under two feet of water at times, but there were no potholes. Starting at the border Ecuador did its utmost to jar my memory of bad roads by violently jarring both the bike and its rider. Perhaps the state of the roads in this part of the country, which had been for years an area of skirmishes with the enemy in the south, is part of their war effort to thwart a possible Peruvian invasion. No *Blitzkrieg* here. At Machala we turned east, and the road climbed steeply into the Sierra. It had not improved. On the contrary, as the result of numerous landslides it had become almost impassable in places. Furthermore, there were virtually no road signs, undoubtedly also part of the war effort, an attempt to confuse the enemy. I had to ask for directions at every crossroad. Thus, what with repeatedly stopping and asking my way, bouncing like on a bronco over the potholes (again I harboured ill will toward Bilstein), and having to rush into the bushes every now and then in answer to a battle cry from within, the ride to Cuenca was not a pleasant one.

North of Cuenca the Ecuadorians succeeded in adding insult to injury by actually introducing speed bumps on a road that was already one continuous succession of speed bumps. They did this without posting any warning signs. These devices would surely throw the chains right off an invading tank. War effort! And no big drain on the defence budget. Clever! A Peace Agreement between Peru and Ecuador was reached in October, 1998. Perhaps now they can repair their roads.

About half-way between Cuenca and Riobamba, as we climbed yet another mountain range, the road was so bad that I thought it could not get any worse. It did, however. It had slipped down the mountainside, and a section of about two miles was gone completely. On the hastily carved-out detour I witnessed a sight so pathetic that it will forever symbolize for me the state of the highways in

Ecuador. Coming around a sharp curve on a steep upgrade I saw three little boys about seven years old kneeling in the dirt in the middle of the road hands upheld in prayer, looking at me with pleading eyes. Briefly I wondered whether they were praying for me to crash so that they could clean me out, or for my safe passage. Giving them the benefit of the doubt, I stopped and handed them some money, thinking that of all the saints in Heaven this would probably be a job for St. Jude, the saint responsible for hopeless cases. It appeared that they had done the right thing. We made it to Riobamba safely and in good time. "Thank you, St. Jude, for favors granted!"

I shouldn't have let the Saint off the hook so easily, for I surely would have liked his intercession in Riobamba. When I booked a room at Hotel Whymper downtown, I was informed that the city was subject to a temporary water problem. There was no water in the hotel at the moment, but it would be turned back on *mas tarde,* later. I asked myself, why do I always fall for *mas tarde* when I should have learned a long time ago that in these latitudes *mas tarde* could mean anything. In my naïveté I assumed that in a city the size of Riobamba, with a population of almost 100,000, a water outage should not last longer than a few hours. Wrong! There was no water later that night, nor was there any next morning. To make sure that this was not just a quirk of Hotel Whymper, I checked in the washrooms of various restaurants downtown; no water. This problem would probably have been beyond the sphere of influence of even St. Jude himself. But I should have asked him to give it a try anyway. As it was, I rode off next morning a bit sticky, but in reasonably good spirits. The real victim here in dire need of the Saint's intercession was the chambermaid, for during the night fierce battles had continued to rage in my intestines, with dire consequences.

To my great relief the nation's capital, Quito, had no water problem, not even a temporary one. Nevertheless, Quito failed to meet the expectations triggered by my visit five years ago. The highway between Riobamba and the capital was consistently bad, and the city itself seemed to have gotten worse since 1992. In the Old City, although designated a World Heritage Site by UNESCO, more buildings were in need of repairs, and an even greater number had become derelict. The only thing that seemed to have improved was security. Even though there was a multitude of panhandlers everywhere, this time I did not feel threatened walking around town after sunset. Was this a sign of better things to come? I hoped so.

After this disappointment I needed some physical comfort. This was provided by a decadent buffet in Café Colón of the Hilton Hotel in the New City. By this time the local militia within my gut had triumphed over the Peruvian invaders, and the time was right to celebrate.

Something was rotten in the state of Ecuador. The whole country seemed to be out of order. The ATMs attached to banks, although boasting that they were hooked up to Cirrus™ and Plus™, refused to cough up money, so that I had to cash travellers' cheques to maintain my cash flow. One could not place international phone calls from hotels. At least one city had no water. The roads were in a terrible state of repair; there was virtually no road maintenance going on; no road workers could be seen anywhere. Ecuadorian motorists were even sloppier drivers than the ones in Peru. Road signs were non-existent. But a dead giveaway that things were not going well in Ecuador was the fact that there were hardly any long-haul trucks on the highways. Perhaps they had all broken down because of the abominable state of the roads. Compared with the other countries in South America I had seen on this trip, Ecuador appeared to be an economic basket case.

Even Otavalo, the little town famous for its Indian market, where the mountain people of the surrounding area meet and sell their handicrafts, was a disappointment this time around. It was rather lacklustre, and the people peddling their wares seemed morose and aloof. They did not seem to care whether they sold anything or not. In fact no one seemed to care in general, and any effort at conversation was thwarted in a short time. In Ecuador I had failed to make contact with any local person, short of ordering something, or paying for something. Making my way through immigration and customs at the border in Tulcán in five minutes flat was a relief. I felt that I had not been welcome in Ecuador.

Perhaps this negative impression of Ecuador was all my fault. Was I comparing apples with oranges? Had the anticipation of entering Colombia, one of my favourite countries on the continent, clouded my judgment? Perhaps—crossing the border seemed like a change from night into day. The roads were excellent. There were road signs, complete with distances. There were road crews to be seen at work everywhere, cleaning, keeping the tarmac in top shape, or laying new pavement. There were no speed-bumps, and no potholes anywhere. No, not quite true. Between Ipiales and Pasto there was one about to develop, but it had already been marked and cut out in a square section, presumably ready to be lifted onto a truck and shipped to Ecuador free of charge under their Free Trade Agreement. Heavy truck and bus traffic indicated that the Colombian economy was booming. And I was looking forward to the adrenalin rush that was sure to come from sharing the Colombian highways with the country's Knights of the Road, its kamikaze truck drivers.

A friendly welcome at the border set the tone. "How did you get into Ecuador, *Señor?*" asked the Colombian Customs Official. "With a *Carnet de passage en douane Señor,*" I replied. "We accept that," he shot back. Stamp. Stamp. Two minutes later we were on our way. There were no hassles with swarthy little men carrying thick bundles of money and calculators. In short, everything was different from just 200 feet and fifteen minutes ago. This country seemed to be in working order.

Even its working girls showed human interest in the elderly traveller. Hotel Bolívar in downtown Popayán, my stopping-place of choice, happened to be next to the red light district (Why am I always so lucky?). On my way to a restaurant I was stopped on the sidewalk by one of the ladies, who, apart from the general hard-sell job-related questions, showed genuine interest in where I had come from, when, why, and how. She even made me promise to come and have a chat with her after dinner. Mulling this over during my meal, I decided that I would have to be unfaithful to my new lady friend. I was certain that at this very

19) *Ecuador: equator monument*

moment my Nemesis back home in Ottawa would be gazing into her crystal ball and plotting all kinds of strategies to make the rest of my trip uncomfortable in order to make me rush home. I could not afford to add fresh fuel to a fire already burning out of control. Hence, my virtue was not to be put to the test in Popayán. "Thank you, St. Jude... ."

*   *   *

Once around the city of Cali, which had taken over one hour of stop-and-go riding, the Pan Am turns into a biker's playground reminiscent of the *Großglockner Hochalpenstraße* in Austria. It twists and turns up and down in hair-raising serpentines, but here without guardrails to impede a possible plunge into oblivion, and always with the possibility of being confronted head-on around the next corner by a bus or a Mack truck. Hundreds of slow-crawling trucks and buses had to be passed. Hundreds were approaching, all trying to pass one another. Many times I was close to having to make a leap for the ditch. But at the last moment the trucker had eased over just a bit to clear my handle bars. It was biker's ecstasy, a full 10 points, an A+, for the road, for the scenery (Juan Valdez coffee country), and for the challenge. Furthermore, at every mountain top there was a little restaurant that sold the most delicious Colombian coffee, to celebrate survival.

I had previously decided to by-pass Bogotá, making my way to Cartagena via Medellín, in order to find a ship that would take us around the Darién Gap back to Panamá. When we arrived on the outskirts of Medellín after dark, circumstances forced me to cheat for the first time on this trip. I had made it a point of honour always to find my own way to my chosen hotel downtown, and again out of town, by simply asking pedestrians for directions. In Medellín the unthinkable happened in the form of a road block and a sign reading *Desvío* Detour. I knew then that I was licked. Even in sign-happy Colombia such signs usually appear only once, at the actual road block. They lead you away, but never back. Once you make your first turn, you're on your own. After riding for an hour in the dark getting nowhere, I gave in and asked a parked taxi driver to lead the way to Hotel Ambassador in downtown Medellín; I would follow him. It took us almost an hour of continuous riding until we finally arrived at the hotel. I must admit that in spite of all the asking I could have done, I would not have made it on my own before midnight. He asked for four dollars. I gladly gave him six. He deserved it.

The next day was to be my last riding day in South America, and the highway north out of Medellín was a fitting climax for over two months of unforgettable riding. Again the conditions were more difficult than anticipated, and again we arrived in town after sunset. Fortunately there was no *desvío* in Cartagena to mess things up, and the city is small enough not to get lost, so finding my way to Hotel Flamingo in Bocagrande was easy. If it had been as easy finding onward transportation, my happiness would have been complete.

Making the rounds of the shipping agencies in Cartagena on this Thursday proved to be an exercise in frustration. They did not ship motorcycles by boat, nor did they know of anyone in town who did. I should try the airlines. Every one of the scheduled air carriers had given up shipping motorcycles, and the cargo lines were not interested. They suggested that I might be luckier in Barranquilla, about 120 km further north. Barranquilla had a much larger airport than Cartagena, and could accommodate larger aircraft, which in turn would "perhaps" take motorcycles. This was again a time for decision-making. If I were to ride up to Barranquilla tomorrow, Friday, it would be too late to ship the bike then, provided that, indeed, they shipped motorcycles. The earliest would be Monday morning. But until Monday I would have plenty of time to ride south to Bogotá, a distance of about 1,000 km, where I was certain we would get a lift. Bogotá it was, a decision easy to live with, since it meant a few more days of riding in a great country, a few more days of enjoying great Colombian hospitality, and a few more days of adrenalin rushes that the Colombian truck drivers could trigger so well.

*   *   *

On Sunday morning at ten o'clock we rolled into Bogotá, elated that we had closed the bottom loop of the figure 8 at Tunja, just north of the city. It was at Tunja we should have turned left for Bucaramanga last November in order to avoid that miserable stretch of road to Pamplona passing itself off as the Pan American Highway. Coming up from Cartagena I learned that there are, indeed, long stretches of bad road and of roads under construction in Colombia. But this did not diminish the good impression I had of the country and of its people. Bogotá itself had turned into a pedestrian-friendly city on this day. The main streets of downtown were closed to motorized traffic and had been turned into bicyclists' and in-line skaters' playgrounds. This seemed to be a good omen for things to come. There should be no worries about flying high tomorrow, or so I thought.

After skipping breakfast so that we could arrive at the cargo terminal before morning rush hour traffic, I found myself the first customer to call at Challenge Air Cargo (CAC). The man in charge remembered me. "Of course you can fly with us," he assured me with a welcoming smile and a handshake. "But from Bogotá we only fly to Miami. We do the route in a counterclockwise direction: Miami—Panamá—Bogotá—Miami." "But Sir," I replied, my face dropping, "we don't want to go to Miami. We want to go to Panamá. What now?" "No problem," he added. "Three warehouses down the line you will see a carrier called Girag. They will take you and your bike to Panamá." Wow! When you thought you had everything worked out and there would be no surprises, sure enough there was some angle you hadn't thought of. Off to Girag, then.

The people at Girag were true professionals. The lady in charge immediately set to work to draw up the required documents, and to send me on my way with detailed marching orders. With my Bill of Loading in hand I was to present myself at Customs, some 600 yards across a very busy Airport Expressway. One of the customs inspectors would have to come over to check out the bike and clear the *Carnet*. This done I had to go to the bank in the Passenger Terminal of the airport to get cash pesos to pay for the airfreight (US$325). While I was there I bought my ticket to Panamá, again on Aces, departure tonight at 17.00. Back at Girag, the bill paid, I had to drain the fuel tank, disconnect the battery, and help them lift the bike up the ramp into the departure hall. That was it. Now I could relax over a leisurely brunch at my hotel downtown. It was 11.30 a.m. The rest of the day would be sheer relaxation, no stress. I would have plenty of time to buy that beautiful pair of emerald earrings I had selected last November as a peace offering for the Lady of the House. I would have plenty of time to take a bus out to the airport. I could even have a drink at the bar before boarding the aircraft. No hassles. Ha!!!

At the airport at 15.30 they had already started to check in passengers for Aces flight AE 516 to Panamá. The lineup of people was long and was hardly moving, for the security officer in charge was taking his job very seriously. He let it be known that our lives depended on his vigilance; no, not only our lives, but that of the airline, that of Colombia. In his frail hands lay the future of the whole of Western Civilization as we know it. He was in charge, and we were not to forget it. Unfortunately ahead of me was the entire ensemble of the Bogotá Symphony Orchestra bound for a tour of Central America. They were travelling with all their instruments, except the grand piano. Our security man had no problem with the stringed instruments, for they could be shaken to detect hidden bazookas. The woodwinds and percussion could be slightly disassembled for easy inspection. The problem was the brass section. He felt duty bound to stick one of his fingers into every little opening to check for hidden explosives or similar illegal substances. This was Colombia! The only thing he did not explore digitally was the conductor's baton. After some forty-five minutes it was my turn. Since I had nothing to tempt his loose fingers, there was no problem. My problem started at the next checkpoint, where we were invited to pay 30,800 pesos departure tax. I gave the lady in charge three 10,000 peso bills, which she put immediately into her cash box, while I was fishing in my pockets for the remaining 800 pesos. When I handed these over she snapped, "*Señor,* it's not 800; it is 30,800 pesos, please." Somewhat taken aback I explained to her that I had just given her 30,000, which she had immediately put into her cash box. This she flatly denied. The more I insisted on my version, the more she became entrenched in hers. It was hopeless. I would have to dig into my stash of U.S. dollars to pay up, or I was not going to go anywhere. At this point I heard a timid voice speaking from my left. It belonged to one of three Grey Nuns in full regalia, who had patiently listened to our argument. The little nun asserted firmly that I was right, and the lady wrong. Her two companions nodded agreement. In a concerted effort they asserted that they had seen her put my money into her cash box. What could she say? This was definitely a case of intercession from a higher power. She quickly threw my receipt at me and said, "Next, please!" I turned and thanked my three guardian angels for their gracious intercession on my behalf, while secretly saying, "Thank you, Saint Jude... ."

Central America and Mexico

20. *From Panama to Honduras*

Comfortably settled in the familiar surroundings of flight AE 516, and having somewhat sedated my frazzled nerves with something tall and cool from the bar, I realized that the time had come to make decisions about the last leg of the trip. A recent telephone call home had revealed that the house was still standing, although weighed down under a heavy load of snow. There had been a severe ice storm with blackouts in the whole region, and a state of emergency had been declared, but the Lady of the House was O.K. She had not blacked out. I felt, then, that I could with a relatively clean conscience chisel away at least another month before I would have to make my grand entrance at home. I would not have to return in a straight line the way I had come down. Instead, I could take the northern route and visit some famous Mayan sites along the way in Honduras, Guatemala, and Mexico. However, this would come a little later. The first thing to do was to get the bike out of Panamanian customs.

A telephone call after breakfast to Girag at Tocumén International Airport Cargo Terminal revealed that the bike had arrived and was ready to be picked up. When I arrived there with a container full of gasoline, it was still strapped to a 10 by 14 foot pallet among boxes of miscellaneous merchandise. The Girag crew allowed me to free the bike myself, and to get it ready for the ordeal that lay ahead. With the documentation from Girag in hand I was sent by Customs from one office to another, until they had run out of offices and had to deal with my case. After two hours of Panamanian bureaucracy we were on our way with a temporary import permit, duly approved, signed, stamped, and copied more times than I care to remember. Welcome to Central America!

With Panama City sightseeing having been taken care of during my last visit, it was strictly business this time around. An oil and filter change was required again, and I needed a visa for Nicaragua. This did not seem like a great workload. But because of the extreme heat and humidity, sweat was running freely by the time it was done. The only places to cool off downtown were restaurants, banks, and large department stores. There seemed to be no shopping malls downtown, strange for a city the size of Panama.

Thursday, the fifth of February, almost proved to be my undoing. The Nicaraguan visa was ready to be picked up at 9.00 a.m. To avoid wasting time I had loaded the bike after breakfast, in order to pick up my visa at the embassy on my way out of town during the morning rush hour. It was a gorgeous day in the high nineties under a brilliant sky. The embassy is located in a residential section between the Old and the New City, in a good neighbourhood with large mansions shaded by stately old trees. Riding from the bright sunshine into the shade of one of these giants with sunglasses on is like riding into a dark tunnel. Keeping to the extreme left on a one-way street I failed to see the protruding root of a tree, made contact with my left cylinder, and was airborne before I knew what had happened. Coming down with a hard thud on our left side in front of an approaching car triggered an adrenalin rush the like of which I had not experienced in Colombia. Fortunately the driver of the car was able to stop in time to allow me to lift up the bike and limp over to the sidewalk to check for damages. The crash bar had been wrapped around the cylinder head, but it had done what it was designed to do. It had protected the cylinder head from being shorn off. The left handlebar grip with the clutch lever was bent, but could be straightened out easily. Nothing was broken, just showing some scrape marks, and the same was true for the rider. I had scraped my left shin against the cylinder head, and my left arm on the pavement. In view of the fact that I was only wearing shirt and jeans, I considered myself lucky. The Nicaraguan visa was ready, and we were off to find our way out of town, only to get shaken up again.

At this time of day traffic was very heavy. As we were going around a roundabout I was hit by a car in the rear right side. The rear wheel slid sideways, but we remained upright. It appeared that the saddle bag of the hard luggage had absorbed some of the impact. The whole thing happened so fast that I did not even have time to give the lady driver of the car a dirty look, and I'm certain that she did not realize what she was missing. This was strike two, I was thinking, and as they say in baseball, "Three strikes; you're out!" It was absolutely mandatory to avoid strike #3, at least for the remainder of the day. Perhaps divine intercession should again be called upon, and I was wondering how to get the helpline of the saint in charge of "avoiding collisions."

But it was difficult to stay on the straight and narrow, so to speak, for the road to the border was excellent, and most of the way a four-lane highway, although that is not to say, an "expressway." Since Panamanian drivers were generally slow and careful, I found myself continuously in the passing lane. I remembered very well that disobeying the speed limits, especially in towns, could get very expensive here. In fact, in almost every little town I could see one of Panama's finest in green, half-hidden behind trees, aiming his little thingy of a radar gun at us. I had to resist giving in to my Colombian driving mode with all the will power at my disposal. This time around I had vowed to slow down and to take it easy. The way we were going was not the way to do it.

However, one sure means of slowing anyone down in these latitudes is a border. I had forgotten what it was like to cross borders in Central America, and the one looming ahead was a rude reminder that nothing had changed since the last time we were passing through.

Having been here on my birthday, almost three months ago, I remembered that this border happened to be one of the easier ones. And yet it took over one hour to cross, even though I was the only one waiting to be processed. The officials were obviously having their early morning "briefing" while slurping large cups of java, and seemed to resent my intrusion. When they finally deigned to cater to my wishes, they managed to involve most of their man- and woman-power, while giving me a good aerobic workout by making me rush from window to window, to the photocopier, and back to another window, only to be told that there was yet another document to be copied. If this was their idea of "civilization," I wanted no part of it. But I wasn't asked my opinion. In fact I did not wish to be asked. All I wanted was to get away from here as quickly as possible. It was a Friday once again, the beginning of the Latin weekend, and I wanted to see the BMW dealer in San José, Costa Rica, before shutdown. Why do I always have to be a victim of deadlines?

Nothing had changed since last November on the road to San José. It was good for some 100 km from the border, became horrible for the next 100 km, with numerous washouts, landslides, and long sections of pot-holed gravel, to improve again on its climb up the Cordillera to an altitude of over 9,000 feet, and down to San José. I found the going very easy this time around, had no trouble passing the many slow-moving, diesel fumes-spewing transport trucks, and arrived in town at 4.00 p.m. It seemed that I must have learned something about riding a motorcycle during the last three months. But had I learned anything about patience and understanding since my last visit? I could hardly curb my curiosity over what the BMW *gerente*, Herbert Von Breymann, had in store for me.

At 4.30 p.m. Herbert was still enthroned behind his large, cluttered desk. He did not appear to have moved from this spot since I had seen him last. He did not seem overly surprised to see me, and told me calmly that he had returned the wrong shock absorber to Guatemala. He had ordered the correct replacement from the United States to be shipped directly to the BMW dealer in Caracas, where it was probably still waiting to be picked up. At my request he sent a fax to Caracas asking that it be forwarded directly to the BMW dealer in North Dallas, Texas, where I would have it installed. That was all he could do. At this point I didn't really care anymore. I had gotten used to riding on a bucking cow, and was worried more about the state of my tires. In view of what lay ahead in Honduras and Guatemala it would be prudent to get a new set put on. "No problem," said Herbert. "I can get a new set of Pirellis for you immediately from one of my friends in town, and you can have them mounted tomorrow morning at another friend's place and be on your way." I thanked Herbert for his help, and for that of his many friends, and retired to the familiar surroundings of the Garden Court, Best Western Hotel, to free Cuba Libres between 6.00 and 7.00 p.m., all the bananas you could eat, and all the coffee you cared to drink. Things did not look too bad after that.

When we arrived at the designated tire shop with my brand new Pirellis next morning my estimation of Herbert Von Breymann received yet another blow. His "friend" informed me that he did not install tires on motorcycles. I should go elsewhere. Where to, he had no idea. I had seen a place down the street on my way over, and decided to give it a try. "Oh, sure," said the young man in one of the bays. "I'll be with you in a few minutes." He himself was the owner of a motorcycle, and obviously knew what he was doing; there was no fifteen-pound sledgehammer in sight anywhere. When he inspected my brand new Pirelli rear tire, he noticed several deep gashes in its carcass, and told me that even though the tire was tubeless, he would suggest putting in a tube to be safe. If it had not been a Saturday I would have exchanged the damaged tire for a good one. But I was stuck with it and went for the tube. No thanks to Herbert and to his friends in the tire business.

Sunday morning was not a good time to be riding out of San José. We had a hard time holding our own among a multitude of tour buses and private cars. It was peak holiday travel season, and everyone seemed to be on the road to prove it. Freshly washed and with new tires installed, we looked our best. But this was probably not the reason we attracted the attention of every policeman Costa Rica could post along the Pan Am. Every one of them, and there were hundreds, was pointing a shiny new radar pistol at us, hoping to nail us for a juicy fine. In Panama the police had brandished dented old clunkers, probably hand-me-downs from Costa Rica, whereas in Costa Rica every one of the boys in black must have received a sparkling new toy in his stocking this past Christmas. Like children they were out on this beautiful sunny day to play with it, enjoying the "high" such a phallic symbol could bestow upon its bearer. Every one of us motorists tried to observe the speed limit religiously, even though at times it was down to a ridiculous 25 km/h. I saw many motorists getting nabbed. In spite of my vigilance I was stopped on the open road by a motorcycle cop. He did not have a radar gun, but he held up his radio telephone accusingly, informing me that his colleague in the last town had informed him that I had been speeding. Now, this was a touchy situation. It was his word against mine. Of course I tried to explain to him good-naturedly that I was incapable of committing such a dastardly crime against the laws of the land, being a gringo tourist and a guest in his country. And wouldn't he agree with me that at my age speed is the furthest thing from a man's mind. He laughed. We compared bikes. We shook hands. There are officers and gentlemen in every country. But I breathed a sigh of relief when we reached the Nicaraguan border at 12.30.

Two hours later, only slightly stressed, we entered the country still vivid in my memory for its undisciplined bovines criss-crossing the highway at will. They had not changed their habits since the last time I passed through.

The combination of an excellent newly surfaced road, the absence of policemen along the Pan Am, no radar traps, no speed bumps, and very light traffic was a welcome relief after the police state of Costa Rica. Having relapsed temporarily into my Colombian riding mode on my way into the capital, Managua, I split the two long columns of cars waiting for the light to change, and was slowly making my way to the front. This did not go over very well with a city policeman at the intersection. He waved me over and informed me angrily that this sort of thing is not done in Nicaragua, and would I please obey the law, which also applied to visiting gringos. And would I please turn off my lights. In Nicaragua vehicles don't have their lights on during the daytime. They had been after me for that on our way down, and again I had difficulties explaining to him that this was impossible. This was the way we were wired. He shook his head and waved us on, probably thinking, *Gringo estúpido!* This was our welcome to Managua.

It got worse. In the centre of the city there are virtually no street names posted. Was this a leftover from the civil war? I had to ask at every street corner to find the hotel of my choice, Casa Fiedler. After lunch I had planned to walk around downtown, but where was downtown? All I saw was wide open fields with over-grown ruins, dilapidated buildings, cheap housing units, and temporary shacks, a mess. The Cathedral was the tallest, best-preserved ruin of them all, but the large cracks in the outside walls made survival doubtful. Two earthquakes and a civil war had done their tricks. Managua looked like the city of Dresden in former Communist East Germany in the late 1950s. It has a long way to go to regain its respectability as the capital of a beautiful country. But there is hope.

A sure sign of which way things are going economically in a country is its highway system. In Nicaragua the main highways were excellent. There was road construction everywhere, and even secondary roads were in good condition. In light of its highways this was not a second Ecuador. There seemed to be a spirit of optimism in the air. Things will get better soon. But they should do something soon about their wayward cattle.

One advantage of there being no downtown area in Managua was that I had no problem finding my way out of town. The road was excellent to the border at Las Manos, where a few minutes before noon, I cleared the Nicaraguan side rather quickly, but had to wait for an hour on the Honduran side until the officials had finished their siesta. Forty-five minutes later and US$30.00 poorer we were back on the CA 6, the now familiar highway into Tegucigalpa.

If Managua was lacking a downtown, Tegucigalpa had too much of it. This became painfully apparent during evening rush hour, and this time we arrived on a Tuesday.   Crammed between high mountains, and built during horse and buggy days without the "benefit" of an earthquake now and then, the city suffers from a serious traffic problem. Practically all streets downtown are one-way streets, too narrow to allow more than one lane of traffic. It is no wonder that after 3.00 p.m. there is gridlock and chaos as everyone tries to gain a small advantage over everyone else just to move a few feet forward. I knew where I wanted to go, and the giant Coca Cola sign up on the flank of El Picacho was my lodestar, but I found myself in a maze, going in circles, which only a desperate move, like going the wrong way in a one-way street, could solve; same maze, same vicious circle, same one-way street as last time, but not the same cop. It took almost two hours to cover a distance that could easily have been covered in fifteen minutes on foot. What a relief to park the bike at the hotel and watch the chaos on the downtown streets from the sidewalk.

Next morning, with good directions from a taxi driver, I avoided entering the downtown maze, and had no problem finding my way out of the city. Once on the CA 5 bound north-west in the direction of San Pedro Sula, I was grateful that I did not have to waste valuable time going in circles, when I could spend it on a road that must rank among the top ten on the ecstasy index for motorcycle riding in Central America. The road winds up and down several mountain ranges, and passes alternately through coffee plantations, or banana plantations, depending on the altitude. It was in excellent condition, but traffic was heavy. Since Honduran motorists are slow and careful drivers, I must have raised some eyebrows by my Colombian aggressive driving mode. However, I had never seen an accident in Colombia either time I had been there. On this relatively short stretch of road I saw three transport trucks upside down in the ditch. Why? The only answer I could think of was that when a driver goes off the road in Colombia he inevitably takes a plunge and simply disappears into space, to be discovered in a thicket hundreds of feet below, perhaps days later, by some passing shepherd, whereas in Honduras wide roadside ditches collect the hapless motorist, who then becomes an exhibit for all passers-by to see. I did not care for either alternative.

Some five kilometers south of San Pedro Sula the road to Copán turned off to the left, and things quieted down considerably, since traffic on the CA 4 was relatively light. As the road rose slowly from sea level we entered tobacco country. Indulgence in the weed here has not yet acquired the social stigma that it has north of the Rio Grande, and the products produced by the cigar factory in nearby Santa Rosa de Copán are flaunted openly on many roadside billboards. This is the *real* Marlboro Country. I had once been an *aficionado* of fine cigars, and upon seeing a colourful display of the locally manufactured goodies in a roadside restaurant, I could not resist the temptation of backsliding—if only briefly—into this politically incorrect habit. Why are so many simple pleasures immoral, illegal, or insalubrious? The local product is, indeed, mild, sweet-tasting, and delicious, and yet it delivers the anticipated punch. I shall always associate the little town of Copán Ruinas with the taste of cigar smoke, and I hoped that my lungs and my cardio-vascular system would forgive me this momentary relapse. Perhaps I should not have bought a whole box of twenty. Pavlovian conditioning seems to have been at work here. But this was just as well, for I found the actual ruins near the little town a bit disappointing.

As every connoisseur of fine ruins knows there is a great variety among them. They range from a collection of piles of mere rubble on the one extreme to an approximation of the sublime on the other. Among the latter I count the pyramids and Karnak in Egypt, the ruins of the ancient cities of Persepolis in Iran, Angkor in Cambodia, Machu Picchu in Peru, and Teotihuacan in Mexico. Some people may argue that on these sites there is not much more than rubble, yet others can sense the spirit of greatness still hovering over the piles of stone. They can sense even today that here once upon a time world history was made. Power was wielded over life and death, absolute power. I did not feel this magic in Copán. To me Copán looked like a Mayan backwater. True, excavation has unearthed only a fraction of what must have been there. But what is there today is not convincing. The restored ball court and the hieroglyphic stairway were interesting, but they were not overwhelming in their grandeur, and the large ugly tarpaulin that was strung over the stairway to protect it from the elements did not help matters either. In short I felt that in Copán there was too much nature and not enough culture. It was fascinating, though, to witness the contest between the two opposing forces, giant trees conquering and destroying the puny products of humanity's endeavour. I had hoped to see more ruins and less jungle. But again, my disappointment was all my fault. I should have come here with an open mind and no expectations, and leave it at that.

As I thought this over that evening in a local restaurant, I was interrupted by a grey-haired oriental-looking lady at the table next to mine, whom I had seen in the morning on the archeological site. "Are you not the man on the motorcycle, who arrived yesterday around four in the afternoon, the same time as our bus?" she asked me. "Since, as far as I know, I am the only foreign motorcyclist in town, it must be me," I replied. "My sister and I were jealous of you and the unlimited freedom you must enjoy on your machine. We have been spending so much time waiting *for* buses, waiting *on* buses for arrival, and waiting for buses to get away. How great it must be to go whenever or wherever you feel like going, to stop whenever or wherever you feel like it, and not to have to worry about the rest of the world," she continued. "The lady over there is my sister Lynne, and my name is Dorothy. We are from New York." This was intriguing. Near the ruins, and later, in town, I had seen a number of same-sex couples, some men with pony-tails and ear-rings, but mostly women, wearing sensible shoes, farmers' overalls or drip-dry cotton dresses, broad-rimmed hats, a rucksack, and no make-up. And here beside me was a prime example of this genre, friendly, talkative, and perhaps willing to be questioned. "'Unlimited freedom' as you called it, unfortunately is an illusion," I replied, trying very hard not to sound like a professor delivering a lecture to a class of two. "Travelling with a motorcycle, as a matter of fact, is like being married. You know the formula, 'for better for worse, for richer for poorer, in sickness and in health...,' and it seems that not even Death can part the two of you, for your bike is written into your passport in every country you are passing through. To leave it, or to abandon it, even if both of you are totalled, would trigger a bureaucratic nightmare that would outlive you and be passed on to your heirs. It is easier to divorce a spouse than to leave a country without your motorcycle. And travelling with a motorcycle is definitely 'for poorer.' At almost every border there are fees to be paid, both legitimate and spontaneous. The bike needs fuel and oil and tender loving care, and may give you trouble at times, just like a spouse. At times it can be like a millstone around your neck. Here, for instance, I would have stayed in a hotel at a fraction of the price I'm paying. But I had little choice. Security of the bike had to be my main concern." I thought that I had lectured enough, and was looking at the sisters expectantly. Did they know what I was talking about? "My sister was never married, so she doesn't know what losing your freedom means," said Dorothy, who seemed to be the spokesperson for the two. "I was married for twenty-five years, and raised two children, who are adults now. Then my husband decided that he needed more space, and gave me back my freedom, though unilaterally. But we parted amicably, and now I'm free to travel with my sister wherever and as long as we want. I know what you mean with 'millstone around your neck.' After what you've told us I don't think we'll opt for a motorcycle," she said smiling, "especially since we are thinking of going to Bali next, one place we always dreamt about. How would we get there on our motorcycle?" she added jokingly. But I think I made my point, and the two ladies seemed to have come to terms with their lot as bus and air travellers. Then conversation drifted to trivial observations. Soon the two world travellers said good night, and I retired to my hotel and to what was left of my box of cigars. Yes, I thought, another aspect of "unlimited freedom" is to be able to smoke one of these cancer sticks wherever and whenever you like, "for better or for worse..."

21. *Guatemala, Belize, Mexico*

The road out of Copán Ruinas to the Guatemalan border and on to Tikal could have been a page out of an adventure motorcyclist's wishbook. What I needed at this point was a challenge to maintain my image as a macho motorcycle adventurer. Not having been robbed in Lima, or shot at in Ecuador, or flattened on the pavement in Colombia, I needed some excitement to bolster my image. On our way over from Tegucigalpa it had been too easy, with good pavement, no floods (unlike exactly one year later during the visit of hurricane Mitch), no rain, since we were in the dry season, not even ill-behaved cattle. We were desperate for some action. The road on the other side of town was gravel, dusty, potholed, and narrow, with steep grades and blind curves set in superb mountain scenery, a good start. Bouncing and sliding with our Bilstein-challenged rear end into El Florido, the border town, we expected the worst, but were disappointed. This border was so laid back that I thought I was back in Chile. At 9.30 a.m. the officials on both sides were just rolling off their cots to face yet another day of boredom. Between their yawns they tried to get rid of us as quickly as possible, but not before having exacted their fair share of "development aid." The Border Curse that had followed us on the way down had finally died and was buried. Or could it be, perhaps, that I had finally mastered the art of border hopping by following this simple formula: Stay cool, smile, and keep paying? The road, on the other hand, got worse.

Just before reaching CA 10 near Chiquimula the macho biker met his challenge, in the form of a construction zone. They had dumped several truck loads of fill, and were about to spread it with a road grader. I saw the deep soft stuff ahead of us, with high ridges between the passes the grader had made, and hesitated. But one of the construction guys waved me on, and on we went, against my better judgment, only to hit one of the high soft ridges. Down we went on the left, which seemed to be our favourite side. It was a soft landing this time, and there were many helpers to lift the Old Cow and the Old Man. The left crash bar was wrapped around the valve covers once again, otherwise there was no damage, not even a scrape on either machine or rider. We duly registered this fall as something required by the script for adventure biking. This was three down on this portion of the trip. I was relieved, however, that our tumble had no serious consequences.

Adventure eluded us again on the CA 9, the Atlantic Highway, which we left for the CA 13 at Morales. According to the maps pavement was supposed to end at Modesto Méndez, but continued for another 46 km to San Luis. I had no complaints. But then the adventure biker again got what he was asking for, in the form of rough gravel, dust, pot-holes, blind curves, steep grades, and heavy truck traffic. At Poptún it was getting dark, and I had swallowed enough dirt for one day. So I called it quits.

We should have kept going, for this little town turned out to be one of the dustiest, dirtiest places in which I had had the misfortune of spending a night on this trip. Pension Isabelita's "rooms" were not much better than the solitary cells in a maximum security prison, and the "lady" in charge displayed all the characteristics of one of the wardens. As a greeting she scolded me because my bike was blocking the entrance to the only toilet and shower on the premises. When I asked her when the water would be turned on for the shower, she bellowed *mas tarde*. She couldn't fool me, however. Even I had learned by now what this expression meant in these latitudes, and I was proven right: there was no running water during my sojourn. But why bother? I didn't really need water anyway. Tomorrow back on the road more dirt would be added to what was there already, so what was the use. What bothered me more, however, was that the electricity was turned off at 6.00 p.m., and the fan stopped turning. From this moment on thousands of mosquitoes sallied forth from the four corners of my cell to embark on a feeding frenzy on this gringo the likes of which I had not experienced since Labrador. But unlike their cousins in Labrador these little pests were stealth fighters. They dived in like *Stukas* but with engines turned off, silently, and took their bite and sip of blood. By the time the itch had started they were far away. I was glad that I had taken my malaria pills. This didn't stop them, of course, but at least it offered peace of mind. I was a little raw and ill-humoured as I packed the bike next morning, only to be snarled at again by the warden. I hadn't paid her yet; and I should have paid her last night, she added. Now I knew why. Undoubtedly in the past they must have had casualties during the night. Some unsuspecting gringos must have bled to death during the attack of the stealth fighters before paying her. Smart lady! She had made me feel as unwelcome as the Reception people at the *President* in Caracas. It's true that feeling unwelcome for US$3.50 was easier to bear than feeling unwelcome for US$150.00. Nevertheless, I got out of there as fast as I could.

The next hundred kilometres, which took us into Flores, were hellish. But the adventure biker endured them stoically, as required by the script. Slowly bouncing around a sharp curve I was confronted by two men, one older, perhaps the father, and a little boy of about ten, perhaps his son. Both men were swinging shovels, pretending to fill one of the large potholes in front of them, while at the same time the little boy was holding out his hand soliciting money. Of course the three little boys in Ecuador immediately came to my mind, and I was disgusted. Whom did these two idiots think they were fooling? What they were doing was like the little bird trying to move a mountain of sand one grain at a time. On this sad excuse of a road they'd do much better to pray, like the boys in Ecuador. This was pathetic; no, this was stupid. They did not deserve any money, I decided, and did not stop. A little way down the road, however, I was having second thoughts. How arrogant of me to belittle their actions. Here I was riding an expensive motorcycle with more money in my back pocket than they could expect to earn in a year. Many of their countrymen were lying on their backs doing nothing but waiting for the coconuts to fall and the bananas to ripen. At least they were

20) Guatemala: Tikal ruins

trying. I should have given them something, if only for their effort. It was too late now, however; I was not going to turn back on this execrable road. But I vowed to atone for my inordinate pride, the sin of Satan, and to make amends somehow soon. Though I still thought that they would have done more good praying. Perhaps I should have told them so.

With my mind on leave, I covered this last section of dirt more quickly than anticipated, and I had to make a choice of either staying in Flores and visit *Ruinas Tikal* the next day, or heading straight for Tikal and staying there overnight. The ruins won out in the end, a decision I did not regret. I had the whole afternoon and evening to explore this magnificent forgotten city in the jungle.

Remnants of a civilization that lasted from approximately 300 A.D. until 1000 A.D., the temples and public buildings that had been excavated were still redolent of power. The magic, which had eluded me in Copán, was still there, tangible. There was visible proof that Tikal must have been the centre of an empire that had stretched its tentacles in all directions. The pyramids, several of which can be climbed, can compare favourably in design, execution, and artistry with the best buildings Angkor has to offer. Looking from the top of one of the highest over an endless expanse of jungle, one wonders where the builders found the vast amount of stones, necessary for the construction of these grandiose structures, and also what spiritual and physical resources supported and sustained their efforts. And finally, one wonders what caused the decline of such a magnificent, undoubtedly highly sophisticated civilization. Here was again the physical evidence of a power struggle between the eternally opposing forces of nature on the one side, and of art, the products of human culture and civilization, on the other, a struggle that holds a particular fascination for the present-day observer. In Tikal the forces of culture had obviously been more successful than those at work in Copán. Tikal did not disappoint. It was worth suffering the bumps and dirt of the track leading into this still remote area of Guatemala. Tikal was a pleasant surprise.

Another pleasant surprise was the border on the Belizean side. "How long do you wish to stay?" asked the immigration officer in impeccable English, his native tongue. I said, "One week, Sir." The officer answered, "I'll give you thirty days. O.K.?" The customs officer did not even want to see the bike. He only entered the data from the ownership into the passport. We were gone in less than fifteen minutes. No helpers, no photocopies, no charge. And there were more surprises in store for us.

All road signs indicated that we had arrived in the capital, Belmopan, but where was the city? Belmopan had been created capital in 1970 by an Act of Parliament. The seat of government had been moved from Belize City to this little fly-blown place in the geographical centre of the country. What the parliamentarians could not do, however, was to stuff the little town with people. Most government employees still commuted daily from Belize City, one hour's drive away. The town had been planned for a population of 40,000, but at present the total population was in the vicinity of 6,000. On this Sunday, though, a marked, but only temporary, increase in population had occured. With my arrival the population had swelled to 6,001. But you would never know. The whole place looked deserted, a ghost town in the middle of nowhere.

It was high noon when I arrived, lunchtime, and I had something to celebrate. The Old Cow's odometer was about to mark 40,000 km (25,000 miles) since leaving Ottawa last October. The Belmopan Convention Hotel seemed to be a suitable venue to celebrate this important milestone in our travelling life. Alice, the waitress, when she finally arrived, obligingly served a suitable liquid for a toast: freshly squeezed orange juice, and the first of an endless series of cups of excellent coffee, the rest of which were self-serve. The chicken dinner I ordered, however, took an endless amount of time to arrive. Eventually becoming worried that they might have forgotten about me, since I was the only guest in the dining room, I went in search of Alice, only to be comforted with the news that the chicken had been captured and plucked, and was at present roasting over a low flame. "You can't rush these things, Sir," she added with a smile. She had a well-developed sense of humour, Alice, which somewhat offset her badly developed sense of duty. I could even forgive her for smooching with the chef (he was a nice-looking young buck), while I was nearing starvation. We were in Belmopan, Belize, at noon on a Sunday, and the passing of time was of little consequence. The meal was excellent, and the tip I left for Alice was more a penance for some of my recent sins committed than a gratuity. We still made it to Belize City on a good road before 3.00 p.m.

As I went from hotel to hotel in downtown Belize City in search of lodging I was painfully reminded of what I had told the ladies in Copán, that part about a bike being "like a millstone around your neck." The places within my budget all seemed to lack secure parking. I could not be sure that my travelling companion would still be waiting for me the next morning where I had left her the night before. In the end we registered at the most expensive hotel in town. Of course we deserved the treat, but if we were to keep this up I would have to ask my wife to work overtime to help pay my VISA bill, a request that she would probably find "totally unacceptable." On foot that evening, with the bike in safe custody, I convinced myself that downtown Belize City is not the place to flash a camera, a watch, or expensive jewellery. Losing the bike, no matter under what circumstances, was not part of the script, according to the motorcycle adventurer's handbook. Happily reunited the next morning with my mount, I looked forward to leaving Central America for the familiar sights and sounds of Mexico, the Latin outpost of the North American continent.

This border crossing was almost like a homecoming. This was the fifth time that we either entered or left Mexico, so the procedure had lost its mystery. It had become routine, and routines are low-stress exercises. As we moved away from the border in the direction of Chetumal I knew that we had arrived when we encountered a fair number of road signs, hit the first *topes* and *vibratores* met the first toll booth without a by-pass for motorcycles, and saw the familiar green signs of the government-owned filling stations, Pemex. Stopping for fuel, I knew that we had arrived when the attendant informed me that they had just run out of *Premium,* but still had some *Magna sin* left. This was Mexico, and this was Pemex. They always gave you good service with a smile, whether they had anything to sell or not. I bought some *Magna sin* Regular, but resolved to keep my eyes open for the red *Premium* sign. I had learned very early that the Old Cow had a distinct aversion to the Mexican fuel and water mixture that at times happened to find its way into the underground tanks of Pemex's *Magna sin plomo.*

North of the Tulum ruins road construction with heavy truck traffic made for slow going. But as we approached Cancun the four-lane expressway under construction was virtually complete, and traffic moved faster. A multitude of billboards on both sides of the road explained in no uncertain terms that this part of the Yucatan Peninsula was destined to become one of the Continent's greatest getaways. Advertised were walled-in retirement communities with single dwellings or duplexes, golf courses, and cemeteries, multi-unit condominiums, time-share apartments, golf resorts, sun-and-surf resorts, or simple vacation home communities in the middle to upper price range; with just a modest down payment, you're in. These were Florida clones in a Latin setting. The only things missing to make one feel truly at home were the trailer parks, the strip malls, and the new and used car lots. Just give them time. The fast-food joints were here already.

Instead of going straight into Cancun, I decided to make a detour through the hotel strip, built on a narrow spit shaped like the letter "J" just off the coast. It, too, lived up to expectations. Massive structures, some looking like Mayan pyramids, others like steel and glass high-rises, still others like concrete grain elevators, all with flowery, bucolic names, invited the sun-hungry gringos to buy the package deal, be dropped off at the airport and delivered to his or her spot in paradise, be fed and entertained, be delivered to the plane and returned to home base, led by the hand like a pre-schooler, all for an all-inclusive price (you get what you pay for); no stress, no hassles, just fun in the sun. The Strip is a copy of Miami Beach, Rimini, Las Palmas, the Canaries, or the Algarve, a holiday ghetto. It seems to be making money in spite of the scare of a thinning ozone layer. Not being on a package tour, I opted to spend the night in downtown Cancun, which I found a little less artificial, and definitely less expensive than the Strip.

Just a couple of hours' drive west of Cancun lies another must-see for connoisseurs of fine ruins, Chichén Itzá. The dozens of tour buses in the parking lot suggested that a tour of the ruins must have been part of the "package." The site was as crowded as downtown Cancun on a Saturday afternoon. However, the presence of a multitude of ruin hounds walking about did not detract from the magnificent remains of this once powerful city. In its centre, and also the centre of attraction, is *El Castillo,* which looks like the centre-piece of a wedding cake. On each of its four sides 91 steps lead up to the base of the top structure. On this day clusters of tourists were like ants trying to huff and puff their way up to the top over the high risers. Inside of the pyramid 61 steep steps lead up to the chamber of the red jaguar, perhaps the throne room of the high priest. A lot of huffing and

21) *Mexico: Chichen Itza ruins*

puffing here as well. Away from the centre-piece traffic was less dense, but there were still many interesting discoveries to be made. Of particular fascination to me was the well-preserved (or restored) ball court with grandstand, with a relief showing the prize of honour being bestowed upon the winning (some claim the losing) captain of a ball game: decapitation. I could not help thinking what would happen if American footballers were to reactivate this rule. This could take the boredom out of some of the interminable bowl games being played around New Year's Day. With this exciting new rule on the books they would probably no longer need cheerleaders, and would thereby save a bundle of money, and even more could be saved on the salaries of the winning (or losing) captains. Perhaps these thoughts were triggered by the unmerciful noon sun beating down upon my unprotected bald spot, or by my violent movements. One of the guards had admonished me that it was forbidden to take photographs with a tripod. But having come all that distance I absolutely needed a picture of myself in the foreground with *El Castillo* in the rear. I must have spent about an hour circling the pyramid trying to find a suitable spot to set up my camera on the tripod shielded from the scrutinizing eyes of the ever-watchful guards, to run into position while the remote control counted down, and to run back quickly to dismantle the whole set-up before being discovered. Outwitting the authorities seems to provide a small sense of satisfaction.

Back at the hotel, a bit smug and very thirsty, I ordered two Coronas (it was happy hour: two for the price of one) to celebrate my achievements on this memorable day, when a voice, belonging to a young lady at the table next to mine, asked me, "Well, did you finally manage to get your pictures?" She was in the process of finishing a melted cheese sandwich, and was on her second bottle of beer. She was nice to look at, a honey blonde, hair in a bun, skinny, with freckles all over, and no make-up. She did not wear farmers' overalls, but a rather loosely fitting sari-like gown, khaki in colour, probably drip-dry, and sensible shoes. I nodded, asking her if I could join her at her table. She had no objection. Her name was Carol, down here from Minneapolis to visit a girlfriend near Cancun. But two days ago her friend had gone to the corner store and hadn't come back. During her absence the apartment was visited by several shady characters, all men, asking for her friend. Getting more afraid after each visit, she packed her bags and left, with the intention of spending the rest of her two weeks elsewhere in Mexico. That is how she ended up in Chichén Itzá. She wanted to see the ruins, where she had seen me sneaking around to take the forbidden pictures. When she heard that I was here on a motorbike, she said, "When I was an undergraduate in college I was so much into motorbikes that I wrote a paper in one of my philosophy seminars on Robert Pirsig's book, *Zen and the Art of Motorcycle Maintenance.* My professor liked it so much that he submitted it to a learned journal, where it was accepted and published under my name. I've had many boyfriends with bikes, but never owned one myself." I was impressed with Carol's academic credentials and with her love for motorbikes. But at the moment I was more interested in Carol as the representative of a stereotype.

In my eyes Carol was part of a phenomenon that I had observed first in Copán, young men, but mostly women, same-sex couples, in her case only half a couple by default, travelling together, single, or single again, in their mid-thirties or thereabouts, women who had forsaken the "beauty myth," who were determined to have a good time on their own, to do what they wanted to do, whenever and wherever they wanted to do it, independent, unconventional, selfish. In fact "selfish" was Carol's own term she used when we came to talk about relationships. She confided that she was afraid of making a commitment to marriage even though at the age of thirty-seven her biological clock was ticking in fast-forward. She had a well-paying job as a paralegal secretary, working from Monday to Thursday. Her hobbies were singing in a dance band on weekends, and travelling, which she could well afford in respect to both money and time, since she had many holidays during the year. She had led a sheltered life in a happy family, mom and dad still alive and not divorced. And yet her three older brothers and she herself had never married and were childless, to the sorrow of mom, who wanted to be a grandmother. Carol had had several relationships, mostly with older men, thus minimizing the danger of becoming too involved. She added that her life was too perfect, that there was no way of improving her situation by changing her status. Then she quoted the words that I had heard my mechanic repeat many times over, with variations, "If it ain't broke, why fix it?" This was her philosophy. And I was not surprised. She had studied Robert Pirsig and evidently had become one of his disciples. I remembered my broken shock absorber, but didn't think that this was the moment to challenge Carol's outlook on life. Back in the olden days she would have been classified as an old maid, or a spinster. Today in more charitable times she is the envy of her "committed" friends, who regard her as a swinging single, a young urban professional lady, forever young, the stuff of many Hollywood productions, particularly of the daily soap operas.

It was a perfect evening. The humidity had abated with the heat. Carol was deep in thoughts about the problems of "commitment." I mentioned to her that I had seen advertised a Sound and Light spectacle tonight at the ruins, first in Spanish, then in English. This made her snap out of her reverie, and she decided that she would like to go if I accompanied her on the thirty-minute walk along the dark road to the site. The show was excellent, both the narration and the special sound and light effects. We agreed, however, that in the hands of a Hollywood director there would have been more special effects. But this was not Hollywood.

Back at the hotel, as we wound down behind our Coronas, we were joined by Christian, in his early thirties, tall, tanned, with a beard and shoulder-length greying and thinning hair, wearing an earring, slashed jeans, and sandals. Christian was from Anchorage, Alaska, here to escape the northern darkness and to get some sun and some good marijuana. He had also attended the Sound and Light spectacle and joined us in our discussion of its merits and shortcomings. Moving on to more personal matters, Christian told us that having recently divorced his wife because of "irreconcilable differences," he was enjoying his new freedom. He was enthusiastic about Mexican history and culture, and also about the easy availability of the home-grown weed. He agreed with Carol that the ruins were worth a repeat visit the next day. I did not fail to see the humour in this chance encounter. Here were these two stereotypical examples of the modern-day Mexican ruin hounds, who were about to form a very traditional not at all stereotypical mixed couple. It was getting late, and I had a long way to go the next day. So I wished them good night and lots of fun tomorrow. Who knows what the spirit of Quetzalcoatl hovering over the ruins will have in store for them.

*   *   *

We made it into Merida just before the downtown area was to be closed to traffic. Along both sides of the city streets scaffolds had been erected to seat the spectators of a parade that was to start at five o'clock in celebration of Carnival. This day was to be the first day of the three-day event, Children's Day. Punctually the first float arrived, followed by many more during the next two hours, trailers, beautifully decorated in fantasy themes, pulled by tractors, music blaring, and children marching, frantically trying to do some kind of dance steps, being coaxed by equally frantic mommies. Some of the kids seemed to enjoy themselves, while others looked dazed, not really understanding what was going on and what was expected of them; they would have preferred to watch the parade from the sidewalk. The whole parade was a symbol of life. I lasted until the very end, and had to tell myself that I had come here to experience Mexican culture. Mexican beer I could drink when I got home to Canada.

Next day in Campeche I experienced what appeared to be an instant replay, again Children's Day, celebrated again with a long parade, almost a copy of the one in Merida. But this one lasted over three hours, and this time I did not last until the end. The town with its ancient sea-side fortifications, built to ward off attacks by pirates, offered too much to see to be passed over in favour of seeing the rerun of a parade. The particular charm of Campeche for me was the fact that so much remained of the small-town atmosphere of colonial Spain; it compensated for the encroachment of modern times in the form of steel and concrete highrises and large luxury hotels. My walk through the deserted backstreets and along the seaward defences was worth the effort. A delicious seafood dinner at *Café Artista* finished off another perfect day.

From Campeche it was only a short ride of some 400 km to my next stop on the Mayan ruins trail, Palenque. I planned to make this my last visit to an archeological site before heading north. The Palenque site is relatively compact. Its setting is idyllic, a jungle clearing with a steep wooded hill on the one side and a large plain on the other. It is bisected by a little cascading creek that at least gives the illusion of coolness. Nature has not been as successful in Palenque as elsewhere in destroying the things that human hands have wrought. The buildings, many of them with their roofs still intact, are glorious examples of the best of

Mayan art. The great number of sculptured wall panels still in excellent condition on the magnificent *Templo de las Inscripciones* and on the other less impressive structures as well, bear witness to a civilization that had attained a high degree of refinement. Palenque was a fitting climax to my Mayan ruins circuit. If I had to make a choice as to which of the sites I had seen (Copán, Tikal, Tulum, Chichén Itzá, Palenque) I liked best, my vote would have to go to Palenque.

*   *   *

Near the city of Villahermosa the next day I was reminded that I was getting close to home. Parked on the side of the highway was a caravan of seven motorhomes, of various sizes, their drivers sitting on the front bumper of the first one to chat while sharing a cup of coffee. This brought back unpleasant memories of Alaska. Since I noticed that each unit was licensed in a different state, I became curious, turned around, parked the bike, and promptly was invited to a cup of coffee. Joe, hailing from the Detroit area, seemed to be their spokesman. He explained to me that they were all retirees following the sun. They found life down here much cheaper than in the Forty-Eight, but, alas, also more dangerous. In order to face the enemy they had found each other on the Internet. They met in Arizona, and decided to stay together until their return to the U.S., sometime next April. I mentioned to Joe and the rest of the gang that I thought their concern with safety to be a little exaggerated. They were not convinced: "Better safe than sorry!" said Joe. "I suppose it's not so bad in your case. You, on a bike, pose no threat (He probably meant to say: You look poor). But anyone arriving with a motorhome down here is seen as immeasurably rich, and fair game to be ripped off." I couldn't argue with him about that point. My cup being empty, I wished them a happy holiday, and thanked my good fortune that I was not condemned to carrying such a super-heavy millstone around my neck as a motorhome. Life seems to be full of trade-offs. Or is there poetic justice? Something to think about on the way to Veracruz.

When I passed through Veracruz on my way north last August, I had liked what I saw, and had made a mental note to return some day in the future and spend at least a night in this delightful Caribbean city of over one million people. The timing of my arrival, the Monday before Shrove-Tuesday, could not have been better. Again I made it to a beachfront hotel just in time before the barricades went up in preparation for the evening parade. This one was to be the highlight of the seven-day Carnival celebrations, the parade of the adults. It began at five o'clock and wound its way along a three-mile course following the beach. There seemed to be no end to it. Float after float passed by, decorated in the most garish colours, its riders dressed in the traditional costumes associated with the local *jarocho* dance culture. There was a lot of stamping of feet as the dancers showed off their artistry doing *bambas* and *zapateados*. Other floats were based on themes from fairy tales, legends, and modern TV soap operas. Every float carried music,

22) *Mexico: Palenque ruins*

some of it live, some amplified to eardrum-bursting intensity. A multitude of young ladies (all of whom looked young, even the ones who had seen a few seasons go by) threw candies and streamers into the crowd, which, because of the good supply of beer at hand, became more and more animated as the show progressed. The last float passed by the hotel sometime after 9.30 p.m., making me think that this was it. Time to have one more beer before retiring. But this turned out to be just the overture of the fun. As I lay in bed trying to fall asleep, the music outside was getting louder and louder. There was only one thing to do, get dressed and join the revellers. All along the three-mile parade route and back into the side-streets, the musicians who had been on the floats had set up shop, playing non-stop to an appreciative audience that was dancing on the sidewalk and in the street. I found the ladies of Veracruz as friendly and as welcoming as those of Rio de Janeiro during Carnival. They seemed to enjoy dancing with the elderly gringo, and they did not refuse the offer of a drink at the bar to heighten their enjoyment. I remembered my New Year's resolution made almost two months ago in Bariloche, and tried to curb my interest in Coronas. It was difficult. I also remembered that during Carnival most laws were suspended for a time, including those associated with resolutions. This was my excuse.

Fortunately the highway to Tampico was in excellent condition and very forgiving. It was now Mardi Gras, Shrove-Tuesday, the day before Ash Wednesday, but Tampico had finished with Carnival, and was already embarking on the sombre lifestyle of the Lenten season. This helped keep me away from further temptation.

It was fitting that my last day of riding in a great country was Ash Wednesday, the first day of the time of Passion, a time of introspection and mourning. The trip was almost over. Tapachula had become just a memory. It was out of my system. I had conquered the ghosts of the past. Thinking about the whole figure eight around the Americas while riding out of Tampico, I almost forgot that I desperately needed to get fuel before doing anything else. But where were the service stations when you needed them? Finally the familiar green sign appeared on the horizon. I pulled in and was received with the usual friendly smile, and with the almost usual shrug, "*Lo siento Señor* we are out of *Premium* but we can give you *Magna sin.*" What choice did I have? Foolishly I told the attendant to fill 'er up. Some ten miles down the road the familiar hiccups started, at first sporadic, then rather intense. I knew immediately what was the matter. The Old Cow, having swallowed a good dose of Mexican *aqua,* reacted in her usual way, and she was miffed. Cleaning out the sediment bowls of the carburetors a couple of times helped a bit. Finally the old bovine returned to normal, bad diet forgiven, and continued her good behaviour the rest of the way into Matamoros and the border. *Addios Mexico* I thought, it is high time you guys privatized your state-owned excuse of a petroleum industry.

Finale

22. *Homecoming*

Reverse culture shock was immediate. On the Mexican side there was a mile-long line-up of cars bumper to bumper on a four-lane highway crawling up to the border at less than walking speed. On the other side, coming into Mexico, traffic was very light. Still in my Colombian riding mode I crossed over into the other lanes, riding against the oncoming traffic, and made my way to Customs and Immigration in a few minutes. No one raised an eyebrow. On the other side of the border, in Harlingen, in an attempt to save a detour of about ten miles to get to my motel, I entered a one-way street the wrong way. Everyone approaching me went hysterical, horns blaring, lights flashing, hands waving. Ahhh...the good ole law-abiding U.S. of A. Time to go back to good road behaviour.

Heading north toward Dallas on a boringly excellent highway in annoyingly disciplined traffic I had enough time to arrive at a decision concerning the last 3,000 km of the trip up to Canada. While it was springtime in Texas at this time of year—the end of February—in Canada there was still some three feet of snow on the ground. On Canadian roads there was slush of the corroding salty type, and snowstorms were not uncommon. It would be a cold ride, the last third in freezing temperatures at 70 mph, not much fun. A "real" adventure biker could handle little things like that, of course. On the other hand, I could leave the bike in the able hands of George at BMW of North Dallas, and let him do the necessary repairs. I could book a seat on a flight home, and earn a good number of merit points from my loving spouse for being home so early. I could pick up the bike in April when the ride up would be more fun, and the Old Cow, having had its surgery done, would be like a heifer in the spring. I did not reach a decision at once, but next morning something occurred that tilted the scale in favour of the latter alternative.

It was time again for a valve clearance check, and the motel in Giddings was the perfect place to do it. Warmed by the already powerful rays of the rising sun, I found the job more pleasure than work. Then the long-expected happened. The bolt holding the right valve cover stripped its thread in the cylinder head and could no longer be torqued. The left one had done this in La Paz, and I was surprised that it had taken so long for its twin on the other side to follow suit. There was not enough of an oil leak to raise alarm, but enough to help me decide to leave the bike in Dallas. Perhaps this was a hint from the Higher Powers. Who knows?

At BMW in Plano, North Dallas, George, the head mechanic, had done a great job guarding my cold weather gear. He could be persuaded to rejuvenate the Old Cow and have her ready by April 1. There was, of course, yet another episode of the epic tale of the shock absorber waiting for me. I was shown a copy of the fax Herbert Von Breymann in Costa Rica had sent to Caracas, asking them to ship the itinerant shock to Dallas. Under the text he had scribbled a note advising me to transfer the necessary freight costs to Caracas, so that the dealer could send the part. What a joke. This would cost me another hundred dollars on top of the import duty at US Customs. I tore up the fax and asked the people in Plano to order an aftermarket shock absorber for me and install it, but please, please no Bilstein. Let Bilstein stick with oxcarts. And there were other little things I asked George to look after. I needed a new crash bar on the left side, since the old one had become non-functional in Panama. The oil seal on the transmission had to be replaced. A Helicoil had to be installed into the stripped thread holding the valve cover bolt. The steering head bearings had to be replaced. They had shown signs of failure as far back as Ecuador. And while he was at it, I asked him to replace the timing chain and the piston rings, and to repack the wheel bearings. We had run up 120,595 km (over 75,000 miles), and I was a firm believer in preventative maintenance. George promised to do all these things, and whatever else he could find. I boarded a flight to Canada with the comforting belief that I had done the right thing. Leavetaking of the Old Bovine was an emotional experience. We had been so close for such a long time. It felt like abandoning a loved one. I'm sure that Dr. Gregory W. Frazier, the author of *Motorcycle Sex* would have a few choice words to say in this context.

*   *   *

There were no fireworks, no colourful "Welcome" banners, no welcoming ceremonies when I walked in the door of my long-time residence. "Hi, Dear, it's me!" were my hopeful and somewhat guilty words of welcome. "Oh, it's you!" was the matter-of-fact reply. Fu Fu the cat gave me his usual dismissive tailwag and walked away sulking. Well, at least the lock on the door had not been changed, and my closet still contained my clothes. My peace offering from Bogotá, the emerald ear-rings, were graciously received. Perhaps Pavlovian conditioning had not been in vain after all. Eventually Fu Fu forgave me and let himself be petted and fed. I was home again.

During the next few weeks as I was acclimatizing, the winter abated, but not before having given us a few more snowstorms. It was time to repatriate the Old Cow. George informed me that they had installed a new shock absorber, no Bilstein this time, thank God, and had done all the work as requested. The crash-bar, which they had not yet received from BMW North America, was on back order. (It would arrive at the BMW dealer in Ottawa, Canada in September.) Otherwise the bike was ready to go.

On April 6 the Old Cow came back to her familiar stable. We had clocked 47,543 km (almost 30,000 miles) since last October on the South American loop. North America and South America together, the figure 8, comprised a grand total of 76,407 km (almost 48,000 miles), in seven months and six days, excluding the two months of the "Interlude" and the bike's one month stay in Dallas.

Asked if I would do the trip over again, I can answer with an emphatic "yes!" It was a great adventure and I have no regrets. What would I do differently the next time? I would not freak out in Tapachula or anywhere else. And I would change my itinerary a little. Instead of going south from Boa Vista, Brazil, I would go east into Guyana, on a road that is difficult, but not impossible in the dry season. From Guyana I would enter Surinam, then French Guyane, and ship the bike to St-Georges de l'Oyapock, Macapá, or Belém, Brazil, since the road between the two countries is still under construction. Otherwise I would follow the same circuit. Yes, and the timing of the trip was perfect. It is to be hoped that there will not be another *El Niño* around for awhile.

*   *   *

Having a totally reconditioned motorcycle in the garage is hard on the man who has been infected with the Adventure Travel Virus. Once you are diagnosed ATV positive it is only a matter of time until the condition develops into full-blown ATES (Adventure Travel Experience Syndrome). At my last self-diagnosis it had become apparent that I have entered this advanced stage of the disease. All the symptoms are present: daydreaming of wide open spaces, of rivers to ford, of deserts to cross; buying an inordinate number of travel guides and reading them furtively while outwardly performing the duties of a designated househusband; phoning and faxing embassies, consulates, and travel agencies; e-mailing places as far away as Beijing. According to the latest edition of a popular medical dictionary my case is the result of a very locomotion- specific mutation of the virus identified by the acronym MATES (Motorcycle Adventure Travel Experience Syndrome). Of course the disease is terminal; there is no cure. Only long extended trips across continents can afford relief, alas only temporary. On my desk are two weighty volumes in which I find myself immersed between chores almost every day. One is a road atlas of Asia; the other contains the collected treatises of Ivan Pavlov on Conditioned Responses. There is a lot of work to be done before riding off again at sunrise for the next experience.

Appendix

Itinerary

Distances are given in km (1.6 km = 1 mile). Odometer readings were taken on the morning of the day of departure.

Campgrounds and hotels listed were in different price categories; all had safe parking for the motorcycle.

North America

Country	Date	Distance	Accommodation
Canada	1 July 97	0	Home, Ottawa, Ontario
	2 July	777	Fred's Half-Way, Timmins, Ontario
	3 July	1,448	Silverwood Park Campground, Nipigon, Ontario
	4 July	1,502	Grann Motel, Pass Lake Corner, Ontario
	5 July	2,344	Portage La Prairie Campground, Manitoba
	6 July	3,080	Saskatoon Campground, Saskatchewan
	7 July	3,751	Bluebird Camping, Athabasca, Alberta
	8 July	4,290	Alahart RV Park, Dawson Creek, B.C.
	9 July	5,290	Downtown RV Park, Watson Lake, Yukon
	10 July	5,760	Hi Country RV Park, Whitehorse, Yukon
	11 July	6,318	Yukon Terr. Gov't Campground, Dawson, Yukon
U.S.A.	12 July	6,940	Trail's End RV Park, Fairbanks, Alaska
	13 July	7,779	Prudhoe Bay Hotel, Deadhorse, Alaska
	14 July	8,180	Arctic Acres Camping, Coldfoot, Alaska
	15 July	8,590	Trail's End RV Park, Fairbanks, Alaska
	16 July	9,190	Chugach State Park, Anchorage, Alaska
	17 July	9,720	Palmer Campground, Alaska
	18 July	10,345	White River Motor Inn Campground, Can. Border
Canada	19 July	10,607	Arctic Studies Camp, Kluane Lake, Yukon
	20 July	11,150	Hi Country RV Park, Whitehorse, Yukon
	21 July	11,700	Jade City Camping, B.C.
	22 July	12,326	Cassiar RV Park, Kitwanga, B.C.
	23 July	12,840	Prince George RV Park, B.C.
	24 July	13,460	Pemberton Camping, B.C.
	25 July	13,708	Home of Sister and Brother-in-law, Victoria, B.C.
	26 July		Victoria, B.C.
U.S.A.	27 July	14,100	Kampers West Kampground, Warrenton, Oregon
	28 July	14,700	KOA Kampground, Crescent City, California
	29 July	15,247	Sonoma State Campground, Sebastopol, California
	30 July	15,723	San Simeon State Park Campground, California
	31 July	16,348	Motel Imperial, San Diego, California
	1 Aug.	16,676	Riverside RV Park, Yuma, Arizona
	2 Aug.	17,429	Hacienda Motel, Deming, New Mexico
Mexico	3 Aug.	17,969	Hotel Parador San Miguel, Chihuahua

	4 Aug.	18,762	La Fortuna Motel, Fresnillo
	5 Aug.	19,358	Motel, San Juan, Del Rio
	6 Aug.	19,880	Hotel, Acatlan
	7 Aug.	20,350	Hotel La Mision, San Pedro Tapanatepec
	8 Aug.	20,694	Hotel Kamico, Tapachula
	9 Aug.	21,151	Hotel Liesse, Palomares
	10 Aug.	21,700	Hotel, Nautla
U.S.A.	11 Aug.	22,535	The Sands Motel, Brownsville, Texas
	12 Aug.	23,230	Ricefield Motel, Winnie, Texas
	13 Aug.	24,077	Dolphin Inn, Fort Walton, Florida
	14 Aug.	24,636	Crystal River Motel, Florida
	15 Aug.	25,486	Bed and Breakfast, Key West, Florida
	16 Aug.	25,967	Farrel's Motel, Fort Pierce, Florida
	17 Aug.	26,590	Garden's Corner Motel, South Carolina
	18 Aug.	27,245	Bluff Shoal Motel, Ocracoke, North Carolina
	19 Aug.	27,656	Owl Motel, New Church, Virginia
	20 Aug.	28,445	North Hampton Campground, New York
Canada	21 Aug.	28,864	Home, Ottawa, Ontario

South America

Canada	20 Oct.	0	Home, Ottawa, Ontario
U.S.A.	21 Oct.	650	Motel 6, Scranton, Pennsylvania
	22 Oct.	1,410	Gateway Motel, Max Meadows, Virginia
	23 Oct.	2,348	Super Motel 8, Memphis, Tennessee
	24 Oct.	3,121	La Quinta Inn, Plano, Texas
	25 Oct.	3,480	Sands Motel, Giddings, Texas
	26 Oct.	3,980	Motel 6, Harlingen, Texas
Mexico	27 Oct.	4,609	Roadside motel near Ozuluama
	28 Oct.	5,154	Hotel Plaza Sol, Lerdo
	29 Oct.	5,679	Hotel La Mision, San Pedro Tapanatepec
	30 Oct.	5,977	Hotel Kamico, Tapachula
Guatemala	31 Oct.	6,356	Hotel Baru, Santa Rosa
El Salvador	1 Nov.	6,536	Hotel Family, San Salvador
	2 Nov.	6,727	Hospedaje, Santa Rosa de Lima
Honduras	3 Nov.	6,888	Hotel MacArthur, Tegucigalpa
	4 Nov.	7,004	Gran Hotel Granada, Danli
Nicaragua	5 Nov.	7,402	Hotel Nicarao, Rivas
Costa Rica	6 Nov.	7,732	Best Western, San José
	7 Nov.		"
	8 Nov.		"
	9 Nov.		"
	10 Nov.		"
	11 Nov.		"

	12 Nov.		"
	13 Nov.		"
Panama	14 Nov.	8,147	Hotel Fiesta, David
	15 Nov.	8,590	Hotel Costa Inn, Panama City
	16 Nov.	8,620	"
	17 Nov.		"
Colombia	18 Nov.		Gran Avenida Hotel, Bogotá
	19 Nov.		"
	20 Nov.	8,640	"
	21 Nov.	9,195	Residencia San Carlos, Pamplona
	22 Nov.	9,305	Hotel Casa Blanca, Cucuta
	23 Nov.	9,355	"
	24 Nov.		"
Venezuela	25 Nov.	9,721	El Bosque Motel, Barinas
	26 Nov.	10,262	Hotel President, Caracas
	27 Nov.	10,847	Hotel Los Viajeros, Ciudad Bolívar
	28 Nov.	11,162	Hotel La Reina, Guasipati
Brazil	29 Nov.	11,834	Hotel Tres Nações, Boa Vista
	30 Nov.	11,840	Hotel Praya Palace, Boa Vista
	1 Dec.		"
	2 Dec.	12,280	Fazenda Santa Clara, near Equator
	3 Dec.	12,641	Pension Sulista, Manaus
	4 Dec.	12,643	M/S Clivia, Rio Amazonas
	5 Dec.		"
	6 Dec.		"
	7 Dec.		"
	8 Dec.	12,647	Hotel Regente, Belém
	9 Dec.	13,105	Hotel Anjos, São Antonio
	10 Dec.	13,814	Truckstop, near Gurupi
	11 Dec.	14,784	Hotel Byblos, Brasília
	12 Dec.	15,340	Hotel Moderno, Uberaba
	13 Dec.	16,011	Hotel Lito Palace, Registro
	14 Dec.	16,638	HP-Hotel, Palmeiras
	15 Dec.	16,945	Hotel Cataratas, Iguaçu Falls
Paraguay	16 Dec.	17,335	Hotel Azara, Asuncion
Argentina	17 Dec.	18,121	Hotel San Justo, San Justo
	18 Dec.	18,875	Hotel Waldorf, Buenos Aires
	19 Dec.		"
	20 Dec.	19,706	Descanso Ceferiniano, Pedro Luro
	21 Dec.	20,766	Hotel Su Estrella, Comodoro Rivadavia
	22 Dec.	21,555	Hotel Comercio, Rio Gallegos
	23 Dec.	21,960	Hotel Atlantida, Río Grande
	24 Dec.	22,202	Hotel Canal Beagle, Ushuaia
	25 Dec.	22,230	"
	26 Dec.	22,432	Hotel Atlantida, Río Grande

Chile	27 Dec.	22,683	Hotel Mercurio, Punta Arenas
Argentina	28 Dec.	23,233	Hotel Kapenke, El Calafate
	29 Dec.	23,498	"
	30 Dec.	24,183	Hotel Covadonga, Río Mayo
	31 Dec.	24,858	Hotel Tehuelche, Esquel
	1 Jan. 98	25,153	Hosteria Sur, Bariloche
Chile	2 Jan.	25,543	Hotel Don Luis, Puerto Montt
	3 Jan.	26,081	Hotel Bio Tourismo, Los Angeles
	4 Jan.	26,604	Hotel Imperio, Santiago
	5 Jan.		"
	6 Jan.	27,260	Roadside hotel, near Incahuasi
	7 Jan.	28,060	Hotel San Martin, Antofagasta
	8 Jan.	28,852	Hotel King, Arica
Bolivia	9 Jan.	29,362	Hotel Copacabana, La Paz
	10 Jan.		"
Peru	11 Jan.	29,635	Hotel Italia, Puno
	12 Jan.		"
Bolivia	13 Jan.	29,850	Hotel Inca Utama, on Lake Titicaca
Peru	14 Jan.	30,463	Gran Hotel Tacna, Tacna
	15 Jan.	30,872	Hotel Jerusalen, Arequipa
	16 Jan.	31,461	Hotel Lineas, Nasca
	17 Jan.		"
	18 Jan.	31,925	Hotel Esperanza, Lima
	19 Jan.		"
	20 Jan.	32,519	Hotel Libertador, Trujillo
	21 Jan.	33,252	Hotel Costa del Sol, Tumbes
	22 Jan.		"
Ecuador	23 Jan.	33,518	Hotel Presidente, Cuenca
	24 Jan.	33,790	Hotel Whymper, Riobamba
	25 Jan.	33,989	Hotel Café Cultura, Quito
	26 Jan.	34,127	Hotel Coraza, Otavalo
Colombia	27 Jan.	34,631	Hotel Bolívar, Popayan
	28 Jan.	35,228	Hotel Ambassador, Medellín
	29 Jan.	35,904	Hotel Flamingo, Cartagena
	30 Jan.		"
	31 Jan.	36,581	Hotel D'Leon, Bucaramanga
	1 Feb.	36,888	Hospedaje San Carlos, Tunja
	2 Feb.	37,038	Hotel Dann Colonial, Bogotá

Central America and Mexico

Panama	3 Feb.		Hotel Costa Inn, Panama
	4 Feb.	37,090	"
	5 Feb.	37,092	"
	6 Feb.	37,524	Hotel Fiesta, David